C000050735

THE OPTIMIST

Stanford Studies *in* Middle Eastern
and Islamic Societies *and* Cultures

THE OPTIMIST

A Social Biography of Tawfiq Zayyad

Tamir Sorek

STANFORD UNIVERSITY PRESS
Stanford, California

STANFORD UNIVERSITY PRESS
Stanford, California

© 2020 by the Board of Trustees of the Leland Stanford Junior University. All rights reserved.

No part of this book may be reproduced or transmitted in any form or by any means, electronic or mechanical, including photocopying and recording, or in any information storage or retrieval system without the prior written permission of Stanford University Press.

Printed in the United States of America on acid-free, archival-quality paper

Library of Congress Cataloging-in-Publication Data

Names: Sorek, Tamir, author.
Title: The optimist : a social biography of Tawfiq Zayyad / Tamir Sorek.
Other titles: Stanford studies in Middle Eastern and Islamic societies and cultures.
Description: Stanford, California : Stanford University Press, 2020. | Series: Stanford studies in Middle Eastern and Islamic societies and cultures | Includes bibliographical references and index.
Identifiers: LCCN 2020008448 (print) | LCCN 2020008449 (ebook) | ISBN 9780804797474 (cloth) | ISBN 9781503612730 (paperback) | ISBN 9781503612747 (ebook)
Subjects: LCSH: Zayyad, Tawfiq. | Politicians—Palestine—Biography. | Nationalists—Palestine—Biography. | Poets, Palestinian Arab—Biography. | Arab-Israeli conflict—History—20th century. | Palestine—Politics and government—1948–
Classification: LCC DS126.6.Z39 S67 2020 (print) | LCC DS126.6.Z39 (ebook) | DDC 320.54095694092 [B]—dc23
LC record available at https://lccn.loc.gov/2020008448
LC ebook record available at https://lccn.loc.gov/2020008449

Cover photo: Tawfiq Zayyad on the Knesset Podium
Cover design: Rob Ehle

Contents

PROLOGUE

IN 1954, PALESTINIANS WHO REMAINED UNDER ISRAELI RULE WERE still recovering from the collective shock of the Nakba (catastrophe): the expulsion of approximately 750,000 Palestinians from the territory that became Israel in 1948 and the destruction of hundreds of villages and most of the Palestinian urban centers. Soon the status of those who remained violently changed from being part of a self-confident majority to a minority living under antagonistic military rule. People lost contact with their expelled family members, and the new rulers were treating them as unwanted intruders in their own homeland while drastically changing the landscape in front of their eyes. Many lost their land and were trying to adjust to their new social status. The new economy was structurally biased against them. Poverty and unemployment were common, and the future seemed uncertain. That same year, a young Palestinian communist activist published in his party literary bulletin's *al-Jadid* a poem directly addressing these sentiments of colonial victimization and economic discrimination. His poem ended with a utopian revolutionary vision:

> The years have taught us
> That you want to change our land into tombs
> And dance over its ruins.
> But your wishes will not be fulfilled.
> And the war monster

Will be crushed by the toilers' fist,

And the Peoples¹ will build a permanent peace, forever.

We would then get rid of our burdens,

And live for our children.

Songs would fill the horizon,

And the mothers' hearts would find peace.²

This anticolonial Marxist rhetoric was compatible with the editorial line of *al-Jadid* and reflected the important role intellectuals affiliated with the Israeli Communist Party (ICP) played in articulating a vocabulary of resistance in those years.³ The optimistic fervor, though, was a trademark of the author of these lines, Tawfiq Zayyad, who would go on to play an important role in the struggle of the Palestinian citizens of Israel over four decades as a leader in the ICP, an admired poet, the mayor of Nazareth, and a member of the Knesset. Above all, Zayyad was a producer of hope: hope for justice for Palestinians, hope for a Palestinian-Israeli reconciliation, and hope for the creation of an egalitarian society based on human dignity and without exploitation. As naively quaint and uncritical the idea of hope might sound today, it was a fundamental aspect of Zayyad's intellectual and political endeavor.

Zayyad's hope was deeply embedded in his Marxist conviction, which in turn maintained a strong link to his struggle for Palestinian rights. His political consciousness and socialization as a communist took shape within the context of the Palestinian struggle against British rule and Zionism through the 1930s and 1940s. After the 1948 war and the expulsion of most of the Palestinians who lived in the territory that became the State of Israel, Zayyad became a member of a colonized ethnonational minority struggling for survival. Israeli citizenship was imposed on him, but his party, the ICP, immediately turned this citizenship into a tool in this struggle, challenging the authorities through parliamentary, judicial, municipal, and cultural channels.

Zayyad is the oldest of a generation of major Palestinian poets (Taha Muhammad 'Ali, Samih al-Qasim, Mahmoud Darwish, Salim Jubran, Rashid Husayn) who reached adulthood in the early years of the State of Israel. Through their poetry, they played an important role in producing and disseminating political ideas and meanings. They came from working-class backgrounds and were deeply invested in improving the lives of the working class and peasants. In the words of the Italian leader and theorist Antonio Gramsci, they were "organic intellectuals."⁴

These poet activists continued a tradition of political poetry with a left-leaning orientation that flourished before 1948, but following the Nakba, the range of potential formal political affiliations available to them was extremely narrow. Due to their anticolonial consciousness,[5] most of them rejected being part of a Zionist political party,[6] yet most forms of politics based on Palestinian solidarity or Arab nationalism were illegal. In the 1950s, the only non-Zionist party that actively and consistently confronted the colonial policy of the Israeli state locally and internationally was the ICP. In addition, the party provided some of the few opportunities for the publication of Arab literature and poetry. As a result, most of the leading poets of this generation were affiliated with the ICP.

As political activists and as poets, Zayyad's generation took part in shaping Palestinian national identity. For Palestinians in Israel living under the military government, which was in effect until 1966, poetry became a major avenue for political expression and mobilization.[7] Yet poetry and parliamentary politics remained divided in the particular and somewhat extreme circumstances of Palestinian politics in Israel.[8] In her discussion of Arab Palestinian members of the ICP under the military government, Palestinian sociologist Honaida Ghanem distinguished between the politicians and the intellectuals, who were usually poets. Politicians worked to achieve equal rights for Arab citizens and integrate them into the state apparatus, and therefore they worked within the boundaries of Israel citizenship. Poets called for a more radical national liberation and presented the state as a colonialist oppressive creation, a temporary deviation from justice.[9] This poetry was embedded in and even shaped the Arab and Palestinian national discourse. The ICP had to navigate carefully between the conflicting goals of Israeli politics and Palestinian poetry.

In this context, Zayyad is a particularly interesting figure. No other poet of his generation became so intensively involved in politics or developed such a long and successful political career as he did. Moreover, as his political commitments grew, politics took priority over his dedication to poetry. During the eighteen years he served as a member of the Knesset, he wrote no poetry. He explained that he lacked the time for writing, but it is also likely that being a member of the Israeli parliament required a state of mind that was incompatible with crafting revolutionary poetry.

Zayyad rose to fame as a revolutionary poet during the heyday of secularism in the Arab world, and many considered the poetry of his generation an emblem of this secularism. To be sure, religion and secularism are flexible categories, and the boundaries between them are the product of historical processes and social construction.[10] While I reject any essentialist understanding of these categories, I do argue that Zayyad himself had a coherent and rather rigid idea about their meaning. In his writing and his political activism, he took part in shaping these categories as central elements in a particular vision of modernity. At the same time, a scholarly analysis of his worldview has to question the rigid distinction between secularism and religion, which is essential in the Marxist discourse of modernity. While God was absent from both Zayyad's poetry and his political vision, his utopian imagination had undeniable messianic dimensions that were anchored in his Marxist faith.

The understanding of Marxism as a form of secularized messianic religion is part of a long tradition in philosophy and sociology;[11] however, some prominent scholars, including Hannah Arendt, harshly criticized it.[12] In this book, I do not examine communist institutions as functionally equivalent to religion and therefore do not engage in many aspects of this controversy. I do argue, though, that Zayyad's subjective experience, as reflected in his rhetoric, leaves little doubt about the eschatological dimension of his utopian vision. This is a key element for understanding his tireless hope, as well as his ability to radiate this hope around him. Indeed, "where there is hope," wrote the original Marxist German philosopher Ernst Bloch, "there is also religion."[13] While this statement both oversimplifies and essentializes religion, Bloch's theory of secularization as a dialectical process between the sacred and the profane helps us conceptualize Zayyad's secularization.[14]

For Bloch, dialectical materialism "hears and grasps the import of the mighty voice of tendency in this world, which it has made its own, has taken hold of the living soul of a dead religion." Although the "fool's paradise of the Other-world has been burnt away to ashes," he wrote, "that remains as a call, signaling the way to the fulfilled This-world of a new earth."[15] In other words, a spiritual vocabulary is what enabled the articulation of Zayyad's godless utopian vision and the mobilization of other believers.

Indeed, one important but underexplored aspect of Zayyad's Marxism was his personal and political secularism. Before the 1980s, religion played a fairly minor political role among Palestinians in Israel, and if the secular politics of ICP was ever contested, it was by the state authorities who attempted to use religion and religious affiliations to undermine the communists. The appearance of the Islamic Movement in this decade and its explicit and assertive demand to use Islam as a political doctrine has made the secular-religious axis one of the most contested issues among Palestinians in Israel today. Zayyad consciously positioned himself as the vanguard of a secular struggle, and his exchanges with leaders of the Islamic Movement were venomous and violent. Adopting Bloch's analysis, though, we can see this tension not as a struggle between the sacred and the profane but between two competing utopian visions. Both parties' inability to compromise was partly rooted in their similarity.

This book follows Zayyad's journey from his anticolonial and Marxist socialization under British rule to his struggle to lead resistance after 1948, his rise to fame as a revolutionary poet in the 1960s, his political career as the first communist city mayor[16] in the Middle East and a long-time member of the Israeli Knesset, his predicament following the collapse of the socialist regimes in Eastern Europe, his conflict with the Islamic Movement, and his optimistic surge amid the Oslo process in the early 1990s, though he did not live to witness its collapse.

POSITIONALITY

I never met Tawfīq Zayyad (1929–1994), and I have only some anecdotal memories, which I probably share with many of my generation, of his appearance in the Israeli media in the 1980s and the 1990s, and especially his turbulent confrontations with right-wing politicians. While carrying out studies of the political challenges of Palestinians in Israel, and especially my work on Palestinian collective memory and commemoration, I paid increasing attention to Zayyad.[17] Interviews and media reports repeatedly highlighted his name, and I gradually developed a deep curiosity about the combination of revolutionary poetry, down-to-earth pragmatic politics, charisma, simple manners, and the talent for drama that made him an exceptional leader. I became galvanized by the potential for his biography to tell a broader story about Palestinians, the State of Israel, and hope in the age of the Nakba.

As I entered this field of study, I felt like an explorer in a foreign land or even a trespasser. I am a Jewish Israeli scholar studying a Palestinian leader, a fact that raises a series of dilemmas related to my position in the power/knowledge nexus and the hierarchy of power between our related groups. From my more than two decades of studying various issues related to Palestinians in Israel, I am aware of the sensitivity surrounding my relation to the field. Historically, with notable exceptions, most Jewish Israeli scholars who have studied Palestinians adopted an orientalist worldview of the Israeli establishment, identified with its political goals, and in many cases had strong formal or informal ties with the government agencies or the intelligence services. Consciously or unconsciously, the body of knowledge they created has been oriented toward or has served the goal of improving the techniques of subjugation.[18]

Even with a conscious effort to distance myself from that approach, my interactions with my interlocutors, their self-presentation in my presence, and the framing and vocabularies they chose to tell their story have inevitably been shaped in one way or another by the power equation. My past studies have been influenced by similar power dynamics. In addition, the reactions of my Palestinian audiences to my self-positioning as an authority to tell the story of the colonized group have ranged from satisfaction that I am providing a scholarly stage for the Palestinian predicament to overt hostility, questioning my right to do so, as well as implicit suspicion about my motivation.

The doubts, however, were also mine: How do I avoid the tropes of my positionality without losing my own voice? This tension is especially pronounced with this book since I am writing the first scholarly biography of Zayyad and therefore bear great responsibility for the way he will be remembered in the future, not to mention his role in the scholarship on Palestinian citizens in Israel. There is no easy way around this dilemma, so I warn readers that this book cannot pretend to be more than what it actually is: an empathic presentation of an iconic Palestinian political and cultural figure by a Jewish Israeli scholar. It is the product of my effort to engage seriously with Palestinian culture and politics by researching Zayyad's life, explicating the context of his political work, and delving into the biographical and political meanings of his poetic oeuvre. It is shaped as well by the historical political moment of its writing, where all paths for justice in Palestine and peace for Palestinians and Israelis seem to be impassable and Zayyad's optimism seems to belong to a distant past. In my previous books, which were partly based on ethnography, I reflected occasionally on my positionality and the way it shaped my interactions in the field. I have avoided that in this book, partly because the nature of biographies is less accommodating of this kind of interruption, but also because I wanted to leave the stage to Zayyad rather than inserting myself into his life story.

The second aspect of trespassing is disciplinary. I am a social scientist by training and my decision to write about a poet has raised some eyebrows among my colleagues in literary studies. Therefore, it is noteworthy that although Tawfiq

Zayyad's regional and international fame is related mainly to his poetry, poetry is not the main focus of this book; rather, I consider Zayyad first as a political leader. Furthermore, During the most dramatic and influential years of his political career (1974–1990), Zayyad did not write poetry. At the same time, his identity as a poet, and therefore the content of his poetry, are central for understanding his social and political status, as well as his life course.

I do not, however, undertake a close literary analysis of Zayyad's poetry, a task that several generations of experts in literary studies have already undertaken (although the vast majority of this scholarship is still unavailable in English). These studies have paid close attention to Zayyad's figurative language and to the kind of allegories and metaphors he used. They have analyzed his diction, meter, and rhythm, and they have also identified the literary legacies that shaped his writing.[19] I do refer occasionally to these studies and their insights, but only to highlight broader biographical aspects, and I do not engage in theoretical debates in comparative literature. The books about Zayyad's poetry usually open with a brief personal and political biography but these introductions are secondary to his poetry and are not based on primary research. As a sociologist, I reverse the order: I treat poetry first and foremost as a biographical document. I consider it as both a window to Zayyad's subjective experience of personal and political events, and a tool that Zayyad used as a political leader.

TAILORING THE STORY

The threads I used to weave the narrative of Zayyad's life are made of diverse sources. I represent Zayyad's childhood from fragments of memories he himself provided in several interviews starting in the mid-1970s, as well as the memories of childhood friends and acquaintances who were interviewed by the journalist Nazir Majali shortly after Zayyad's death in 1994. As a result, for this period more than any other in his life, my raw materials are limited to mythologies already processed by Zayyad himself or by the guardians of his memory. Nevertheless, I tried to contextualize these stories in their broader historical, social, and political backgrounds.

For later periods, I rely heavily on interviews and conversations with family members, friends, and acquaintances, as well as with political partners and rivals. While human memory is always the result of selective attention and subjective interpretation, stories told after a long period of time are more likely to be shaped by the experience of the narrator since the event and by contemporary social and political circumstances. Under these conditions, it is very difficult to distinguish fact from fiction. Furthermore, given that Zayyad was a prominent and frequently controversial political leader, every contemporary reference to him is likely to be shaped at least partly by contemporary political agendas and rivalries.

The relative weight of dependence on information obtained from these interviews declines as I move forward in time when a variety of other sources become available. Among these, one major source is press coverage, mainly local Arabic press coverage but also, though to a lesser extent, the Hebrew and international media. Most of the materials from the Arabic press was based on the organ of the Israeli Communist Party, *al-Ittihad*, which until the early 1980s was the only non-Zionist Arabic newspaper in Israel. As the party's main media outlet, it covered party activity most extensively, yet it rarely revealed internal disagreements in the party or anything that might have harmed the party's image. In addition, the communist collectivist political culture discouraged a close look at the individual personalities of activists.

The Hebrew media, which provided a mirror image of *al-Ittihad*'s qualities, were important sources for learning about issues the ICP preferred not to discuss publicly. At the same time, it is noteworthy that some of the journalists in the Hebrew media who covered the ICP had close ties with the security establishment and frequently relied on anonymous sources in this establishment. For that reason, it is difficult to tell when a piece of information was accurate, based on some truth but filtered through the surveillance lens, or intentionally fabricated as part of a psychological warfare campaign. In most cases, I provided the story and juxtaposed it next to any competing version of the story from other sources, if available. The advantage of the Hebrew media was their greater interest in personality issues, a topic absent from *al-Ittihad*. After his election as Knesset member and mayor of Nazareth in the mid-1970s, Zayyad fascinated many Jewish Israeli journalists. While the common reference in these media to Zayyad was paternalistic or even racist, some of the reporters took seriously the journalistic task of providing an in-depth portrayal of him.

Diverse archival sources are also central to this project. I rely on letters, reports, and recorded interviews with Zayyad held at the Tawfiq Zayyad Institute, as well as the institute's video collection that includes raw footage from public events or unpublished interviews. I turned to the Israel State Archive to understand state policy, and in the municipal library in Nazareth I found protocols of the Nazareth Municipal Council. The archive of the Israeli Communist Party at

Yad Tabenkin and the Communist Party Archive at the National Library of Israel were valuable for understanding internal party dynamics. The Knesset Archive documents, and especially the Knesset Plenum minutes, allowed me to trace Zayyad's parliamentary activity. Moreover, Tawfiq Zayyad's brother Musbah provided me with an invaluable source: personal letters Zayyad wrote from Moscow while he was living there in the early 1960s.

Finally, I rely on Zayyad's own written words. Zayyad did not leave much autobiographical material or explicitly self-reflective texts. Therefore, my *verstehen*, my interpretation of the meanings Zayyad gave to the events and processes in his own life, heavily relies on other texts he wrote: political speeches, sporadic political commentary, short stories, and, above all, his poetry. Fortunately for a biographer, Zayyad often overtly connected his poetry to concrete political developments, and at least one literary critic described his poetry as "more biographical than artistic."[20] It is noteworthy that Zayyad himself considered poetry to be embedded in biography, and biography to be inherently political. In a 1966 critique of Mahmoud Darwish's poetry, he commented, "In order to understand Mahmoud Darwish as a poet, we have to know him as a person, as a political entity."[21] Even so, the reliance on poetry to tell a life story is a creative process, and not without risk. As the literary scholar and biographer Mutlu Blasing commented about the use of poetry for biographical purposes, "A biographer attempts, at her own peril, to unravel the complex fabric of the myth he [the poet] made of his life."[22]

The sources I have listed do not represent an exhaustive list of possible sources about Zayyad; they are only those to which I had access. As a political activist who lived in three countries—Israel, the Soviet Union, and Czechoslovakia—Zayyad surely has a surveillance file in the archives of the secret security services in each of these countries. Among these, I was able to obtain only his file at the Czechoslovakian secret services (which turned out to be quite thin and without substantial information). The Israeli Security Service (Shabak) closely followed the activities of Arab activists, and the Soviet KGB surely took great interest in the activities of foreign nationals on Soviet soil. One day, when scholars gain access to Zayyad's files at these agencies, we might learn even more about him.

Chapter 1

COMMUNISM AND ANTICOLONIALISM

TAWFIQ ZAYYAD WAS BORN ON MAY 7, 1929, IN NAZARETH. OUR knowledge about his childhood and adolescence is very limited because he left no written memoir referring to this period. In interviews, he sometimes shared anecdotes, but most of what we know about his youth comes from testimonies that the journalist Nazir Majali collected from childhood friends and classmates and that the Nazareth Municipality published in a memorial book shortly after Zayyad's death in 1994.[1] Most of what I heard from people in Nazareth about Zayyad's youth echoed the memorial book with minor deviations. These stories have become canonical—pieces of the mythology on which his public image rests. It does not necessarily mean that they are wrong. Rather, they provide only a partial view that is colored by the perspectives and agendas of those who told the story and edited the book.

Majali writes that Amin Zayyad, Tawfiq's father, was a self-made man whose father died in his childhood. He went to Damascus to study medicine, and while a student, he made a living by transporting commodities between Palestine and Damascus on a donkey he had purchased. Political and economic circumstances forced him to give up his dream to become a doctor, and when he accumulated enough money, he settled in Nazareth, opened a vegetable store, and married a local woman named Nazha.[2] Tawfiq Zayyad's poetic flair might be traced back to his father, who had a "picturesque poetic language."[3] In 1958, following the detention of Tawfiq and his younger brother for their political activism (see chapter 2),

Amin Zayyad was interviewed by the Jewish communist poet and journalist Haya Kadmon. A translator assisted the interview, but Amin Zayyad was frustrated by his inability to transfer the full meaning of his words into Hebrew. He told Kadmon that a precondition for her next visit was that the translator would be a poet, because he himself was speaking a poetic language and he wished a Jewish poet would listen to his words, as well as to his son's poetic words, in their full power and authenticity.[4]

Nazha and Amin Zayyad's first son, Subhi, died shortly after his birth (an event that was not so rare at the time; infant mortality among Palestinian Muslims in 1927 stood at more than 20 percent).[5] They named their second son after the first, Subhi, and his birth was followed by the birth of a baby girl, who died as well at a very young age. To end the bad luck, the family elders decided to change Subhi's name to Tawfiq.

Tawfiq's classmates whom Majali interviewed remembered him as a highly articulate, sharp-tongued boy with a sense of humor. Samih Rizq described him as a good political commentator. His classmate and friend Hassan Mahmud Khatba remembered his consistent stand on the side of the oppressed, his modesty, and his love of people. He added that unlike other students from the city, Zayyad was not arrogant, and he cultivated friendships with classmates from the villages. His neighbor and friend Ibrahim Taha said that as a child, Zayyad spent a lot of time playing and valued fairness. We know as well that Zayyad began writing and publishing poetry as an adolescent. Though later in life Tawfiq Zayyad was renowned for his politically committed poetry, in his youth, he wrote love poetry and in the mid-1940s, he published under a pseudonym in the Haifa-based *al-Mihmaz* and the weekly Jaffa-based *al-Hurriyya*.

Majali's narrative identifies three broad social and political issues as central to Zayyad's worldview: the national anticolonial struggle, communism, and religious tolerance. Majali's focus on these themes partly reflects the political competition in the 1990s between the communists and two predominant internal political challenges: nationalists, who criticized what they considered to be the communists' insufficient emphasis of Palestinian national identity, and the Islamic Movement, which attacked the communists' secularism. Majali's text is a tacit response to these criticisms, emphasizing Zayyad's patriotism (and, by extension, that of his party) and implicitly criticizing the Islamists' intolerance. Regardless of Majali's short-term political calculations, though, his account does in fact capture the three interrelated ideas that shaped Zayyad's political consciousness.

NATIONALISM AND COMMUNISM

National identification among the Arab residents of Palestine emerged with and was shaped by the anticolonial struggle against Zionism and was further developed through popular movements that crossed class, religious, and regional differences.[6] Although some articulations of socialist ideas were evident in the rhetoric of Palestinian nationalist intellectuals and poets from the 1920s,[7] communism as an explicit articulated political plan was marginal among Palestinians, at least until 1948. Those Arab Palestinians who embraced communism frequently had to contend with fundamental tensions between nationalism and communism.

The question of the compatibility of nationalism and communism has occupied communist intellectuals and politicians since Karl Marx.[8] The tension between the universalist aspirations of communism and the strong in-group orientation of modern nations has nurtured immense scholarship and many political attempts to bridge this gap. In Nazareth, however, communist activism was embedded in nationalist activism. Their linked early evolution in the city formed the backdrop to Zayyad's childhood and adolescence, and he and other young activists experienced nationalism and leftist politics as a package deal.

Nazareth residents were involved in the Arab Palestinian national movement from the beginning. To the First Palestinian Arab Congress, which convened in Jerusalem in 1919 as a response to the Balfour Declaration (the 1917 British official statement of favoring the establishment of a Jewish national home in Palestine), the city of seven thousand people sent two delegates. In 1920, its representatives to the congress issued a letter of protest that condemned the Zionist movement while also proclaiming solidarity with the Jews of Palestine,[9] a position indicative of how both anticolonial and universalist tendencies in Nazareth predated the Communist Party.

In its early years, communism in Palestine did not show any signs of the future alliance with Arab Palestinian nationalism, and indeed the Palestine Communist Party (PCP) that formed in the 1920s was a worker-based group among Jewish immigrants. Since 1921, the party's activity was considered illegal, and therefore its recruitment was done secretly. Throughout the British Mandate period, major Palestinian newspapers such as *Filastin* and *al-Karmil* launched frequent attacks against communism and what they saw as its ideological bedfellows, Judaism and Zionism. In the context of 1920s Palestine, the association of communism and Jews had a basis in social reality. In the words of Najati Sidqi, the first Arab Palestinian member of the PCP, "Jewish immigration to Palestine carried with it habits, ideas, and social customs which were foreign to the Arab Palestinian environment. It was then, in the early 1920s, that we heard about Bolshevism, anarchism, Marx, Lenin, Trotsky, and Herzl." The first Arab member joined in 1924, and in 1925 there were eight. The party invested in their ideological socialization, and in 1927, it sent four Arab members to receive political training in the Soviet Union.[10] It was only after the al-Buraq uprising (known also as the 1929 riots), however, and under heavy pressure of the Comintern, that Arabization of the party's demography became a major official goal.[11] In spring 1930, about twenty out of the approximately one hundred party members in the country were Arab, and six or seven more Arab members were studying at the Communist University of the Toilers of the East in Moscow. In mid-1931, about fifty out of its approximately three hundred members were Arabs. Following British persecution and a financial crisis, the total cadre shrunk, and in summer 1932, there were only twenty-five Arab members. An intensive recruitment effort doubled the number of Arab members by the end of the year.[12] In 1934, the party appointed its first Arab secretary, Ridwan al-Hilu.

COMMUNISM IN NAZARETH

The first documented communist activity in Nazareth dates back to 1932, and its context was the efforts of the PCP to Arabize its ranks. At the time, the PCP leadership believed that a communist revolution in the country was imminent.[13] It aspired to sparking the revolution, and the Arabization efforts were compatible with both the Comintern universalist policy and the anticolonial sentiments of the local Arab population. As part of the recruitment efforts, the Haifa branch was assigned to establish several subbranches, including in Nazareth.

In 1932, the party leadership secretly sent two of its activists, Jacob Herzenstein and Tanhum Tulchinsky, to the Galilee to recruit Arab activists.[14] Herzenstein, who was under the surveillance of both the British police and the Haganah intelligence, arrived at Nazareth disguised as a local Arab and tried to recruit members. There is no evidence of any success of his effort. At approximately the same time, a communist cell was established in Nazareth by eight local miners who were recruited by the Jewish activist Yehush'a Shnitzer while he resided in nearby 'Afula. This cell, however, did not survive after Shnitzer moved to Tel Aviv.[15]

The turning point was the Great Revolt, which erupted in 1936. For three years, Arabs in Mandatory Palestine rebelled against the British administration, demanding Arab independence and the end of Jewish immigration and land purchases. The active involvement of the PCP in the revolt contributed to the party's credibility and popularity among Arab Palestinians. Although Nazareth played only a minor role in the uprising, contributing a small number of rebel commanders,[16] one of them, Fu'ad Nassar (1914–1976), was especially important in connecting the anticolonial struggle to labor mobilization and communism.[17] Nassar was arrested at the beginning of the revolt and spent six months in the Acre prison, where he was radicalized by Jewish communist jail mates. After his release, Nassar joined the rebels in the Hebron and Jerusalem areas.[18] He left Palestine toward the end of the revolt, was jailed in Iraq, and returned to Nazareth in January 1943. On his return to the city, he played a significant role in mobilizing the labor movement by establishing a Marxist study circle, which provided a crucial base for many of the activists involved in the labor movement.[19] For this purpose, he used the bookstore of a Catholic priest, his brother Sam'an, to which he ordered Marxist scholarship.

Both the Great Revolt and emerging Marxist presence in the city affected the young Zayyad. Later in his life, he would act as a curator of the popular memory and poetry of the revolt, and the mythology constructed around Zayyad consistently emphasizes his early involvement in the national struggle. Majali describes his father, Amin Zayyad, as one of the rebels, though we have no information about the extent of his involvement. During the revolt, British troops entered Nazareth several times in search of weapons and wanted individuals. As an adult, Zayyad would recall that his first encounter with British troops was when they raided his family's house. Amin Zayyad denied having any weapons, but the officer interrogated Tawfiq, who knew where the gun was hidden. They tried to convince him gently, then to bribe him, and then to threaten him with detention and beatings, but Tawfiq rebuffed each advance.[20] Tawfiq's father was nonetheless arrested, and Tawfiq's mother sent him daily to take food to his father at the detention center in the city.[21]

Another central childhood memory of British forces that Zayyad publicly spoke about several times relates to an incident he dated to the late 1930s. Then around ten years old, he went with his classmates to watch British police playing tennis on a court adjacent to their school. "Well, we wanted to look at the British female officers, so we said to each other [let's go watch] 'tennis,'" Zayyad smiled in a 1992 interview.[22] When the players lost a ball, they accused Zayyad and his classmates of hiding it, and then beat and detained the children. Zayyad referred to this incident as his first prison experience.[23]

While the direct encounter with British occupation left a big impression on Zayyad, school became a more consistent site of political socialization. During the Great Revolt, high school students organized demonstrations, and children Zayyad's age threw bitter-vetch kernels under the British horses to make them slip on the asphalt.[24] Majali ascribes much of young Zayyad's political socialization to three of his teachers, all of them graduates of the Arab College in Jerusalem: Rushdi Shahin (1920–1997) from Nablus, who was among the founders of the National League for Liberation (NLL) and a member of its Central Committee; Fu'ad Khuri (1919–1968) from Yafat al-Nasira, who was active in the Association of Arab Teachers and joined the National League for Liberation in 1945; and Jamal Sakran from Rayna (birth and death dates unknown).[25]

The poet Hanna Abu Hanna (born in 1928), who studied in Nazareth from 1934 to 1943, also mentioned the same teachers as influential and credited them with inspiring national sentiments in his generation. However, Majali and Abu Hanna give slightly different descriptions of the pedagogical orientation of the three. Majali emphasizes both their patriotism and their communism. According to Majali, the three introduced their students to the communist newspaper *al-Ittihad* (published from 1944 and still in publication) and the communist journal *al-Mihmaz* (published 1945–1947). Abu Hanna, however, mentioned only their patriotic education, especially through the poetry of nationalist poets like Ibrahim Tuqan. This difference might reflect the different political biographies of Zayyad, Abu Hanna, and Majali. Majali, born in 1952 in Nazareth, is the youngest among the three, and like Zayyad, he has never denounced the Communist Party. Abu Hanna left Nazareth in 1943, before the major developments that made the city a bastion of communist activity and trade unionism in the mid-1940s. In the 1990s, Abu Hanna left the Communist Party and joined the National Democratic Assembly, which emphasized Arab national identity.

The political socialization of Zayyad and his generation was affected as well by global developments. With the outbreak of World War II came the expansion of war-related industries, and the size of the Arab workforce in the country increased tremendously, which led to a significant development in trade unionism among Arabs in Palestine.[26] Most Nazarenes employed in a war-related industry went to Haifa, where they worked in oil refineries, Palestine Railways workshops, and army installations.[27] These economic developments contributed to the workers' development of class consciousness, which "was informed by an understanding of one's class, a suspicion of the colonial authority, and an aspiration for workers' solidarity."[28] Although Nazareth was a relatively small city in Mandate-era Palestine, it became the center of a strong labor movement in the 1940s, highly involved in both the countrywide labor movement and Palestinian national politics.[29]

In October 1942, communist activists in Nazareth established a trade union, the Arab Workers' Society–Nazareth (which would later change its name to the Arab Workers Congress in Nazareth [AWCN—Mu'tamar al-'Ummal al-'Arabi— al-Nasira]).[30] In May 1943, the PCP split approximately along ethnonational lines, and shortly after, the Arab members who had withdrawn from the party established the National League for Liberation (NLL). In Nazareth the AWCN activists established the local branch of the NLL.

As historian Joel Beinin writes, working-class activists created a self-conscious alliance with the young intelligentsia, particularly urban Christians, to form the NLL, since both groups were marginal to the traditional political system and did not belong to powerful landed families.[31] Although the NLL was established by former members of the PCP, the absence of Jewish members enabled them to emphasize the group's Arab-Palestinian nationalist orientation, and the declarative NLL program, published February 1, 1944, did not include any reference to the principles of socialism or revolution.[32] Nevertheless, in future publications, the Marxist ideals were not absent, and the potential tension between communist ideals and nationalist goals played out across the pages of *al-Ittihad*, the NNL organ. Many of the dilemmas that the NLL was engaged with were similar to those that other communist movements, acting in colonial settings, faced during times of war and conflict,[33] and *al-Ittihad* discussed these dilemmas, suggesting unambiguous solutions. On October 1, 1944, for example, it published an article titled "Communism and Nationalism [*qawmiyya*]" by Khalid Bakdash, the influential leader of the Syrian Communist Party, whom many Palestinian communists considered to be an ideological authority.[34] Bakdash's position is clear: the internationalist dimension of communism was expressed in the principle of equal rights for all nations and in the mutual solidarity of oppressed people.[35]

In Nazareth, there was significant overlap between the leadership of the Marxist AWCN and the NLL.[36] Fu'ad Nassar, for example, served simultaneously as the secretary of the AWCN, the editor of *al-Ittihad*, and a member of the Central Committee of the NLL. This was the climate in which Zayyad's political consciousness took shape. During these years, he could frequently be found at Sam'an Nassar's bookstore, reading literature and books on politics and science.[37] According to Majali, one of his favorite books at the time was the Arabic translation of *Physics of Entertainment*, a physics textbook by the Jewish Russian science writer Yacov Perlman. Zayyad could not afford to buy books, but Sam'an Nassar was so impressed by his dedication that he offered Zayyad free access to his shelves. Though Zayyad may have been too young to attend Fu'ad Nassar's Marxist study circle, which convened at the bookshop, it is likely that he was at least influenced by it. Mun'im Jarjura, with whom Zayyad would later work closely, was one of the regular attendees of the reading circle.[38] In 1981, Zayyad told a journalist that he started to read Marx when he was seventeen or eighteen. At that same age, he started working in construction (as a painter) and in agriculture, and his memories from that period allude to the hardship of the working experience: "Many nails stuck in my feet in the British military bases in Haifa," he said.[39] Among the communist leadership in Mandatory Palestine, and later in Israel, this authentic proletariat background was not the rule but the exception. While Arab communists gained support from the urban working class, the leadership was mostly populated by the relatively affluent and disproportionally Christian, educated strata.

SECULARISM

While the guardians of Zayyad's public remembrance explicitly discuss his relation to the national anticolonial struggle and communism, the role of secularism in his life is more elusive and has not been openly identified. More generally, this reflects a broader trend in the historiography of Palestine. Whereas secularism in Palestine has gained limited attention among scholars and writers, nationalism and communism in Palestine have been studied extensively, and therefore Tawfiq Zayyad's communist and patriotic stands are easily understood as embedded in broader social developments. Majali, for example, mentions briefly that Zayyad was "not religious," as if it was an arbitrary personal choice. In this book, I argue that Zayyad's secular politics and lifestyle were just as embedded in broader social and cultural developments as his communism and nationalism.

During the late nineteenth and early twentieth centuries, a new discursive grammar related to religion emerged in the Arab Middle East. While the normative implications, the extent to which this was a drastic break from the past, as well as the historical genealogy of this process are controversial, there is little doubt that various Arab intellectuals, mainly in the Levant, called to limit the political power of religion and that some Arab nationalists rejected it as a basis for political solidarity.[40] These intellectuals identified the restriction of religious authority with modernization and as a major marker of social progress. Toward the end of the nineteenth century, the common Arabic term for secularism, *'almaniyya* or *'ilmaniyya*, was coined as a translation of the French term *laïcité*, the separation of religion from politics.[41]

The emergence of this new discursive order in Palestinian cities has not been well studied. In many of the studies of Ottoman or British Mandate Palestine, the adjective *secular* is used in reference to institutions, processes, or individuals—for example, *secular schools*,[42] *secular education, secular party*,[43] *secular thinker*,[44] and *secular nationalism*.[45] Such terms indicate an implicit understanding that a broader social, cultural, and political process related to the place of religion in social life was underway in Palestine at the time, but rarely do the studies delve into what that process was.

Most scholars of secularism distinguish between personal secularity, which in the ideal form means the absence of personal religious beliefs, and institutional-public secularity, which means religion lacks a political role.[46] Regarding the first meaning, the movement toward secularity in the private case of Zayyad's family is evident. Majali depicts Tawfiq's father as a religious person who could recite the Quran by heart, and despite his modest background and education, people in his community informally sought his opinion on religious matters. According to Majali, Amin Zayyad rejected religious extremism and believed that Islam is a religion of tolerance. In the value they accorded to tolerance, argues Majali, Tawfiq Zayyad and his father resembled each other and differed significantly from religious extremists.[47] Writing in 1994, Majali clearly attempts to distance Amin Zayyad's religiosity from contemporary Islamic movements, and his rhetoric is a direct reflection of the growing tension between the communists and the Islamic movement in the 1990s. It is possible as well that the emphasis on the strict adherence to Islam ascribed to Amin Zayyad is part of the communists' attempt to gain legitimacy among the more traditional parts of their potential constituency in the 1990s. However, a press report in Hebrew from 1958, long before the appearance of the Islamic movement, similarly refers to Amin as a "pious Muslim" and mentions the religiosity gap between him and his sons.[48] Tawfiq Zayyad's family members confirmed the difference between Tawfiq and his father regarding religion, but they emphasized Amin's tolerance by noting that Tawfiq would drink alcohol in the presence of his father. Thus, it is quite certain that Tawfiq Zayyad's lifestyle differed from his father's, though it does not appear to have created a schism between the two. Zayyad's friend As'ad Kanana from

Yafat al-Nasira similarly abandoned his father's religion for communism (and later became the first communist to chair a local council in the country).[49]

Did the two friends' distance from religious practice represent a broader phenomenon? As Talal Asad has argued, because the secular is so much a part of our modern life, it is best pursued through its shadows.[50] An important shadow in this context is the establishment of the Muslim Brotherhood in Egypt in 1928 and its regional spread in response to the erosion of the status of religion. The movement's founder, Hasan al-Banna, protested the decline of religion in the public sphere: "Wine-shops are found on the roads of the cities. Drinking is freely propagated. Passion-arousing paintings on huge boards for publicizing wines [...] These activities are prohibited by our religion [...] in the strongest language."[51] During the Great Revolt in the 1930s, the Muslim Brotherhood sent volunteers to Palestine to support the uprising, and in the early 1940s, branches of the movement were opened in Palestine, evidence of the relevance of their message in the local context.

As a decline in the political and institutional role of religion, secularization in Palestine is a documented phenomenon that can be traced back to the emergence of secular educational institutions that were unaffiliated with any religious organization in the late nineteenth century. These institutions provided education at least partly aimed at preparing students for the economic market or developing ethnonational identity rather than religious socialization. In Jerusalem in 1909, Khalil Sakakini opened al-Madrasa al-Dusturiyya, the first secular school designed for Arab Muslim and Christian students.[52] Sakakini was highly influenced by the atheist and secularist Syrian intellectual Shibli Shumayyil (1850–1917),[53] who preached for excluding religious studies from public schools.[54]

Sakakini's sentiments of Arab national identity were conditioned on keeping it religiously neutral, as he wrote in 1915: "If nationalism means to love life—then I am a nationalist. But if it means to prefer one religion over the other, one language over the other, one city over the other, and one interest over the other—then I am not a nationalist, and that is all."[55] After World War I, several Palestinian newspapers became proponents of Arab nationalism, the most notable among them *Filastin* in Jaffa and *al-Karmil* in Haifa. As champions of this emerging political identity, they did not abandon religion as a source of inspiration and a reservoir of politically effective symbols, but they rejected it as a source of moral authority in the political realm.

Talal Asad observed, "The basic thrust of Arab nationalist ideology is of course supra-denominational [...] In brief, 'religion' is what secular Arabism specifies and tries to set in its proper social place."[56] For both Muslim and Christian Arab nationalists, Islamic history has played a major role in defining identity and collective memory; Christian symbols have also been part of the discursive canon, especially among the Palestinian elite. Intellectuals in Palestine frequently have drawn on mythology across religions. The Christian-owned newspaper *al-Karmil*, for example, celebrated the birth of the prophet (*mawlid al-nabi*) by portraying him as an Arab hero rather than the messenger of God and founder of Islam, and the paper's editor saw no contradiction in celebrating the prophet's birth under an advertisement for Amstel beer.[57]

According to Asad, this discourse of "Arabian prophet" was not unique to Arab nationalists in Palestine, and it was an inversion of the classical theological view according to which the Prophet is not the object of national inspiration but the subject of divine inspiration.[58] Similarly, in 1930, both Christian- and Muslim-owned newspapers used the metaphor of crucifixion to refer to the British execution of Palestinians.[59] This "deconfessionalization" and nationalization of religious mythology reflected a growing cross-confessional anticolonial alliance, which also had some concrete institutional expressions, such as the Muslim-Christian Associations (MCA), formed as a response to the Balfour Declaration.

At the time, this political secularism in Palestine had a narrow meaning, still far from denying religion any political role. Its proponents aspired to marginalize religion as a basis for political solidarity, but at least *Filastin* and *al-Karmil* did not aspire to deprive religion of any public status. For example, although many of the Palestinian elite regarded the founder of modern Turkey, Mustafa Kemal, as a hero who defied European colonialism, his political program of eliminating the institutional power of religion was much less welcomed. The abolishment of the caliphate triggered widespread dismay throughout the Arab and the Muslim world, including in the Palestinian press. Both *Filastin* and *al-Karmil*, the two Christian-owned publications, protested the abolishment of the Ottoman caliphate. *Al-Karmil*'s editorial expressed the opinion that "it is the interest of the East to be supported by the wise clerics and the enlightened persons worldwide. If not, it is to seek the installation of religious authorities in a satisfactory manner—before the spread of intellectual chaos."[60] *Al-Karmil* went on to suggest convening an interconfessional Muslim-Christian-Jewish conference to discuss the new circumstances. Frequently, *Filastin* and *al-Karmil* attributed the abolishment of the caliphate to foreign influence and intervention, with communists and Jews as the major suspects. *Filastin* explicitly ascribed it to hidden socialist-communist-Jewish forces.

The Jews, *Filastin* argued, have always been interested in separating religion from politics in order to gain equal rights. Relying on the forged Protocols of the Elders of Zion, *Filastin* identified a Jewish hand in every major revolution, including the recent abolishment of the caliphate.[61]

It is noteworthy that Palestinian demands to reinstate the caliphate had instrumental aspects. It was partly motivated by the aspiration to crown the Hashemite Sharif Husayn as caliph, hoping by that to enhance Arab national demands over Palestine and challenge the Balfour Declaration.[62] It might have related as well to lingering Ottoman loyalty after the collapse of the empire.[63] However, even if instrumental, the demand shows that although these newspapers aspired to build a supraconfessional political solidarity in Palestine, they nevertheless were not interested in disconnecting politics from religion. This tendency had a terminological expression. Proponents of Arab secularism adopted in the late nineteenth century the term *'almaniyya* or *'ilmaniyya*, as a translation of the French term *laïcité*, which means the separation of religion from politics,[64] and they avoided using the term *ladiniyya*, meaning nonreligious, so as not to antagonize Muslim believers.[65] *Filastin* and *al-Karmil*, however, preferred the term *ladiniyya*[66] and its negative connotations, signaling a certain distance from the outright secularist intellectuals in other parts of the Levant.

The communists suggested a different and a much more radical form of secularism than the very soft version that Arab intellectuals like Khalil Sakakini, Najib Nassar (founder and editor of *al-Karmil*), and 'Isa al-'Isa (founder and editor of *Filastin*) advocated. The radicalism of the communist version is anchored in its aspiration to replace religion with an alternative secular theology. Before the Arabization of the party in the 1930s, communist activists not only sought to remove religion from politics but also were explicit that recruits were expected to abandon any personal practice of religion.

Najati Sidqi, who joined the PCP in 1925, was one of the first Arab Palestinians sent to study at the Communist University of the Toilers of the East in Moscow. In his memoirs, he describes the heavy pressure to abandon religion:

> One of the Palestinian students did not forget to bring with him from Jaffa his prayer rug. He was caught "red-handed" and was brought to a "self-criticism" trial. He argued a lot and defended himself, claiming that Islam is the religion of socialism and that praying is a spiritual exercise that does not contradict the idea of getting rid of exploitation and colonialism. The folks were lenient with

him because he was a beginner student and one of the teachers was assigned to explain to him the history of the emergence of the religions.[67]

In 1974, Ridwan al-Hilu, the first Arab secretary of the PCP, explained that the party was not against religion; its criticism of religion was directed instead toward the religious establishment and the mufti Haj Amin al-Husseini. However, in the same statement, he acknowledged the antireligious environment of the university in Moscow: "I remember that during the cell meetings that took place on the beach in Jaffa, I was going aside to pray and I kept doing that until I traveled to Moscow in 1930."[68] While in Palestine the PCP tolerated prayer, the Soviet indoctrination contributed to legitimizing the abandonment of religious practice. After returning from Moscow, al-Hilu lived for a period with his Jewish girlfriend, Simha Tsabari, in an apartment in Tel Aviv,[69] perhaps another indication of his distancing himself from practicing religion. These stories of gradual secularization echo Zayyad's abandonment of his father's religion.

The public position of the party in Palestine, though, was far from hostile to religion. In its early years, the party adopted a neutral stance toward personal religiosity and religious traditions; it did not attack these traditions, but neither did it attempt to harness their symbolic power for its purposes. As Arab participation grew, however, the party's approach to religion gradually became more sympathetic, and in its Arabic pamphlets in the 1930s, the party referenced the Quran and Islamic literature.[70] This sympathy became more obvious after the 1943 split. Unlike the Jewish PCP, the Arab NLL reaffirmed Islam as a positive component of the national movement. One of the movement's publications, *al-Ghad*, was careful to present itself as part of the continuous cultural tradition of Islam. *Al-Ghad* found in Islamic tradition and history an early tradition of socialism and a history of struggle against foreign oppression and for national independence.[71] In other words, the newspaper shaped Islamic tradition to fit the NLL political ideology. Similarly, it was important for *al-Ittihad* to emphasize that the Soviet Union was not antireligion.[72]

Because the production of Zayyad's historical memory has focused on his role in the national struggle and neglected other aspects of his adolescent years, we have few tools to evaluate the impact of these sociohistorical developments on him. Nevertheless, we know that his favorite author at the time was Abu al-'Ala' al-Ma'arri (973–1057), a philosopher, poet, and writer who was accused of heresy because of his questioning of religious dogma and his refusal to accept one religion's monopoly on truth. Al-Ma'ari was critical of clergymen who disrespected people's minds and manipulated them.[73] He was not an atheist, but he regarded Islam, like any other religion, as a human institution. As such, he believed it was false and rotten to the core because its founders sought to procure wealth and power for themselves.[74] His work was rediscovered by Arab intellectuals in the late nineteenth century, and his rationalist critique of religion influenced modernist Arabic writers and poets.[75] Because of al-Ma'arri's social justice advocacy and denunciation of dogmatism in religion, his work had a special resonance among Marxists. It is not surprising, therefore, that it was available at the Marxist collection Fu'ad Nassar established in his brother's bookstore in Nazareth. In high school, Zayyad borrowed al-Ma'arri's *Risalat al-Ghufran* (*The Epistle of Forgiveness*) from Sam'an Nassar's bookstore and copied it word for word.[76] We know also that later in his life, Zayyad did not observe religious practice, married a Christian woman, did not raise his children as religious Muslims, and that in the last years of his life, led a confrontational approach toward the Islamic Movement and its attempt to impose its interpretation of Islam on Arab politics in Israel. It is likely that these choices were shaped in part by the secularizing spirit of Zayyad's environment as an adolescent.

NAKBA

During the last years of the Mandate period, Nazareth was becoming a center of mobilization for leftist forces.[77] By 1946, Tawfiq Zayyad had already taken part in high school students' demonstrations against British rule and Zionism, and according to some accounts, he even led them.[78] In December 1947, after the UN General Assembly approved a plan to divide Palestine into Jewish and Arab states, the NLL Central Committee met in Nazareth to discuss the partition plan.[79] With the Soviets in support of the plan and the Palestinian leadership and leaders of other Arab countries almost unanimously opposed, the NLL was deeply divided on the issue, and the meeting was tense. Among the notable supporters of the plan were prominent figures of the Nazareth NLL branch who had greatly influenced Zayyad, including Fu'ad Nassar, Emile Habibi, and Tawfiq Tubi.[80] Zayyad's former teacher Rushdi Shahin also voted in favor of the plan.[81]

About his own position, Zayyad said in an interview in October 1976, "Although I was a young, inexperienced communist without special political consciousness, I accepted this because it could really solve the Palestinian problem and prevent negative developments, which we have witnessed since 1948. Developments since

1948 have proved that the communists were correct. What we accepted in 1948 and the other recognized leadership rejected, now all Palestinian People are struggling for: an independent Palestinian state."[82]

In the war that erupted following the UN decision, Israel occupied territories beyond the area allocated to the Jewish state by the UN, uprooted 750,000 Palestinians, and depopulated hundreds of villages. Commonly, the occupying forces would gather the young men for interrogation and sometimes deportation or even execution, as happened on July 16, 1948, in 'Aylut, a village near Nazareth. Later that day, the Haganah forces, the main paramilitary Jewish force at the time, occupied Nazareth as well. Tawfiq's brother, Musbah, who was nine years old at the time, remembers that when the soldiers arrived near their house in Nazareth, his mother, anxious about the news from 'Aylut, asked nineteen-year-old Tawfiq to bend his knees so the soldiers would not identify him as a grown-up man.

In the end, Tawfiq Zayyad and the other men of Nazareth were more protected than their neighbors: Nazareth was the only city in the Galilee that was not massively depopulated throughout the course of the war. The Jewish Canadian officer who commanded the Seventh Brigade that captured the city, Ben Dunkelman, disobeyed the order of his commander, Haim Laskov, to evacuate the city's population.[83] Dunkelman's defiance forced Laskov to ask for approval of the expulsion from a higher authority. However, Israeli Prime Minister David Ben-Gurion vetoed the order, probably due to the city's religious significance to the Christian world.[84] Another possible reason for the nonexpulsion of Nazareth's residents may have been the firm stance of the mayor, Yusuf al-Fahum, who called on residents to stay in their homes and not be scared of rumors of mass rape elsewhere in the region.[85]

During the war, about one-fifth of the city's population of sixteen thousand became refugees—a much smaller ratio than any other Palestinian city that fell under Israeli rule—while a much larger number of refugees poured into the city from nearby villages and other northern cities. Following the war, Nazareth was home to the largest concentration of Arab Palestinians within the armistice line (known also as the Green Line) and turned into a major site for political activism. For this reason, Israeli authorities came to regard Nazareth as a substantial security threat and a city to keep under close surveillance.[86]

At the end of the war, about one-quarter of the city's twenty thousand residents were refugees from other localities,[87] and many did not have an Israeli identification card since they were not in their homes when the State of Israel took its first census in November 1948. The state subsequently targeted these "internal refugees" for expulsion beyond the armistice lines,[88] and several waves of expulsion campaigns took place in Nazareth after the war.[89] Most of the internal refugees who were candidates for expulsion resided in Nazareth's Eastern Neighborhood, where Tawfiq Zayyad lived. In a 1988 interview, Zayyad said he could "still see the images of pregnant mothers taken on trucks to be thrown beyond the border, and men and children as well. I can still see the images of groups of people throwing themselves in front of the trucks carrying the expellees to stop them from leaving."[90] Large protests and a general strike organized by communist activists might have reduced the scale of expulsion.[91]

The collapse of Palestinian society and economy and the major demographic shift in the country in the aftermath of the Nakba had far-reaching implications on Arab Palestinian communism. In October 1948, the NLL activists who remained within the armistice line remerged with the PCP to establish the Israeli Communist Party (ICP). In Nazareth, the AWCN became an organ of the ICP. From that point on, Palestinian communists in Israel would have to follow a narrow path between resisting the military regime and remaining within the boundaries of legality and legitimacy, as well as between their revolutionary ideology and the mundane urgent needs of their constituency.

One early example of this tension was related to the dire need for employment in Nazareth. Even before the war ended, the Israeli government opened labor exchange offices throughout the country where the unemployed would register to receive public jobs. In Nazareth, the AWCN established a labor exchange, which was recognized and partly funded by the Israeli government. At the same time, in areas of the country where mass expulsions took place, the newly established Israeli authorities faced a shortage of labor for some urgent needs, such as collecting the harvest from lands whose owners had become refugees. For the AWCN, this was an opportunity to provide temporary employment for workers from Nazareth, eight hundred of whom were recruited by the military government through the AWCN-run labor exchange[92] for work in the Lydda and Ramla region.[93] Tawfiq Zayyad and some other communist activists were among them.[94]

How did Zayyad and his the communist activists feel about being forced to make a living by working for the Israeli authorities while literally replacing Palestinian refugees? While we cannot answer this question directly, we do know that they tried to protest. Their political activism among the Ramla workers, their open use of communist slogans, and their call for the return of the refugees concerned the military government.[95] Presumably the alcohol they introduced to the work camp provoked some of the other workers.[96] The military government eventually decided to send all workers from Nazareth back home.

The Ramla incident encapsulates the tension in the ICP activity under the military government. Navigating between mundane urgent needs and dreams about freedom and equality frequently led to painful compromises that maintained the appearance of a certain "order." As we will see in the next chapter, Tawfiq Zayyad was frequently there to disrupt this order.

Chapter 2

STEADFASTNESS

WHEREAS PRIOR TO 1948, ZAYYAD WAS PART OF AN ESTABLISHED majority in Palestine that struggled against the Zionist movement, after the war, when Zionist forces expelled approximately 750,000 Palestinians from their homes to beyond the armistice lines, the 156,000 Palestinians who remained behind experienced a drastic and sudden devaluation of their status. Officially they became citizens of the new state, but as historian Shira Robinson has pointed out, in the first years of the state's existence, citizenship became a "category of exclusion" that enabled Israel to legalize Palestinian expulsion and prevent Palestinian return.[1] In other words, the citizenship of those who remained was a tool in denying the return of those who were expelled. The former became a subjugated minority within the newly created State of Israel and until 1966 lived under strict military rule that dictated many aspects of their lives.

According to the UN partition plan, Nazareth was supposed to be included in the territory of the Arab state, but Israel occupied the city during the war and later annexed it entirely. The local members of National Liberation League, including Zayyad, became a member of the Israeli Communist Party (ICP), which in those years was the only organization that could legally and publicly mobilize political resistance among Arab citizens under military rule. The ICP recognized Israel as the national homeland of the Jewish-Israeli People (not necessarily as the homeland of every Jew) and therefore was tolerated, even if the military government made many efforts to minimize its power. Although its leadership was mostly and overproportionally Jewish, the party attracted Arab Palestinian support because it was a legal political party represented in the Knesset (it gained four seats in the first elections, held in 1949) yet strongly defended Arab rights. The party demanded the return of Palestinian refugees and opposed dominant Israeli positions in both foreign and domestic affairs. In addition, because most of the Palestine political, economic, and intellectual elites were exiled, the Palestinian communists constituted a rare continuity with Palestinian leadership from before 1948. Hence, although the communists were a marginal political group among Palestinians under British rule, they gained a leadership position among the Palestinians who remained in Israel following the establishment of the State of Israel.

The Communist Party was the major engine for mobilizing resistance, and its fuel was poetry. Revolutionary and anticolonial movements have a long tradition of political poetry.[2] The rhythm, the conciseness, and the strong emotive orientation have made poetry a genre suitable for political mobilization. The work of Zayyad and other Palestinian writers belonged simultaneously to two major artistic currents: in its diction, imagery, and form, they were part of modern Arabic poetry, and especially Palestinian classic and romantic poetry of the 1930s and 1940s.[3] At the same time, they adopted social realism as a literary stand.[4] They were influenced by communist authors and poets such as the founding father of socialist realist literature, Maxim Gorky, as well as his followers, the poets Vladimir Mayakovsky, Nazim Hikmet, Pablo Neruda, and Louis Aragon, among others.[5] As historian Maha Nassar has indicated, Zayyad and other poets affiliated with the party "emphasized a leftist, anticolonial discourse that sought to link Palestinians in Israel to a rich and dynamic Arab literary and political heritage, as well as to contemporary populist mobilizations in the region and the world."[6]

Indeed, Palestinian poets under the military government were major public intellectuals, producing and disseminating political ideas.[7] Zayyd himself objected to the idea that poetry is like a mirror that reflects life, because, as he put it, "a mirror does not create even a single job," and he frequently referred to poetry as a "weapon."[8] Accordingly, his poetry was rarely personal and almost always related to his political action. Because the raison d'être of his poetry was the political mobilization of the masses, his style and vocabulary were accessible, and it is evident that he wrote his poems bearing in mind that he would recite them on stage.[9] Similarly, the need to mobilize action is reflected in the bright, optimistic endings that characterized Zayyad's poetry.[10]

Literary critics agree that in his poetry written in the early and mid-1950s, Zayyad sacrificed artistic quality for the instrumental purpose of reaching the masses, and some commented that his poems from that period lack poetic maturity.[11] Nevertheless, this poetry is crucial for understanding the two major dimensions of Zayyad's political activism in the 1950s and 1960s: class-based struggle with a cosmopolitan orientation and a struggle for the particular rights of the Arab Palestinian People. These two dimensions do not contradict each other, but their relative weight changed following Zayyad's personal experience, as well as broader political developments.

LABOR STRUGGLES

Zayyad's early political activism was as a member of the Arab Workers Congress in Nazareth (AWCN), which was established in the mid 1940s[12] and then renewed its organization of workers shortly after the city's occupation in 1948. Zayyad's activism was based on his class identity, developed as he was growing up in a poor family and unemployed in the first years after the war. As an emerging leader in the party cadre from the mid-1950s, he received a modest salary, which was sufficient for him as a single man. Still, his city was in a dire condition. Throughout the military government period, Nazareth suffered from a high rate of unemployment as a result of government-imposed travel restrictions, policies prioritizing Jewish employment, and the general economic hardship that Israel experienced during the early years of its existence. In Nazareth, this problem was aggravated by the large number of unemployed refugees who had found shelter in Nazareth during the war and could no longer work in their former area of employment.[13] Labor issues and job shortages therefore were major concerns in the city. Zayyad himself was unemployed after the war and took part in demonstrations and organized struggles for work. In one of them in 1949, he was arrested by Israeli authorities for the first time and detained for a week.[14]

On the morning of February 22, 1950, a large group of workers seeking jobs (four hundred according to the ICP mouthpiece *Kol ha-'Am*, fifty according the police) gathered in front of the Labor Exchange office to protest the dire economic situation.[15] From there, the demonstrators marched through the market to the military governor's office, where they clashed with the police. Reports on who started the violence obviously differ, but eventually the police opened fire, injuring two demonstrators and arrested five of the leaders, including Tawfiq Zayyad. Six days later, the five detainees were tried before a military court—the first military trial of civilians since the state was established. They were convicted of "impeding people who were busy in a vital task from fulfilling their job," and each was sentenced to seven days in prison, including time served.[16] In 1952, Zayyad became the secretary of the Nazareth AWCN branch,[17] and in the same year he was arrested again, this time for three weeks, for posting illegal notices.[18]

Organizing the workers for collective action under military rule was a difficult task, and leaders had to be creative. According to popular lore, one day Zayyad and his AWCN colleagues spread a false rumor that a contractor from Tel Aviv was coming to the square near the Labor Exchange office in order to hire workers. When hundreds of unemployed men arrived at the square, they instead heard a speech by the AWCN chair, Mun'im Jarjura, who mobilized them for struggle. The demonstration then proceeded to the city hall, where they heard Tawfiq Zayyad's speech. According to Nazir Majali, Zayyad told them that whoever wanted a job should not wait for God's grace but fight for it.[19]

The combination of class struggle and anticolonialism made Zayyad attentive to similar struggles in the region, such as the one taking place in Iran. In March 1951, Iranian authorities had decided to nationalize the oil industry, and in early April, the Iranian Communist Party (Tudeh) led strikes and riots protesting delays in its nationalization, as well as the industry's low wages and poor housing. In the riots that took place on April 12 in Abadan, the police opened fire, killing six demonstrators.[20] *Al-Ittihad* reported these events with much sympathy to the strikers. In June, Zayyad wrote "'Abadan," a poem full of revolutionary pathos:

Abadan! Do not be scared of their bullets' roar,
Do not celebrate the death on the field.
You are stronger than the crowds of their armies,
And you are more protected from the blaze of their tyranny.[21]

In October, when a delegation of Iranian communist youth visited Nazareth, Zayyad recited parts of this poem at the official reception.[22]

Zayyad was active in the AWCN until the early 1960s and during that time, he published multiple articles in *al-Ittihad* about the conditions of workers in Israel, especially Arab workers. Poverty and class struggle have an important place in Zayyad's poems during that period. In a 1988 interview, he reflected on these aspects of his poetry: "Not for even one moment has what I wrote ever been detached from the political and ideological struggle—the struggle of common people against political, social, and class oppression, and for the victory of the fundamental human values and principles. My first dream since I became aware was, and still is, that bread would be provided for any hungry mouth, a warm home for every human being, a flower for every hand, and joy for every human society."[23] This attitude is reflected in Zayyad's "Where Are Our Payments Going?" (later known as "Taxes"), a poem first published in September 1954 in *al-Jadid*, the ICP's literary bulletin. In the early 1950s, the burden of taxes was a source of continuous frustration among Palestinian citizens, and protests against taxes and discriminatory tax policy were common.[24] Protesting taxes was more than a class issue; it was closely related to the protest against national oppression. Nevertheless, the poem articulated the rage over national oppression in the materialist vocabulary of class struggle:

> Taxes, left and right
> All kinds of taxes
> Stealing the last penny in the pocket
> Leaving our children hungry.
> Our children roam in the midst of the garbage piles,
> Gathering the leftovers of the wealthy's meals.
> Their children shine like dolls,
> Balls of fat, and no bones.
> They do not talk, or laugh,
> But they always eat.
> They grow inside their coops like chicken.

In his protest against injustice, Zayyad did not refrain from including an explicit atheist message:

> And where would the money come from?
> And these heavens, despite the plea
> And despite the prayer day and night
> Refused to provide, even a bit of
> The redeeming gold.[25]

Zayyad's activism in the field of labor struggles and his politically committed poetry in the early 1950s were precursors for his decades-long involvement in municipal politics. When "Taxes" was published in fall 1954, he was a newly elected member of the Nazareth municipal council and turned this seemingly modest position into a stage of protest against the military government.

THE STRUGGLE OVER THE CITY COUNCIL

On April 12, 1954, ICP supporters in Nazareth stayed up all night celebrating their success in the municipal elections with dancing and singing.[26] For several years, Israeli authorities had delayed local elections in an attempt to prevent the communists from gaining a foothold in the municipal council.[27] After the war, they allowed Yusuf al-Fahum, the pro-British mayor who was elected in 1946 in a controversial election, to remain in his position.[28] Facing an economic crisis and a general strike in the city organized by the communists, al-Fahum and the entire municipal council resigned in July 1953, and the Interior Ministry appointed a temporary acting mayor, Moshe Ruah.

Facing public pressure and concerns about the image of Israel abroad, the Israeli government reluctantly allowed elections to proceed in 1954.[29] Although the military government and the Interior Ministry heavily intervened in the election process in order to minimize the ICP's power,[30] the party still became the largest municipal faction, winning six of fifteen seats on the city council. Zayyad was among those elected to serve on the council, an important milestone in his career in local politics. Even at this early stage, he was merging local politics with broader struggles for civic equality and collective rights.

Only three years earlier, the Nazareth branch of the ICP had been in crisis. Personal conflicts between the branch secretary, Saliba Khamis, and two other senior members, Mun'im Jarjura and Fu'ad Khuri, which had lasted for many months, hindered the branch's activity. In addition, in the election to the second Knesset in July 1951, the party had lost a significant number of votes in the city compared with the previous elections. Nazareth was crucial for the ICP. Not only was it home to the largest concentration of the Arab population inside Israel, the local branch also led the Nazareth District (which included the city of Nazareth and the other localities in the Galilee), where most of the party members resided,[31] and it was responsible for maintaining contact with the district's villages. Therefore, the party Politburo (the narrow body of nine decision makers who met once a month) appointed a committee to investigate the situation in Nazareth.[32]

On August 22, the Politburo committee members, Meir Vilner, Tawfiq Tubi, and Pnina Feinhouse, met with all members of the ICP Local Committee in Nazareth and later wrote a thirteen-page report analyzing the crisis. The production of the report reflected the party's characteristic principles of organization "in which discussion is compartmentalized and secrecy is maintained at the leadership level," and a body of paid professional party activists held leadership positions and maintained a strict hierarchy of command.[33] Tawfiq Zayyad was the only member of the Local Committee whose words were directly quoted in the report, which recorded his complaint about "a complete division between the party leadership and the cadre." It appears that the report's authors took his criticism seriously (or at least used it to promote their own agenda), as they commented that "this creates a very fertile ground for the promotion of the bureaucracy and small dictators."[34] Aside from criticizing the "petty bourgeois personal relations" among the members, the committee made some concrete recommendations.

One was to make Fu'ad Khuri, Zayyad's former teacher and close ally, responsible for leading the party's activity in the district villages. This development might explain the extension of Zayyad's geographical activity. In this period, he appeared in "dozens of Arab villages in the Galilee," according to a report about Zayyad published in the Hebrew newspaper *Ma'ariv* in 1957.[35] Suggestive of access to a source from within Israel's security services, the reporter, Y. Kinarot, displayed detailed and unique knowledge about Zayyad's activity:

> Ignoring the Military Government's rules that ban entrance to closed areas without permit from the security authorities, Zayyad used to "hop" freely from one Arab village to another, gathering peasants in the village square, and delivering fiery hate speeches against the government, the authorities, and the Military Government until the security forces ambushed him and in one of his last "dashes" in 1955 arrested him in 'Arraba, the notorious Arab village in the central Galilee. In the middle of his speech they loaded him into the police prison-car and took him to the nearby police station.[36]

Kinarot is most likely wrong about the date. Zayyad's famous visit to 'Arraba took place on April 24, 1954, when four residents of the village were released from jail after being administratively detained for their political activism against a discriminatory tax policy.[37] Tawfiq Zayyad went there to celebrate their release and delivered a speech against the military government in which he described the village mukhtar, Fawzi Yasin, as "an employee of the Military Government."[38] According to the ruling party's newspaper, *Davar*, he also called for a tax revolt and a student strike.[39] After his arrest, Zayyad received an order to report twice a day to the local police station, was confined to house arrest from sundown to dawn, and was banned from leaving Nazareth for six months. From his arrest in 'Arraba in 1954 until he became a member of the Knesset in 1974, the military government and the police frequently restricted his freedom of movement,

The 1954 restriction should be considered in the context of the military government's broader fight to block the ICP's attempts to form a coalition in the Nazareth city council. Zayyad was quick to note this connection. In a letter translated into Hebrew and sent to Jewish and Arab mayors throughout the country, he protested his travel restriction: "This act, now implemented toward Arab municipal council members, might hurt Jewish council members as well, if this will be the will of the military governor or if his partisan interests would require this. The injustice, like justice, is not limited to national classifications."[40] At least in Jerusalem, Zayyad's letter found receptive ears, and a Jerusalem City Council member representing the socialist Zionist Mapam Party, Avraham Koblanov, proposed that the council protest the arbitrary decision against Zayyad.[41] Beyond this reaction, though, we do not have evidence that Jewish local politicians took steps to support Zayyad.

The travel restrictions on Zayyad coincided with turbulent developments in his city as the authorities sought to prevent the election of a communist mayor by the council members at their first meeting on June 8, 1954. After they failed to unite the noncommunist members behind an agreed-on candidate, they tried to delay the election by various other means. For example, hoping to provoke a harsh reaction from the communists, the military governor attended the first council meeting.[42] The communist members prepared for a confrontation and invited their own supporters to attend the meeting. The military government intended to allow only journalists to attend, but the police force that was supposed to implement this decision arrived late, and the room, as well as the adjacent yard, was already packed with ICP supporters.

Zayyad, in his first appearance as a council member, was the first to speak. According to the official council minutes submitted to the Interior Ministry, he stated, "We protest the invitation of the Military Governor. We do not recognize the Military Governor, we do not want him in the council and, in fact, we do not want him in the city."[43] The acting mayor, Moshe Ruah, wrote in his own report that Zayyad "spoke brazenly in a venomous and hateful tone."[44] Zayyad reprimanded Ruah: "You are not allowed to take the authority of the entire council. You were appointed temporarily and you are not allowed to convene an open session, and you are especially not allowed to invite the military governor, hated by the residents of Nazareth. What you want is that the governor will scare the people so they elect whoever he dictates."[45] The two versions of the minutes of this meeting (Ruah's and the Interior Ministry's) are the first detailed documentation of Zayyad's appearance as a public official. His sharp tongue, boldness, and daring were evident from the start. His harsh verbal confrontation with state representatives and political rivals would become one of his trademarks as a public figure.

As Zayyad and Ruah continued to argue, the head of the ICP in the municipal council, Fu'ad Khuri, intervened and began his own prepared speech against the military government, while ICP supporters in the audience echoed him and cheered. When Ruah failed to silence the protest, the Nazareth police chief entered the room and told the audience to leave the meeting. Tawfiq Zayyad confronted him: "What are you doing here? This isn't your place. Your place is at the police [station]. Get out of here. If you came to scare us with your three crowns [probably referring to the three lines marking the captain ranks] know that we will not pay attention to you and not even to nine crowns."[46] When Ruah told the communist members that he managed the elections in good faith, Zayyad commented, "We know what good faith is. [Doing things in] good faith is to report [to the police station] twice a day."[47] The acting mayor eventually ended the meeting without a vote for a new mayor. While the ICP succeeded in mobilizing protest and challenging the authorities, the military government succeeded in obstructing the ICP's longer-term political purposes. No new mayor was elected, an outcome that prolonged the influence of the Interior Ministry in the municipal council.[48]

A second meeting was scheduled for June 17 at 10:30 a.m. Because the authorities were still unable to organize a solid anticommunist coalition, they sought a way to obstruct this meeting as well. That morning, Zayyad and the other communist council members were on their way to city hall when a mob armed with sticks blocked their way. Fu'ad Khuri phoned Ruah and asked him to postpone the meeting to 11:00 a.m. Ruah agreed, but the roads to city hall remained blocked. Meanwhile, a bottle of ink was thrown at Tawfiq Zayyad, and the local reporter of the Hebrew Communist daily, *Kol ha-'Am*, sustained a hand injury. The council members found shelter at the house of council member Khalil Khuri. Later, at 2:30 p.m., Zayyad, Fu'ad Khuri, and Mun'im Jarjura arrived at the police station and protested the police's failure to stop the violence against them. At 6:00 p.m. all six ICP council members returned to the police station with a lawyer and submitted an official complaint. Two historians who closely examined these events did not exclude the possibility that the attack was a result of a government initiative. Jeremy Forman suggested that the involvement of government authorities is "not a far-fetched proposition,"[49] and Leena Dallasheh concluded that their involvement was clear.[50] That same day, the meeting was canceled, which gave the government more time to build the anticommunist coalition.

The turmoil in Nazareth triggered the first interest of the Hebrew media in Tawfiq Zayyad. A *Davar* reporter who came to the city to cover the struggle over the city hall interviewed him and quoted him, stating that the economic condition in Nazareth was worse than in other cities because of the military government and that granting freedom to the Arabs in Israel would bring peace between Israel and the Arab countries and create a Jewish-Arab brotherhood.[51] Speaking to the newspaper of the ruling party, Zayyad was probably trying to quell the fears of Israeli decision makers and influence their decision, but he was unsuccessful. The government intended to cancel the next meeting too—scheduled for mid-July, three months after the municipal elections—if it turned out that a communist mayor might be elected.[52] This time, however, the government was able to impose its preferred candidate, Amin Jarjura.[53]

For the next twenty years, the ICP members in the Nazareth council functioned as an opposition bloc. In January 1957, for example, the new military governor of the Galilee region was invited to the city hall for an "introductory meeting." The governor faced sharp criticism, especially from the ICP members, who were led by Tawfiq Zayyad. Zayyad called for abolishing the military government and demanded that the residents of Ma'lul, Mujaydil, and Safuriyya, who had found refuge in Nazareth in 1948 be allowed to return to their villages (allowing the internal refugees to resettle on their land was a consistent demand of the communists in those years). Their presence in Nazareth, he argued, both aggravated the crisis in the city and was unjust for them.[54]

TORTURE

For Zayyad, the violent events of June 17 were only a precursor for harsher attacks. On October 25, 1955, a military judge sentenced him to forty days in prison for his speech in 'Arraba eighteen months earlier, which the prosecutor described as "causing danger to public safety." Five days later, he was taken to the prison in Tiberias. While Zayyad left very few autobiographical materials for most of his life, he provided a detailed description of that prison experience in a report aimed at mobilizing protest against his ill treatment.[55]

In the report, Zayyad said he came to the prison already weak because of ulcers. When he sat down on a bench, a prison guard ordered him to stand up, but he refused, after which two guards forced him to stand while swearing at him. They then sent him directly to solitary confinement. In the evening, Zayyad was served a dinner of bread and water, which he refused to accept. The following day, after he mopped the floor of his cell, the guards told him to clean the toilet, the shower, and the hallway—orders Zayyad refused because he considered them harassment. Then the guards hit him until his nose bled, took him to the solitary confinement cell, and continued to beat him until he lost consciousness. When he woke up, he began singing. The Hebrew press reported that he sang "The International," as well as Arab folk songs from the 1936–1939 revolt.[56] In his own report, Zayyad wrote that he sang the following lines: "They dispersed us in exile / and filled the prison with us / but nights will come / whose lightning will herald your demise."

Zayyad's line quoted in his report are taken from the song "Peoples of the East," which was written as an Arabic adaptation of the "Partisan Song," widely performed in Russian by the Red Army Chorus. Communist activists in Nazareth were familiar with these Arabized Soviet songs, and the local communist chorus, al-Tali'a, incorporated them in their repertoire. That Zayyad selected these lines from "Peoples of the East" registers his immersion in a universalist revolutionary communism and probably aimed at countering the accusations made by the guards in their own version of the story: that Zayyad used Arab nationalist slogans.

The guards responded to his singing by beating him more and locking him in the solitary confinement cell. After an additional round of beating and several hours in the cell, Zayyad was taken to the Tiberias police station, where he was interrogated and accused of attacking and swearing at a guard and praising the Egyptian president, Gamal Abdel Nasser (The image of Nasser, who came to power in 1954 was highly contested. While being a source of hope for the Palestinians for liberating Palestine, Jews in Israel considered him the archenemy). When Zayyad denied the accusations, two guards held him and tied his hands while a third one slapped him until his nose started bleeding again. Zayyad's report recounts his exchange with the interrogator: "Have you declared: 'Long Live the Israeli Communist Party'? 'Yes,' said Zayyad, 'and I also called out 'down with police terrorism' and 'down with fascism.'" His answers were followed by more beatings. After Zayyad refused to give his fingerprints and successfully resisted attempts to force him to do so, the guards beat him until he lost consciousness. He recounted that he recovered after they splashed water on his face. One told him that he would never get out of prison and that "tomorrow there will be a war with Egypt and the other Arab countries and then the ICP will be outlawed and we will jail all of you." In the evening, Zayyad was taken back to the prison, and in the middle of the night, a guard entered his cell and hit him with a baton while he was shackled until he lost consciousness again.

The beatings continued the following day. Zayyad resisted physically (as much as he could) and verbally, loudly decrying fascism. Describing the morning of the third day, he wrote, "They forcefully tied my arms and legs to the window like a cross, and increased their beating, and I was bleeding until I lost consciousness. They continued for two or three hours, and each time I lost consciousness they splashed water on me."

On the fourth day, November 3, Zayyad was transferred to the Damun prison, where he finally was allowed to meet his lawyer, Hanna Naqqara, but only in the presence of two officers who prevented Zayyad from telling Naqqara about his experience in Tiberias. Unlike the other inmates, Zayyad was not allowed to bring newspapers and books into his cell, and he was allowed to meet a doctor only after four more days. After a week in Damun prison, Zayyad was returned to Tiberias, where he spent most of his time in solitary confinement. He was released on November 29.

Zayyad's reference to "a cross" to describe his torture was further elaborated by *al-Ittihad* (then edited by Imil Tuma, a communist with a Christian Orthodox background). The article published after Zayyad was released and telling his story was titled, "They Crucified Him on the Window Bars."[57] From his later writing, we know that Zayyad was familiar with and inspired by the mythology of Palestinian national martyrs from the 1930s, who were occasionally referred to as being "crucified" (although it was only a metaphor).[58] The theme of crucifixion would continue to be evident in the poetry of major Palestinian national poets, including Zayyad.[59]

The report about his torture was the first time Zayyad's name appeared in the main headlines of *al-Ittihad*, which until then had virtually ignored his activism in Nazareth, probably due to his low rank in the party. Through that painful experience, Zayyad gained popular recognition as a fighter in his party, as well in larger circles among the Palestinians in Israel and, later, the Arab world. His torture became one the best-known episodes of his life and a point of future reference. Months later, after a group of detainees from Umm al-Fahm were tortured in the same prison, *al-Ittihad* titled its report, "The Detainees from Umm al-Fahm Suffer the Same Experience as Tawfiq Zayyad in the Tiberias Prison."[60]

The police version of the story described Zayyad as the aggressor, leading in December 1956 to his indictment for attacking two guards and causing them physical injury. According to the case the police presented to the military judge, when Zayyad was asked to clean his cell, he attacked a guard, knocked him down, and "trampled him with his feet," and then proceeded to attack the other guards who had come to their colleague's aid, after which other guards intervened and moved Zayyad to the solitary confinement cell. The two guards claimed that Zayyad swore at them and said that soon there would be a war and Nasser would liquidate Israel.[61] The Magistrates Court in Acre convicted Zayyad and sentenced him to nine months in prison. Zayyad appealed to the district court, which partially accepted his position and instead gave him a suspended six-month sentence and a fee of three hundred Israeli lira (at the time, approximately the average monthly wage for an employee in a public office). Both sides appealed to the Supreme Court, which rejected both appeals.[62] By the time this appeal was rejected, however, and as the following sections discuss, Zayyad was in jail again—this time without a trial.

MASSACRE AND RESISTANCE

> Has the news of this epic reached you?
> The slaughter of the people, slaughtered like beasts?
> And the story called: Harvesting of the Skulls?
> Its stage
> Is a village
> Called
> Kafr Qasim?[63]

Kafr Qasim is an Arab village located in the Triangle, an area running along the Green Line from its western side that was annexed by Israel following the 1949 Israeli-Jordanian armistice agreement. On October 29, 1956, a group of peasants from Kafr Qasim returned home from their fields, unaware that their village had been placed under curfew by the military government. Forty-seven villagers were executed by the Israeli Border Patrol troops. The massacre triggered long-term political protest and became a major mobilizing and unifying political symbol for decades.[64] Tawfiq Zayyad was highly shaken by the event and took an active part in turning the massacre into a political symbol. His poem "Harvesting of the Skulls," whose first lines appear at the start of this section, written in November 1956, remains one of the most famous texts grieving and protesting the massacre, although only several lines of the six-page-long poem are popularly known. The title refers to the order given by First Private Shalom

Ofer—*ktsor otam* ("mow them down" or "harvest them")—before the execution of the first group of victims.

The first line, "Has the news of this epic reached you?" is a paraphrase of the first line in the Quran, Sura 88: "Has the news of this overwhelming event reached you?"[65] In that Sura, the "overwhelming event" is Judgment Day, and Zayyad's reference loads the massacre with apocalyptic connotations. It is an early example of Zayyad's use of religious vocabulary and Quranic references, evidence of his intimate familiarity with Islamic sources as well as his tendency to use them creatively. After describing and protesting the atrocity, Zayyad referred to it as a catalyst for action:

> This story has awakened the town's people,
> At first they thought it was a nightmare
> But . . .
> A night watch ended and another watch began
> It froze our sleepy eyes
> And our delusional ears were struck
> By the crying of the bereaved mothers,
> The crying of the girls and of the pregnant women.
> The crying of the slaughtered young men
> Is loud and overwhelming[66]

Rather than wallow in helplessness, however, later in the poem, Zayyad explicitly called for action:

> Unite, workers
> Unite, loyal people
> Unite your ranks and be determined
> To erase a regime founded on injustice
> A regime of betrayal, blood, and crime.[67]

The calls for unity were written amid another important regional development: a coordinated attack by Israel, Britain, and France on Egypt following Nasser's decision to nationalize the Suez Canal in summer 1956. Throughout the Arab Middle East, Nasser's determination, accompanied by his anticolonial rhetoric, inspired revolutionary dreams.[68] For Palestinians, in particular, Nasser's aspiration to unite the Arab world against the West was considered a first step toward liberating Palestine and was a great source of hope. The tripartite attack in 1956 resulted in a quick military defeat for Egypt and short-term occupation of the Sinai Peninsula, yet the moment was also a great political victory for Nasser because the US and the UN confirmed Egyptian sovereignty and ownership of the canal. Indeed, this pan-Arab Nasserist momentum fueled Zayyad's hope for radical change, and later, in "Harvesting of the Skulls," he reminded his Arab readers that they were not the minority, as their oppressors argued. Rather, they were the majority in the region and could rely on the power of Arab countries, especially the strongest among them who liberated the canal: "And in Egypt we will burn the tyrant's army / And we will drown it in the canal's water."

Nasser and his disciples in the Arab world cultivated a triumphant mythology around the war, especially around the defense of Port Said, which became a symbol of anticolonial struggle, though fighting there was sporadic.[69] Zayyad's poem "Port Said" contributed to this mythology, glorifying the Egyptian resistance: "A people who fight with their own hand against a legion / with cannons, airplanes, and helicopters." These pan-Arab sentiments were somewhat at odds with the official stand of the senior ICP leaders,[70] although Zayyad and other poets (especially Samih al-Qasim) expressed these sentiments frequently.

Another dramatic Nasserist moment was the declaration on February 1, 1958, of the unification of Egypt and Syria, presumably the first practical step toward uniting the Arab world into one powerful Arab political unit. These regional developments interacted with local dynamics to intensify political tension, as the Israeli authorities accelerated their efforts to "Judaize" the Galilee, namely, to diminish Arab majority in the region by constructing new Jewish settlements while at the same time restricting the physical expansion of Palestinian communities.[71] Although the state had confiscated 1,200 dunam (about 300 acres) of Nazareth's lands in 1954 in order to establish a Jewish neighborhood,[72] the first Jewish residents settled in Qiryat Natseret only in 1957 (in 1963, the neighborhood became an independent municipality, Upper Nazareth). Al-Ittihad protested the policy of dispossession and exclusion in Nazareth and compared it to the policy of racial segregation in South African cities.[73]

Protest over the massacre in Kafr Qasim also continued as the trial of the perpetrators, which began in January 1957, entered its second year. Together with Nasserist momentum in the region and the frustration over land confiscation and Judaization policies, 1958 was a time of accelerated politicization among

Palestinians in Israel. Furthermore, the ICP aspired to counter the government's effort to use the tenth-anniversary celebrations of the establishment of the State of Israel by promoting its image among Arab citizens.[74] These multidimensional political unrests found an outlet in that year's First of May celebration.

FIRST OF MAY, 1958

After the Histadrut[75] and Mapam[76] turned down the ICP's suggestion to have a joint march on May 1, the international workers' day, the ICP submitted a request for a permit to conduct a separate march. The police rejected the request to conduct the march in the morning, the traditional time for this event, and approved only an afternoon march. For the ICP in Nazareth, the First of May events were aimed particularly at Arab high school students who had come from all over the country to study in Nazareth,[77] and therefore the morning slot was crucial. In fact, it is unclear whether the authorities intended to allow the demonstration at all. When Mun'im Jarjura and Tawfiq Zayyad spoke with a local police officer, he admitted that it was possible to allow all three demonstrations to march in the morning but that his superiors objected to that.[78]

The local party leaders in Nazareth decided to march in the morning without a permit and, according to at least one scholar, even without the approval of the party's Central Committee.[79] They invited people to attend their morning demonstration, using large speakers at the ICP offices and on a car that drove through the streets. What might have been especially worrying for the authorities were the songs they played, such as songs by the famous Lebanese singer Fayruz, in which she sang of the return of the Palestinian refugees with terms such as *raji'un* (those who return) and *sanarja'u yawman* (we shall return one day). Zayyad was proud to report these songs in his own account of the events.[80] On the evening of April 29, the police broke into the local ICP office with a search warrant, confiscated the speakers, and arrested MK Emile Habibi and *al-Ittihad* editor Saliba Khamis, who happened to be there. The rumors about their arrest spread quickly in the city, and a crowd gathered in front of the police station in a spontaneous demonstration, which evolved into a violent clash with the police forces.

The report about this event on the front page of the Hebrew newspaper *Ma'ariv* began by identifying the leader of the protest and accusing him of instigating the violence: "Several policemen were injured yesterday in demonstrations and riots of the ICP members, under the leadership of Tawfiq Zayyad, a member of the Nazareth city council. The demonstrators used bats and threw rocks at the policemen."[81]

Zayyad was arrested, and later that night, the police raided coffeehouses and private homes and placed dozens of communist activists under arrest.[82] Zayyad spent the next several nights in the Jalama detention center, at the foot of Mount Carmel, in the same cell with twenty other detainees—and, as Zayyad put it, also with "brigades of fleas."[83] The detainees shared the circumstances of their arrest, and the stories, wrote Zayyad, were "funny and painful, fueling the revenge in our chest, and strengthening our faith in the future." That story sharing would later assist in shaping a relatively coherent and unified narrative about the development of the so-called 1958 uprising. Zayyad himself, for example, provided detailed information about the entrance of the police into the ICP offices, though he was not present.[84]

A devoted communist, Zayyad regarded the First of May as the most important holiday on his calendar, so spending it behind the bars with his fellow communists took on special meaning. With a tone of exaltation, he described that morning in prison: "Even though the barbed wire fence and the prison wall separated us from our People, and from humankind outside, the sun of the First of May did not exclude this corner from the rest of the world. With the awakening dawn the entire prison arose . . . our voices exploded in singing 'The International' anthem to celebrate First of May. And our voices were closer to the horizon than the tops of the tallest trees on the summit of Mount Carmel."[85]

Meanwhile in Nazareth, the police were determined to prevent the march and deployed large forces in the city and on the adjacent roads. Their attempts to prevent the march led to violent clashes in which demonstrators and policemen were injured. Hundreds of people, including thirteen minors aged twelve to sixteen, were arrested in Nazareth, as well as on the roads leading to the city.[86] The wave of new detainees was the first evidence for Zayyad that demonstrators in Nazareth had ignored the ban and went to the streets despite the absence of most of the party leadership. He was joyful and proud to see them: "Didn't I tell you that we left behind us a People who know the way?"[87]

Later, Zayyad was sent to the Ramla prison with fifteen other activists, including Saliba Khamis, Mun'im Jarjura, and the poet Hanna Abu Hanna. Sixty-one other activists were detained in other prisons, and sixteen were sent to internal exile in the northern city of Safed. They were all placed under administrative detention (detention of individuals without trial), waiting for their trial in a military court. On May 22, they sent a letter to the prime minister threatening to begin a hunger strike if the state refused to try them in a civilian court.

On June 2, Zayyad and other members of the Nazareth branch arrived at the military court in Acre, where they faced the charge of participation in an "illegal demonstration." When asked whether he pled guilty, Zayyad answered, "I refuse to answer this question, or any other question, because I do not recognize this court."[88] When the detainees were allowed to make their own declarations, Zayyad said:

These trials are orchestrated in order to scare the Arab People and to deter them from fighting for their legal rights [. . .] Our only guilt is our love for our homeland, our People, and our loyalty to the rights of every People. In the same way that in 1948 we went to jail because of our struggle for the right of the Jewish People for self-determination,[89] we will not abandon our struggle for self-determination for the Arab People. We are being persecuted because of our just struggle. This is how Jews were persecuted in Nazi Germany.

When the judge interrupted him by commenting, "The mufti was Hitler's guest of honor," Zayyad replied:

We fought against the mufti and we went to jail for that. Hitler's attempt also proved the impossibility of oppressing the Jewish People's spirit of freedom. The same will happen with my People. I am convinced that my friends and I will gain the sympathy of the Jewish People, who will eventually stand up against the entire campaign of terror imposed on us.[90]

Zayyad failed, however, to gain the sympathy of the court that day. Because of his past conviction, his punishment was the harshest: the military judge sentenced him to five months in prison.

One of the exiled activists in Safed was Tawfiq Zayyad's teenage brother, Sabih. The Jewish communist poet and reporter Haya Kadmon interviewed their father, Amin, and quoted him in *Kol ha-'Am*: "'Death is better than oppression,' he said proudly. 'I prefer to see my sons sitting in prison because they defended the People's interests than to see them taking care of themselves only.'" The father's exuberance and charisma impressed Kadmon:

With his shriveled face, adorned with beard and gray hair, and his feverish eyes igniting, he looks like a reproving prophet—"they looked at us, the Arab People, as slaves. We feel as servants serving arrogant masters yelling at us, go clean here, go scrub there! How can we keep on like that?"[91]

Kadmon then explained:

> Many times in the past the father quarreled with his sons because their po-
> litical articulations did not fit the religious law and his worldview, but now
> he acknowledges that their incarceration is firm evidence that they are those
> who fight for national freedom and human uprightness, which he appreciates
> so much."[92]

Even if we take into consideration the communist political agenda of *Kol ha-'Am*,
Amin Zayyad's words might be indicative of a tectonic cultural-political shift in
the status of religion. The struggle for national liberation had become so central
in Palestinian society that it provided ways to gain moral legitimacy, even for
people who rejected religion.

One of his fellow inmates and comrades, the poet Hanna Abu Hanna, recalled that a poetry book of the tenth-century poet al-Mutanabbi smuggled into
the prison was "Tawfiq's closest friend."[93] Even when the other inmates played
basketball, Zayyad remained on the sidelines reading his book. Al-Mutanabbi
inspired Zayyad to write his own poems in jail, and some of them became part of
the Palestinian canon. "Many of my poems were written in prison," Zayyad said
in a 1992 interview, and then added half-joking, "and many times I wished to be
arrested so I could have all that time to write, but unfortunately, the authorities
did not always respond to that wish."[94]

Indeed, while in the Ramla prison, he wrote the well-known poem "Behind
the Bars," which reads in part:

> When they jail us
> They do not jail the fire of the struggle
> They do not imprison the determination of the free youth
> That blows like the wind.
> They do not imprison a song
> That rises over the plain
> Eastern with Arabic tunes and red wings.
> It arose on the fertile land
> Like the morning gods.[95]

The poem was first published in *al-Jadid* while Zayyad was still in jail.[96] After his
trial, he was transferred to the Damun prison, where he wrote "The Reward for

the Victory (for the 1958 Uprising)":

> Can you hear it ululating in my blood,
> The Arab greetings for the flag,
> Fluttering, colored with the blood of the victims,
> Over cedar trees that resemble the columns of the sky?[97]

Some readers interpreted it as a poem glorifying the First of May demonstrators in Nazareth,[98] and others saw it as a salute to the left-leaning pan-Arab-oriented coalition that in 1958 struggled in Lebanon against the pro-Western president, a confrontation that took place when Zayyad was in prison.[99] Sent from Zayyad to comrades outside the prison, it was recited by his friend the poet Hanna Ibrahim on July 11, 1958, at a poetry festival in Acre. Zayyad conveyed a similar triumphal enthusiasm in his poem "Fahd," a reference to the nom de guerre of the Iraqi communist leader Yusuf Salman, who was executed in 1949. The July 14 revolution in Iraq that ended Hashemite rule there took place when Zayyad was jailed and gave him much hope and meant that Fahd's sacrifice had not been in vain.

Beyond poetry, Zayyad invested effort in the political education of other inmates. In Damun, he shared a cell with approximately twenty other people, including Tawfiq Kana'na from 'Arraba, who remembered Zayyad as a political leader who delivered political and theoretical lectures from behind bars.[100] In early September 1958, after spending four months in prison, Zayyad was finally released, and afterward he wrote the poem "Night Chatting in Jail." In the late 1970s the Damascus-based music band Firqat Aghani al-'Ashiqin turned the last two verses of this poem into a popular song known as "Oh My People, Oh Branch of My Peers":

> Oh my People,
> Oh branch of my peers,
> You are dearer to me than my own life.
> We keep our promise,
> We do not accept the suffering in the cell
> And the shackles of injustice and its bars.
> We endure hunger and deprivations
> Only to untie the shackles of the crucified moon
> And give you back your stolen right,
> And rescue tomorrow from the night of greed,

So that you won't be bought and sold,

And to make sure that the boat does not remain without a mast.[101]

In these lines, Zayyad reminds Palestinian refugees that he did not forget them and their rights, and at the same time, he highlights the pain and hardship of the Palestinians who remained in their homeland. This message of transborder Palestinian solidarity, sent from behind bars to a People beyond the sealed border, is probably what made these lines so popular in the Palestinian diaspora.

Zayyad's relatively long incarceration and the well-received poetry that he published following it increased his popularity as well as his status in the party. Weeks after his release, the Politburo discussed the possibility of sending him to Poland to represent the party in a formal event, an indication of his emerging leadership status.[102] His public appearances drew attention and large audiences. A month after his release, Zayyad appeared at a poetry festival in Kafr Yasif,[103] reading his recently published poem "Behind the Bars." The author Muhammad 'Ali Taha remembered this festival, which took place illuminated by candles and flashlights due to the lack of electricity. Because of Zayyad's heroic poetic images and fierce lyrics, he expected to meet a sturdy man and was surprised to see instead a "skinny boy" (Zayyad was then twenty-nine years old). Taha recounted that when Zayyad started to read his poetry, his small size made his performance even more impressive.[104]

From an almost anonymous local activist at the beginning of the 1950s, Zayyad emerged by the end of the decade as a natural leader whose charisma, poetry, and police record made him popular far beyond Nazareth and marked him as a promising future party leader. Until late 1958, communism and Arab national sentiments were closely connected, especially in Nazareth, and for Zayyad, there was never any doubt that the two complemented, rather than contradicted, each other. However, when the leading advocate of pan-Arabism, Gamal Abdel Nasser, shifted his treatment of communism from ambivalence to outright hostility, communists like Zayyad found themselves in an unprecedented predicament, as their urge to defend their ideological brothers in neighboring countries clashed with the Nasserist sentiments of their constituency.

Chapter 3

BADGES OF MODERNITY

AFTER THE 1956 WAR, COMMUNISTS IN EGYPT WERE UNITED IN THEIR enthusiastic support for Nasser's anti-imperialist foreign policy,[1] and Arab members of the Israeli Communist Party followed them. After Syria and Egypt formed the United Arab Republic in 1958, Fu'ad Khuri, Zayyad's political father, even dared to suggest that Arabs in Israel would join the union.[2] Nasser, however, considered communists a threat. He developed an anticommunist policy and rhetoric, which drastically intensified in late 1958 with his attempt to extend the union to Iraq and the opposition of Iraqi communists to this move. Communists' lukewarm response to the United Arab Republic deteriorated into overt conflict when Nasser arrested communist leaders in Egypt and Syria on December 31, 1958.[3]

The ICP had to pick a side in this conflict, and its Arab members aligned half-heartedly with the communist side. Zayyad's protest, though, was clearer than that of most of his colleagues. In January 1959, he wrote the poem "Communists" in defense of the communists in the Arab world:

> They said: "Communists." I said: I salute these
> Red ones. With their determination, all Peoples will be free.
> They said: "Communists." I said: it means death
> For the tyrants is a matter of time.
> They said: "Communists." I said: They are flowers
> Perfuming the worlds with their fragrance.

They said: They are a mob. I said: This is my origin,
an honor that decorates my Arabness and lights it.
[...]
Not everyone who claims Arabness is right
Not everyone who has shining fangs is a lion.
[...]
And for you who asked me, I say: our situation will not be settled
until the red flag is spread above us.[4]

The line "not everyone who claims Arabness is right" is an implicit criticism of the Nasserists, who were gaining momentum in 1958. In March 1959, however, the Nasser-backed revolt against the communist-backed revolutionary government in Iraq failed. Nasser blamed the communists for being agents of imperialism, while communists in the region defended the Iraqi regime in its ruthless suppression of the pro-Nasserist revolt. Arab members of the ICP sympathized with the idea of Arab unification, and Nasser's anti-imperial stand was compelling; they therefore criticized Nasser reluctantly and carefully.[5] Their caution stemmed as well from the immense popularity of Nasser among Palestinians. Salah Baransi, one of the founders of the al-'Ard movement (an Arab national group active in Israel from 1958 to 1964), implicitly compared him to the Prophet Muhammad.[6] Palestinian sociologist Honaida Ghanem has argued that for many secular Palestinian intellectuals in those years, Nasser replaced God.[7]

Zayyad represented a rare exception to this restraint. While his January poem could still be read as a protest against Nasserists rather than against Nasser himself, his rhetoric became harsher and directly aimed at Nasser following the confrontation in Iraq, displaying the same bald criticism and self-assurance that characterized his attacks on Israel's military government: "They hung me from an iron rod and claimed, 'Nasserite,' 'enemy sympathizer.' And today, oh Gamal, I am the 'agent' whose 'sins' fill the earth and sky? Today I am the 'partisan,' the 'mercenary,' the 'enemy' of your People and mine? Shut up! Your words are mere lyrics, planting poison in hearts and minds. We have heard it all before, long ago in recent times."[8] In a period when Nasser's voice from Cairo "nailed" Palestinians in Israel in place, and many became "huge ears, sitting on the edges of their chairs,"[9] it is hard to overstate the courage of those who signed their name below these lines.

In terms of realpolitik, attacking Nasser was probably a mistake. The anger toward the ICP even led to physical violence. In Acre, the local ICP club was torched, and according to the Hebrew weekly *ha-'Olam ha-Zeh*, Tawfiq Zayyad himself was slapped in the face in the streets of Nazareth following his anti-Nasserist stand.[10] The immediate and dramatic drop of support for the communists in the Arab community was apparent from the sales figures of *al-Ittihad* in Nazareth and surrounding villages.[11] The ICP also lost 38 percent of its support in the November 1959 Knesset elections and half its seats in the Nazareth Municipal Council. It is hard to believe that Zayyad, with his sharp political senses, was not aware of the potential implications of the venom he directed toward the Egyptian leader. Something else probably overpowered short-term rational political calculations. What was it?

Maha Nassar believes that Zayyad felt betrayed by Nasser's charge that communists were Zionist agents.[12] This is probably true, but if we look at Zayyad's reaction from a decades-long perspective, we can identify a pattern in his reactions to perceived threats on his Marxist faith: a tendency to protect his beliefs at all cost. His agitated response provides an extreme expression of the clash between communism and Nasserism that many Palestinian communists experienced at the time. It was a clash between two secular sets of beliefs, two self-proclaimed modernizing projects with different utopian orientations. Communism was a relatively coherent ideology and vision, aspiring for universal salvation through the creation of a classless society. Nasserism was an amalgamation of aspirations for Arab national liberation and political unification and a personality cult around Nasser himself. This relative incoherence did not make the Nasserist community of believers less enthusiastic. Palestinian communists had hoped that these two movements could coexist, but Nasser's assault on the communists in Egypt, Syria, and Iraq shattered that hope. Zayyad's reaction was one of the most poignant expressions of that disappointment. He expressed the rage of a person whose most sacred principles were attacked and desecrated. This chapter delves into the basic elements of Zayyad's worldview as a communist and how it was shaped and expressed in the 1950s and 1960s.

ZAYYAD'S INTERPRETATION OF MODERNITY

The French scholar Pierre Clermont has interpreted the communist project as a revolt against modernity, an attempt to revive the premodern gemeinschaft in the twentieth century.[13] Other scholars, though, have located it within the framework of multiple modernities.[14] For Zayyad, communism was, without any doubt, the ultimate expression of modernity, and this modernity came as a bundle of mutually connected visions. His rhetoric in political speeches, as well as in his poetry, reflected the idea that history progresses toward a utopian future in which politics is secular, economic exploitation is eradicated, political civil rights are disconnected from ethnic identity, and women are equal to men.

One major element in this matrix of modernity was cosmopolitanism, or, in the Marxist vocabulary, "the fraternity of Peoples." Since the beginning of the twentieth century, various Palestinian intellectuals have drawn a connection between establishing cross-confessional frameworks (in, for example, politics, education, and sports) and being modern.[15] This model of secular politics had its Arab-nationalist version calling for Arab Muslim-Christian fraternity,[16] but it appeared also in its communist universalist version, which included Jews as well.[17] Although a Jewish-Arab partnership was almost necessary for Palestinians in order to practice a legitimate and legal politics under the military government, Marxist ideology provided a strong moral legitimacy for it.

Only partly overlapping with cosmopolitanism, secularism was another element in the communist vision of modernity and progress, and the communists offered a secular alternative to the communal model of organizing encouraged by the Israeli state authorities. The revolutionary zeal of the communists remained extremely marginal among Palestinians before 1948, but the impact of the Nakba on Palestinian society led to a questioning of old traditions. As the ex-communist poet Hanna Abu Hanna wrote, "It was the time to reject everything—the leaders and the rulers, the words and speeches, the masks torn and dropped."[18]

Political philosopher Charles Taylor has argued that a secular society is defined by three qualities: limiting the role of religion in public spaces, by excluding it from their own private beliefs and practices, and by making religious commitment optional.[19] Communists in Israel took steps to realize every one of these qualities. They nurtured secularized public spaces where political organization was explicitly disconnected from religious communities, and they established a secular calendar in which socialist holidays and political memorial days were dominant. Similarly, in their private lives, communist leaders did not observe any religion and frequently married outside the religious communities of their families. By enabling secular public spaces and providing personal examples of nonobservance, they created cultural conditions in which unbelief was a viable option for the broader circles of party sympathizers.

FRATERNITY OF PEOPLES

When Zayyad took his first steps as a communist in the mid-1940s, the Palestine Communist Party had already split along national lines and the National Liberation League in Nazareth did not include any Jewish members. Hence, his encounters and collaboration with Jewish members of the party after 1948 were new experiences for him. His torture and frequent arrests by the Israeli authorities did not interfere with his basic attitude toward the necessity of joint political action with the Jewish citizens of the state or with his attempts to cultivate ties with Jewish activists.

During the Thirteenth ICP Congress (May 29–June 1, 1957), Zayyad met the Iraqi-born Jewish poet David Tsemah (Da'ud Samah). Tsemah was highly impressed by Zayyad and wrote about their meeting in *Kol ha-'Am* under the title "To My Friend Tawfiq." "For only four days," he wrote, we met and discussed our common interests, and we already struck up a deep brotherly friendship." Tsemah and Zayyad discovered that on almost the same day, both wrote an "outcry poem" about the Kafr Qasim massacre. Zayyad told Tsemah about his torture in prison in 1955, and Tsemah wrote that he was proud that Zayyad did not break and represented his People and the party with dignity. Two days after the congress, Tsemah traveled to Nazareth to visit Zayyad, and they walked together in the streets. Tsemah was moved by the trust and love that the city's residents expressed toward Zayyad. Zayyad read some of his poems to Tsemah, and, tellingly, Tsemah was especially impressed with the as-yet-unpublished poem about the 1956 battle in Port Said, which Tsemah called "the glory of the reviving East."[20] At an Arabic poetry festival held on July 11, 1958, when Zayyad was behind bars, Tsemah read "My Brother Tawfiq," his poem praising his friend, using indirect references to Zayyad's own poetry. The poem was subsequently published in *al-Jadid.*[21]

It seems that the basis for the friendship was not only personal chemistry and shared communist ideology but also the love of Arabic poetry and even a similar sense of Arab anticolonial pride. Their friendship represented a broader rapprochement among Palestinian poets who remained in Israel and leftist Iraqi Jewish intellectuals who had arrived in the country recently. The former, who became isolated from the Arab world, relied on the latter for learning about innovations in the poetry movement in Iraq.[22]

Writing for *al-Ittihad* later that summer, Zayyad published "My Brothers in Struggle," a poem dedicated to "Ata's striking workers." Ata was a large textile factory, most of whose workers were Jews. In summer 1957, the workers opened a strike that lasted 103 days and apparently inspired Zayyad:

> He who stole your bread stole my bread.
> We are both the victims of the oppressors.
> We walk the same path, so raise your hands,
> Companions of class struggle.
> We form a new world, we are for peace,
> And for overcoming the reactionary forces.[23]

Kol ha-'Am published a Hebrew translation of this poem two weeks later.[24]

As happened frequently among communists at the time, this universalist ideology gained a personal dimension in the romantic field when Zayyad developed a relationship with Tamar Sneh, the daughter of Moshe Sneh, a Jewish leader of the ICP at the time. Tamar was herself a communist activist who was arrested and interrogated several times in the late 1950s. Zayyad's love for her inspired him to write the poem "A Visit," which was published only in 2016. According to an interviewee who was active in the party at the time, Tamar's family wanted to distance her from Zayyad, and for this purpose, they sent her to study in East Germany. As we will see later in this chapter, sometimes there was a gap between the political commitment of Jewish and Arab communists to cosmopolitanism, on the one hand and, on the other, their reluctance to cross ethnoreligious boundaries within their own families.

Zayyad's cosmopolitan orientation is evident as well in his poetry. In September 1961, Israeli troops killed five Palestinian citizens who were attempting to enter the Gaza Strip. The event triggered wide-scale, turbulent protest throughout the country, and tens of thousands of Palestinians attended the funerals. Zayyad himself addressed a protesting crowd in Nazareth. Among Jews, the protest was marginal, but it still provoked harsh reactions. After Jewish protesters who distributed flyers in Tel Aviv were attacked and their flyers burned, Zayyad wrote "The Burned Flyers," which reads in part:

> Friends of our struggle,
> My spilled blood is dear, it is.
> I am a worker—a human being
> My humanity is my capital
> I know history,

I lived the tempestuous power of the sea

I am a worker—this is my class.[25]

While in his poem, as in many others, Zayyad highlighted the struggle against the Israeli authorities, two times in his life he found himself supporting the policy of the Israeli government. The second time, during the Oslo process, is discussed in detail in chapter 9. The first was in August 1960, three months after Mossad agents kidnapped Adolf Eichmann in Argentina and brought him to Israel for trial. Zayyad wrote a poem calling explicitly for Eichmann's execution:

There is no escape for any terrible cutthroat

Push him toward the rope ... this monster ... the butcher of Peoples

[...]

Auschwitz is still telling stories about their crimes

And on its sides the remains of the death are piling,

A bone here ... a bone there ... scattered between the corners,

And the furnaces' chimney stands like the goddess of Germany,

A swamp of death ... for the killing that was not revenged from bend-
ing.

Hang him! And the souls of the victims might rest

And spread your struggle ... so these troubles would never repeat.[26]

SECULAR PILGRIMAGE

By the early 1960s, Zayyad had gained significant public prestige. His unapol-ogetic style, his courage to confront the authorities, and his fierce nationalist poetry earned him respect among large and diverse circles. The ICP leadership understood his potential for mobilizing support for the party, and they had an instrumental interest in nurturing him as a leader. The Arab senior leaders of the party were almost exclusively upper-class Christians, and the local leader-ship in Nazareth came almost exclusively from the Greek Orthodox community. Zayyad was from a working-class Muslim family in the poor Eastern Neighbor-hood in Nazareth, and his simple manners and interpersonal skills gained him much popularity among the urban working class and villagers.

In order to prepare Zayyad for leadership positions, the ICP Central Committee included him in a group of Arab and Jewish communist leaders sent to study at the Higher Party School in Moscow,[27] an experience that sealed his loyalty to the Soviet Union and to communism as an ideology. Zayyad left for Moscow in August 1962, together with his mentor, Fu'ad Khuri, 'Ali 'Ashur, Jamal Musa, As'ad Kanana, David (Sasha) Hanin, Uzi Burshtein, and others. On his way, he stopped for two days in Paris, where he visited the classic tourist sites such as Notre-Dame Cathedral, the Louvre, and the Eiffel Tower. But for Zayyad, who was leaving his homeland for the first time, the most exciting part of his Paris visit was related to his identity as a communist. In his book *A Nazarene in the Red Square*, he writes that he realized an old dream when he visited the Communards' Wall at the Père Lachaise Cemetery. Zayyad then educated his readers about the history of the Paris Commune, which he glorified as "the first beacon in the storm of life, the first station, the real history of humanity,"[28] and about the "Bloody Week" when it was crushed, culminating in the execution of 147 communards on May 28, 1871, at the wall.

Zayyad's visit to this site may have been an old dream, but being in Russia was an experience of a different order. Moscow was not just another city for a devoted communist like Zayyad, who in Nazareth had made the utmost effort to touch the hem of the garment of the Soviet Union. When the Association of Friendship with the Soviet Union opened a branch in Nazareth in June 1949,[29] Zayyad attended its events, including film screenings about the heroic victories of the Red Army over the Nazis. Years later, he told his deputy, Suhayl Diab, that the war movies made an immense impression on him and contributed to his pro-Soviet world-view.[30] When the Soviet Union launched Sputnik, the first artificial earth satellite, Zayyad and other members of his party in Nazareth sent a telegram to the Soviet ambassador to congratulate him on the achievement.[31] Throughout his stay in the Soviet Union, and even after he returned, Zayyad continued to be impressed by what he regarded as the Soviet Union's great achievements. In a letter he wrote from Azerbaijan during his visit there in early 1963, he praised "the role of culture, televisions, electricity, telephone, and other things that indicate the long stride Azerbaijan made after the [establishment] of the Soviet rule toward civilization, which reminds me of our cities and villages that still lie beneath backwardness and oppression."[32]

The Higher Party School, which Zayyad attended in Moscow, offered its students a full-time two-year course to prepare them for being party officials.[33] The curriculum included Marxist philosophy, political economy, and the history of the workers' movement and communism. The students also heard lectures by prominent communist leaders from the Soviet Union and abroad, including

Nikita Khrushchev, Nikolai Bulganin, and Alexei Kosygin.[34] For the Palestinian students, the most exciting encounters were the meetings with the Syrian communist leader Khalid Bakdash, as well as the rebel and exiled Palestinian leader Fu'ad Nassar from Nazareth. In his letters from Moscow, Zayyad avoided providing any substantial information about his studies, such as the curriculum or names of famous speakers—perhaps a reflection of the communist culture of secrecy and compartmentalization, or of Zayyad's awareness that his letters would be read by both Soviet and Israeli security services. The letters do, however, tell much about his leisure time. For example, in a letter to his parents, he wrote, "Yesterday I went for the first time in my life to the gardens and ice-skated. It was a quite impressive experience. I tripped at least fifty or sixty times on the snow, which was soft like cotton. I will keep sliding at least once a week until I master this. But the question is: When I return, on what I will slide?"[35] Zayyad also expressed some homesickness, and in a December 1962 letter, he complained that only his brother wrote to him. In the same letter, he complained about his busy schedule, the excessive amount of assigned reading and writing, and his struggle with English, the language of most of the texts. He liked the snow but was concerned about his ability to cope with the extremely cold temperatures predicted for the weeks to come.

Zayyad left few detailed descriptions of his personal experience, and his memoirs from Moscow are no exception; they are dedicated mostly to glorifying the Soviet Union with only marginal information about his own interaction with his environment and his subjective experience. Among the rare exceptions to this rule is Zayyad's visit to Lenin's tomb on his first day in Moscow in fall 1962. His exuberant detailed testimony conveys the excitement of a pilgrim who attended his holiest site for the first time in his life:

All the ways lead to Moscow, and all the ways in Moscow lead to the Red Square.

The first moment in Moscow—a dream that came true! I left all my belongings, except my clothes I wore, in the room.

The second moment . . . I locked the door quickly and left. There are moments in the life of a person in which he cannot concentrate on anything because of his all-encompassing passion.

The "metro," they said, "is the shortest way." And they said: "One station, two, three, and then the fourth. And then . . . one hundred meters and you will be in the Red Square." Equipped with this knowledge, I arrived to the metro [. . .] One station, two, three, and in the fourth I got off. It was not difficult . . . one hundred meters. There is no need to ask, the place is well established in my mind.

I climbed in the right direction. The Lenin Museum to your left, and then . . . the Museum of the Revolution to your right. And then . . . the square, in its length and width, flash and blood, in front of you.

Zayyad then described all the objects he saw on his way to his real destination and the moment of his arrival at the tomb:

The heart of the square, which is the heart of Moscow, which is the heart of the world and the spirit of the era: the tomb.

The same image curved in the imagination. You see it for the first time, in your own eyes. But you know, beforehand, every detail of it.

There is nothing strange here. Everything is closer to you than yourself. The same image that you know and you do not know since when . . . your knowledge of it stretches, vertically, to the depths of your soul, along your class affiliation. You, through this image, see your first ancestor. The slave who, centuries ago, raged, and stood upright in front of his master.

In Zayyad's yearning for a distant revolutionary past, which fueled a revolutionary future vision, we might see an illustration of Walter Benjamin's insights that "in the idea of classless society, Marx secularized the idea of messianic time."[36] Zayyad clearly internalized this secular messianism, which has a salient universalist orientation and also—in his version of it—echoes Islamic imagery:

And you come closer . . .

The tomb. The red stone, brought from the Kuril Islands in the north, the honor guard, standing like a rock without moving an eyelid. He knows to where leads the gate, in which he stands, guarding.

And you come closer . . .

And you stand. The people gather quickly. One hundred, two hundred, they assemble. Hundreds . . . of all ages, they stand like you in front of the tomb, they wait like you for the same thing.[37]

Although Zayyad never visited Mecca, his words evoke descriptions of the hajj. The Kaaba, the Black Stone, is replaced with a red stone; the transcendental exuberance is transferred from God to the class struggle; and the enthusiastic discovery of fraternity between Muslims, frequently described by first-time pilgrims, is replaced with the discovery of the large and diverse crowd of visitors to the tomb. Zayyad might not have been a religious person in the popular or traditional meaning of the term, but his political activism was surely fueled by a certain spirituality. The poem Zayyad wrote following this visit, "In Front of Lenin's Tomb," leaves no doubt about it:

> As if I am born anew
> All the suns and the most beautiful roses are in my hand.
> I stood before it, my head bowed
> Your tomb that lives in our hearts,
> Oh Lenin.
> I felt, I, the tortured, miserable being
> The destitute, whose only share of life is a mud hut, I felt as if I
> Owned everything,
> That I was stronger than time and fate,
> That I could plunge into the sky.[38]

Decades later, some orthodox Muslims would consider Zayyad's enthusiasm in front the tomb to be idolatry and his replacement of Islam with an alternative secular theology infuriating.[39] Arguably, the poem is exemplary of the declaration of the Syrian poet Adonis that "Arab poetry has always been against God,"[40] but at the same time, the poem has a clear transcendental orientation. We might best understand these tensions in the poem through Ernst Bloch's theory of secularization as a dialectical process between the sacred and the profane, as Zayyad challenges religious conventions, but at the same time, he perpetuates the basis premises of a religious worldview by evoking eschatological imagination.

Zayyad's distance from Islamic religious practices is illustrated in his letter to his brother Musbah that he wrote from Baku, Azerbaijan, on February 25, 1963. According to the Hijri calendar, it was the last day of the Ramadan, the eve of 'Eid al-Fitr, one of the central Muslim holidays. Zayyad, writing from a city with a Muslim majority, did not congratulate his brother or even mention the holiday. The letter is imbued with enthusiasm about Azerbaijan's modernization, and Zayyad seemed to associate its prior backwardness with Islam: "What we see here is very interesting. This formerly backward Islamic country today outruns many of the finest European countries in many domains." In a letter two weeks later, he did make a passing remark about the holiday. After asking his brother to thank some of his friends for sending him greeting cards for the new civic year (by itself a clearly secular practice in an Islamic context), he continued: "Greetings for the holiday [*kul 'am wa-antum bi-khayr*]. How was Ramadan and the holiday? Here we celebrated 8 March, International Women's Day. On this occasion I attended a festive gathering with the mother of the famous Soviet hero Zawia." Zayyad's interest in the holiday was distant and reserved, and he made it clear that he was observing an alternative calendar.

Creating alternative calendars is a common revolutionary practice,[41] and Zayyad seemed to have fully internalized the communist one. In his book, Zayyad dedicated an entire chapter to the holiest date of the calendar, First of May, as it was observed at the holiest space, Red Square. He began with a detailed description of the preparations and the ambience in Moscow on the holiday eve: "All of Moscow was one glowing unit running on rays of electricity. A fabulous symphony of flags, signs, gushing vitality, and confident invigoration."[42] Zayyad went once again to Lenin's tomb: "I felt that I want, with all my heart, to embrace everything and accept it. And in front of Lenin's tomb I felt more than once a sweeping desire to say something . . . to exclaim to the full extent . . . but the silence was stronger than anything I could say."[43] Zayyad continued to wander the streets of Moscow for hours, intoxicated by the sights: "I felt a sweeping desire to suck this magnificence and revolutionary glory drop by drop! I returned to my place of residence shortly before dawn."[44]

After providing a detailed description of the First of May ceremony the following day, he wrote,

> At the exact same moment, thousands of workers and peasants in my city, Nazareth, and the neighboring villages, were flocking to the city's main street to celebrate the same eternal anniversary. In the Red Square a People who smashed the yoke of capital's slavery was celebrating, and in Nazareth it was a People victimized by two elements, national oppression and capitalist oppression, a People who has not achieved yet its political and social liberation. Nevertheless, a big joy filled my heart: our People also, despite the oppression and terror, did not give up on the parade of class struggle.

Zayyad expressed excitement about communist fraternity on other occasions as well. In a letter to his family on May 30, 1963, he described his experience during the "unforgettable" occasion of Fidel Castro's speech at the Lenin Amphitheater in Moscow, where a crowd of over 125,000 gathered, overflowing the amphitheater's 100,000 capacity. "This [size of the crowd] is not the important thing," he continued, "but the deep love and the stormy and enthusiastic atmosphere among the attendees. Obviously, it could be understood that this deep love is not only for the Cuban People but for every People fighting for their freedom and independence. I cannot forget the storms of applause and the 'hurrah' cheers that were shouted continuously from the throats of the myriads."

EXPLICIT HERESY

When Zayyad returned from Moscow in summer 1964, he launched an ambitious project. Reflecting his populist tendencies and his ideological belief in the power of the masses, he collected popular Palestinian stories from elders and translated popular poems and stories from colloquial Arabic into standard literary Arabic. He did it, however, with his own Marxist and atheist interpretation. Although his early poetry occasionally contained heretical ideas, heresy is much more common, explicit, and consistent in his two collections of short folk stories.

It is especially evident in the collection of short stories, *Hal al-Dunya* (*State of the World*), published in 1970. While many of the volume's folk stories echo Quranic stories, Zayyad's versions seem antagonistic to their original theological message, and some of the protagonists even make explicitly atheist arguments. The protagonist in the title story, for example, is a heretic tailor who "rejects the divine will, which stratifies people into classes."[45] The tailor muses, "If God created everything, he also created evil. Therefore, why did he create it and make people busy with it? If he is not the one who created evil—why doesn't he get rid of it? If he doesn't want to, then he is evil, and if he cannot, then he is helpless."[46] When the patron complained about the pace of his work and said, "The entire world was created in six days, why can't you make a cloth in three months?" the tailor answered, "and look at the state of the world."[47]

Similarly, in the story "Facing the Dead Cow" the protagonist is a poor peasant named 'Abdallah (servant of God) whose cow became sick. He prayed for her life, and in his night dream, he offered his donkey instead. But the following morning, he found the cow dead, and in his disappointment, he stopped praying and changed his name to 'Abd al-Zift—literally, Servant of Tar, though its colloquial Arabic meaning might be untranslatable (similar to "crap" or "trash" in reference to an object or "moron" in reference to a person). Thematically, the story seems to a play on the Quranic tale of Abraham's "great sacrifice," in which God orders Abraham to sacrifice his son and then, just as Abraham is getting ready to do so, God provides a ram to be sacrificed instead.[48] In Zayyad's version, the wish for exchange by divine intervention did not materialize.

"The Heretic Bee" ("al-Nahla al-Mulhida") is an allegory about Third World revolutionaries, represented by the heretic bee, and their struggle against US global domination, represented by a king hornet named Last Sam. While the word *mulhida* could denote a person who rebels against a legitimate caliph in Islamic tradition, its contemporary usage is usually in reference to someone who rejects religion or is an atheist. It might be also a reference to the heretic tendencies of left-leaning revolutionary movements in the 1960s. In all cases, Zayyad's choice of terms to describe his hero is a political statement.

As Zayyad was the mediator between the readers and these old folktales, it is hard to tell whether the heretical elements were included in the original story Zayyad heard or represent his own addition. These aspects of Zayyad's work are not easy for many of his readers to accept. Tellingly, although his work has increasingly gained attention among Palestinian literary scholars,[49] almost all of them have avoided the discussion of heresy in his writing. Those who do discuss it are critics affiliated with Islamist political movements, who seize upon it as a way to denounce Zayyad and his political views.[50]

CROSS-CONFESSIONAL MARRIAGE

Shortly after Zayyad's return to Nazareth, he became close to Na'ila Yusuf Sabbagh, his future wife. Na'ila had grown up in Nazareth's Eastern Neighborhood, as had Tawfiq, and was the daughter of two prominent communist activists of Christian background, Lulu and Yusuf Sabbagh. In 1958, Zayyad had been in prison with her father when Na'ila, then twelve years old (she was seventeen years younger than Tawfiq), accompanied her mother to the prison for a visit. Her father gave her a piece of paper and asked her to hide it in her shoe and give it to her mother later. At the time, she did not know that the paper included a poem Zayyad had written behind bars and wanted published, but a few years later, she became aware of Zayyad's poetry and admired it. She became active in the party and also had a record of several police arrests, including on October 29, 1964, when she was arrested alongside her mother, two of Tawfiq's brothers, and other activists marching in Nazareth to commemorate the Kafr Qasim massacre and protest the state's recent confiscation of land. In the trial that took place ten months later, Na'ila and her mother were sentenced to seven days in prison.[51]

The boundaries between personal life and public life in the Communist Party at the time were blurred, and many activists expected their fellow party members to take into consideration the public consequences of their personal decisions. Na'ila and Tawfiq's intention to cross confessional lines to marry therefore was much more than a personal matter. Mixed marriages in the Communist Party were not uncommon, but many Christians in Nazareth did not see the marriage of a Muslin man and a Christian woman favorably. Although their families supported the marriage, the young couple faced severe criticism in Nazareth, and even from within the party. Most disappointing for Zayyad was the opposition to the marriage expressed by Fu'ad Khuri, his teacher and longtime political companion. His wife, the communist activist Samira Khuri, even visited Na'ila's parents trying to convince them to cancel the marriage. These pressures turned out to be futile, and the couple married on March 31, 1966. Because of their objection to marrying in a religious ceremony and because Israel has no legal option for civil marriage, the wedding took place in Cyprus. The event shook the local branch of the party. The Khuri couple did not attend the wedding reception conducted after Tawfiq and Na'ila returned from Cyprus. Some Christian members of the Nazareth branch left the party in protest, and various official forums of the party, including the secretaries of the Nazareth branch and the Nazareth District, discussed the marriage. Secretary General Vilner had to reject the request of a Politburo member from Nazareth to discuss the marriage at the party's Politburo meeting.[52] According to Nazir Majali, the tension in Nazareth led Zayyad to temporarily move his center of activity (but not his residency) to Haifa, where he was appointed the editor of the literary journal al-Jadid.

Once again, a rift was revealed between the communist cosmopolitan ideology of senior party leaders and their practical approach toward religiously mixed families. The objection might have been related to instrumental political calculations: although religiously mixed marriages were common in the party, communists were aware that political rivals could use their atheism to discredit the party within traditional circles, which resented the party's encouragement of boys and girls mixing freely and frowned on intermarriage between Christians and Muslims.[53] What was tolerated in Haifa, where most of the party's mixed couples lived, was probably less acceptable in the local context of Nazareth.

Meanwhile, the couple lived with Zayyad's parents in their house in Nazareth for five years. In that period, their daughter, Wahiba, and their son, Amin, were born. The family celebrated both Muslim and Christian holidays as social traditions, but they divorced them from their religious content. The living arrangement and close quarters required household members to be mutually considerate. For example, when Na'ila wanted to walk from her bedroom to the kitchen, she preferred to take the long way, going outside and entering from the house's main entrance rather than walk through the main living room. When Tawfiq hosted his guests and served alcoholic beverages, he closed the room's door out of respect for his religious father.

Zayyad's modernity was inseparable from his Marxist vision, calling for economic equality, secular politics, and cosmopolitanism. It seems that his years in Moscow sealed his commitment to this vision, as well as his belief in the linear development of history that guarantees its realization. Zayyad's attraction to the sublime and the utopian was evident in his earlier poetry, but after his return from Moscow, he gained international recognition as a Palestinian national poet, a development that reaffirmed for him the political relevance of his poetry and its messages. While both Marxist vision and national revolutionary poetry pulled Zayyad toward inspirational ideals, he ascended to a leadership position in the party and in Nazareth politics—a development that forced him to apply constant pragmatic compromises. His careful navigation between the exaltation of poetry and the grayness of quotidian politics, as well as between Arab Palestinian liberation narratives and concrete demands of the Israeli political sphere, is the topic of the next chapter.

Chapter 4

IN THE CROSSFIRE

UNTIL THE MID-1960S, ZAYYAD WAS A LOCAL LEADER KNOWN MAINLY among Palestinian citizens of Israel. Among Palestinians outside Israel, he was only beginning to be noticed in literary circles as an important poet. Similarly, low-ranking Jewish party members who were active in the early 1960s and with whom I spoke did not have any recollections of Zayyad's activity at the time. The Jewish Israeli public would have read only occasional reports about him in the press. This relative marginality allowed him to maintain what sociologist Erving Goffman called "audience segregation"¹: he had a certain degree of freedom to emphasize different aspects of his political perspective according to the address-ees' identity. His Arab Palestinian national discourse was rarely translated into Hebrew. The ICP and especially the small number of Arabic-speaking Jewish poets affiliated with it were the only translators of his poems, and the few translated poems emphasized his cosmopolitan side (such as the poem dedicated to the Ata strikers discussed in chapter 3). With his gradual ascendancy into a position of national leadership and the growing circulation of his poetry in the Arab world, it would be increasingly difficult for him to speak differently to different audiences, causing sporadic confrontations between Zayyad and Jewish Israeli, as well as Palestinian, audiences.

SPLIT IN THE PARTY

Soon after Zayyad returned from Moscow equipped with theoretical and practical knowledge about political mobilization, he was reelected secretary of the ICP Nazareth branch and was frequently invited to speak at party events throughout the country. Most of the party's senior leaders had a reserved rhetorical style, and Zayyad quickly became known as an exciting and vibrant speaker who made use of examples from real life.[2] He emerged as a dominant leader in the party as it was in the process of adopting Arab Palestinian national rhetoric, a shift that followed a split in the ICP. Reflecting the fundamental failure of communist ideology to bridge the gap between competing conceptualizations of Zionism and the Israeli-Palestinian conflict, the Israeli Communist Party split into two factions in August 1965. The Zionist faction, which continued to use the name ICP, was led by Shmuel Mikunis and Moshe Sneh; it defined the conflict primarily as a clash between two equally legitimate national movements. The faction that later became known by its Hebrew acronym, Rakah, was led by Meir Vilner and Tawfiq Tubi and held that the conflict was, first and foremost, a struggle of a legitimate Arab Palestinian liberation movement against imperialism. While accepting the post-facto existence of an Israeli nation, this faction's leaders did not consider the two movements as having equal historical rights.[3]

The historical importance of the split is far-reaching. The Sneh-Mikunis faction was almost exclusively Jewish in its leadership and constituency, and within a decade, it would vanish. Rakah was diverse in its leadership, with a clear Arab majority comprising its constituency—a majority that kept increasing to the point where Jewish support for the party became quantitatively negligible, making the sizable Jewish presence in the party leadership an extreme overrepresentation of the party's Jewish base. Thus, there ceased to be a political party with numerically balanced Arab-Jewish partnership and a stable parliamentary representation

Zayyad reacted to the split in a poem he wrote that same summer. Titled "On the Strawberry Bush and the Oak Tree," the poem likened the Sneh-Mikunis faction to a strawberry bush, while the oak represented the real, ideologically committed Vilner-Tubi faction. Referring to the split's ethnonational dimension, Zayyad wrote, "I never hated a Jew, the hate of a People never penetrated my arteries." For Zayyad, the only painful aspect of the separation was the fact that the poet Alexander Pen went with the Sneh-Mikunis faction. Since the 1950s, Pen had been the most prominent Hebrew-language poet identified with the Communist Party, and Zayyad had special sympathy for him. Following Pen's death in May 1972, Zayyad wrote a long obituary, parts of it published in the Hebrew-language communist bulletin *Zo ha-Derekh*, describing Pen's poetry as "the pillar of the progressive humanistic culture of the People of Israel" and, in his characteristic optimism, asserting that "there is no doubt that this culture will be the dominant culture in this country in the not-so-distant future."[4] Zayyad's expression of admiration for Pen is notable, given that after the split, rarely did anyone have something positive to say about individuals in the other faction. (Pen was an extreme nonconformist and eventually left the party entirely.) In the Central Committee meeting following Pen's death, Zayyad said, "I do not think he betrayed us. Historically, he belongs to us."[5]

POETRY OF RESISTANCE

Tellingly, the split in the party coincided with the Arab world's discovery of Zayyad and other poets among the Palestinians in Israel, who were then celebrated as national heroes. The post-1948 armistice line had severed the cultural exchange between Palestinians who remained under Israeli rule and the rest of the Arab world, leading to many misconceptions and misunderstandings. "We suffered a lot from the Arab world considering us not patriotic," said Zayyad in a 1993 television interview. Suppressing an ironic smile, he added, "just because we stayed in our homeland."[6] Zayyad's poetry, especially its treatment of the collective predicament of the Palestinian People, decisively contributed to a drastic change in that image. His poetry's combination of classical Arabic poetic form with free verse and contemporary language—with some poems simulating the Palestinian vernacular and the rhythms of folk poetry[7]—surely contributed further to its popularity.

On February 12, 1966, *al-Ittihad* published for the first time one of his patriotic poems, "I Clasp Your Hands" ("Ashuddu 'ala Ayadikum"), which would also become one of his most famous poems. Nine years later, the communist Lebanese musician Ahmad Qa'bur turned the poem into the popular song "I Call Upon You" ("Unadikum"), which has since been performed by various singers and bands across the Arab world. The poem-song became a major anthem of Palestinian resistance and part of the repertoire of many Palestinian political demonstrations, especially in the 1980s. It is a passionate expression of the collective Palestinian experience and the poet's solidarity with his refugee compatriots. It also implores the diaspora Palestinians not to forget their brothers who remained under Israeli rule and suffered as well:

I call upon you
And clasp your hands.
I kiss the dust under your shoes
And say: I'll lay down my life for you,
Grant you the gift of eyesight in my eyes.
The warm love in my heart I give to you,
For the tragedy I live
Is but my share in your larger tragedy.
I call upon you
And clasp your hands.
I never stooped in my country
Nor will I ever be humbled.
Orphaned, naked and barefoot
I confronted my oppressors,
Carrying my blood in my palms.
I have never lowered my flags,
And have always tended the grass over my ancestors' graves.
I call upon you, and clasp your hands![8]

When the poem was first published, the party was in the midst of a public debate about the content and meaning of Arab revolutionary poetry in Israel, a debate in which Zayyad was involved as both a subject of analysis and an active participant. The debate itself was shaped partly by the split in the party, the internal divisions (political and personal) inside the Rakah faction, and Rakah's evolving relations with the Palestinian diaspora. Zayyad and his fellow revolutionary poets were alternately criticized for being too bitter and commended for their patriotic stand.

The debate had started in January 1965 when *al-Ittihad*'s editor at the time, Imil Tuma, published an article in *al-Jadid* in which he criticized revolutionary Arab poets in Israel for being too desperate and bitter in their recent poems and demanded that the poets observe the developments "from the point of view of the fighter."[9] The following issue of *al-Jadid* published two rebuttals by the journalist Muhammad Khass and the poet Salim Jubran. The biggest support for the criticized poets, however, came from beyond the border. In February 1966, the Palestinian journalist Ibrahim Abu Nab published an article, "The Poetic Ember in the Occupied Land," in the literary journal *al-'Ufuq al-Jadid*,

based in East Jerusalem, then under Jordanian rule. The author aimed to ed-
ucate his readers about the Palestinians who remained under Israeli rule and
criticized the general ignorance about their poetry. He stated, "Maybe the real
Nakba poetry today is written in the occupied land of Palestine," and the article
included poems by Mahmoud Darwish, Samih al-Qasim, and Tawfiq Zayyad.
From Zayyad's repertoire, he chose "Here We Shall Stay" ("Huna Baqun"), a poem
glorifying the steadfastness of the Palestinians under Israeli rule that combined
national and class protest:

> As though we were twenty impossibilities
> In Lydda, Ramla, and the Galilee,
> Here we shall stay
> Like a brick wall upon your breast
> And in your throats,
> Like a splinter of glass, like spikey cactus
> And in your eyes,
> A chaos of fire.
> Here we shall stay
> Like a brick wall upon your breast
> Washing dishes in idle, buzzing bars
> Pouring drinks for our overlords
> Scrubbing floors in blackened kitchens
> To snatch a scrub for our children
> From behind your blue fangs.[10]

That same year, on Nakba Day (May 15), the newspaper *Filastin* (previously
published in Jaffa and since 1948 published in East Jerusalem) published three
poems by Zayyad under the title "Songs of 15 May." The newspaper introduced
Zayyad as follows: "All the terror, the injustice, and the oppression were unable
to prevent these revolutionary whips from scorching the aggressors' skin. These
three poems of a poet who still lives in our looted land, behind the walls of the
big prison in Palestine."[11]

The reference to imprisonment is compatible with the newspaper's selection
of poems. The first among them was the well-known "On the Trunk of an Olive
Tree," depicting surveillance and detention as the author's existential experience.
It conveys the difficulties under the military regime of maintaining visible resistance in the public sphere:

Because I do not weave wool,

And daily I am in danger of detention,

And my house is the object of police visits

To search and "to cleanse,"

I shall carve the record of all my sufferings,

And all my secrets,

On the olive tree

In the courtyard of the house.[12]

The real turning point in the status of Zayyad and his fellow poets in the Arab world was a seminal essay published in June in Beirut by the Palestinian author Ghassan Kanafani. Titled "Resistance Literature in Occupied Palestine 1948–1966," the essay praised the Arab literature and poetry in these territories and "crowned" Zayyad, Jubran, Darwish, and al-Qasim as the "poets of resistance" among the Palestinians in Israel.[13] Kanafani wrote, "The poetry in the occupied land, contrary to the poetry of the exiled, is not weeping, lament, or despair, but a constant revolutionary inspiration and a hope inducing the inconceivable."[14]

When a year later, Israel decisively won the 1967 war, the Arab world grew even more interested in quotidian forms of resistance, and the Palestinian poetry and literature written in the 1948-occupied territory became a new model of Arab power. In October 1967, the Beirut-based journal *al-Adab* published a scholarly essay analyzing Zayyad's poetry.[15] The journal of the Lebanese Communist Party, *al-Tariq,* dedicated an entire issue to the literature of resistance inside Israel.[16] In April 1968, another icon of Arab national literature, the Syrian poet Nizar Qabbani, dedicated a poem of praise to the "poets of the occupied land" in which he specifically mentioned Darwish, Zayyad, and Fadwa Tuqan.[17] In December that year, a group of Fatah[18] leaders in a refugee camp in Jordan also expressed admiration for Zayyad and his fellow poets in an interview with the French newspaper *Le Monde.*[19] Rakah took pride in these "over the border" praises of the poets in its ranks and highlighted them in its own press.[20]

Zayyad's appointment as the editor of *al-Jadid* in 1966 allowed him to bring further public attention to themes highlighted by Kanafani, such as how the Nakba separated the Palestinians in Israel from their pre-1948 revolutionary poets, but nevertheless the revolutionary poetry of his generation is a direct extension of the prominent poetry of the 1920s and 1930s. In an October 1966 article, shortly after the publication of Kanafani's essay, Zayyad wrote, "We fight the same battle, in the same trench, for the love of the land and the People; we fight the same enemy: colonialism and its soldiers; we fight for the same goal: social and national liberation; we fight with the same weapon: courageous words shining bright."[21]

Zayyad's article was met with a response by the Mikunis-Sneh faction of the party, which had almost no Arab followers, though its leaders did not give up on the potential constituency and established a bulletin in Arabic, *Sawt al-Sha'b* (*Voice of the People*). Only a year after the split, they were determined to prove that Rakah was an Arab nationalist party that had abandoned the universalist communist principles. In a text signed "Y. A.," the bulletin criticized Zayyad for his repetitive use of the term *Nakba*. According to *Sawt al-Sha'b*, Zayyad's article was the first time the term had been used in this way in *al-Jadid* or *al-Ittihad*. It is legitimate, the anonymous author argued, to use the term in reference to the tragedy inflicted on the Arab Palestinian People by "both Arab and Jewish colonialism and reactionism." In the Arab states, though, it had already gained another meaning: the establishment of the State of Israel on part of the Arab homeland, an event that led to the expulsion of the Palestinian People. Zayyad was aware of this political meaning, the author claimed, and he knew that "Nakba Day" was May 14, the day the State of Israel was established. The author also wondered what Zayyad meant when he used the expression "revolutionary poetry": "Is this the communist revolutionary poetry, or rather the national revolutionary poetry? Or rather Tawfiq Zayyad does not distinguish between communist poetry and national poetry?"

The article also attacked Zayyad's claim that Arab revolutionary poetry in Israel called for Arab-Jewish brotherhood: "But the brother Tawfiq Zayyad, unfortunately, does not support this opinion with any evidence from the poems themselves."[22] Though *Sawt al-Sha'b* had very few readers and Zayyad did not seem to have bothered to respond to these accusations, the article is evidence of the growing importance of Zayyad himself and the awareness of this importance among Jewish communists, as well as of his emerging role in Rakah as the voice of Arab Palestinian national trends.

At the same time, among the "poets of resistance," Zayyad was probably the most significant advocate of a Marxist perspective and class consciousness, as can be seen in his engagement with other poets. Because for a long time they had no access to literary critics in the Arab world, Palestinian poets inside Israel developed a habit of reviewing one another's work.[23] In December 1966, Zayyad published a review of Mahmoud Darwish's collection, *Lover of Palestine*. Zayyad admired Darwish's poetry but asked for a stronger proletarian approach and global perspective: "I consider the poems included in *Lover of Palestine* among the best poetry written today in Arabic, and not only in our country. We are all looking forward to the next collection. Until then, we deserve to demand from him basic principles: to engage more with the struggle of other Peoples [. . .] and to develop his vertical perspective [namely—referring at class stratification]. In order to do so, it is necessary that he deepen his class orientation."[24]

NEW FRONTIERS

The morning of June 5, 1967, Na'ila and Tawfiq Zayyad were at home with their two-week-old daughter, Wahiba, listening to the radio news about the war that had just begun. Experienced in the Israeli authorities' practice of preemptive arrests, detaining Palestinian leaders inside Israel, whom the security services considered a potential "fifth column," Zayyad told his wife that he would be arrested soon. Indeed, several hours later, the police came and took him, together with other party members, and he remained in administrative detention throughout the Six-Day War.

The unquestionable military victory of Israel in the war triggered euphoric sentiments among the Jewish Israeli public and melancholy among the Arabs. In Zayyad's messianic Marxist perspective, however, the war was only a twist in history's progress, as he wrote in his short poem "One Step Backward, Ten Steps Forward" (alluding to Lenin's famous booklet, "One Step Forward, Two Steps Back"):

> Merely a tumble
> That could happen to any gallant knight,
> It is one step backward
> For ten steps forward.[25]

Even what looks like an Israeli victory was actually a Pyrrhic one, as Zayyad warned when addressing Israeli Jews: "Do not tell me 'we won' / This victory is worse than a defeat."[26] The assessment of the war's impact on the occupier, he wrote, should be examined in the long term:

> You build for today
> We for tomorrow erect our buildings
> We are deeper than the sea below
> And taller than the lanterns of the sky above

In us you find a breath,

Longer than this extended range

In the heart of space.[27]

The Israeli conquest of the West Bank and the Gaza Strip brought the majority of the Palestinian People under Israeli rule. These circumstances had complicated, and sometimes contradictory, implications for Palestinians in Israel. On the one hand, they now were much better connected to Palestinians in the newly occupied territories. Party members were able to renew their contacts with former comrades like Fu'ad Nassar and Rushdi Shahin. The communist bulletin *al-Watan*, published illegally in the West Bank, was accessible to party members within the Green Line, and segments of it appeared frequently in *al-Ittihad*.

The difference in political status for Palestinians on either side of the Green Line meant different experiences, political strategies, and collective self-images. In December 1966, the military rule imposed on Palestinians in Israel since 1949 had been officially lifted, and although some restrictions remained in effect, Palestinians in Israel had more freedoms than those who came under Israeli military occupation in June 1967. In addition, after the war, it became clear that Israel was not going to disappear, and Palestinian citizens of Israel gradually turned to the Israeli political sphere to cope with their predicament, becoming active participants in the Israeli political system.[28] Zayyad's insistence on the legitimacy of his active Israeli citizenship would lead to sporadic tensions with Arab Palestinian nationalism.

These tensions played out in the public arena because of the strengthening of Zayyad's status in his party. Israel uses the closed-list method of party list proportional representation, in which citizens vote for their preferred party and not for any individual candidates. While in 1965 Zayyad was positioned in the thirteenth place on Rakah's list for the Knesset election, making him unlikely to be seated, in the following election in 1969, he was ranked fifth (though the party won only three seats). In addition, parallel to his activity in the Nazareth Municipality, he became increasingly involved in the party's central institutions and in 1968 began to participate in the regular meetings of the Central Committee after being appointed to its advisory committee. The growing involvement of Palestinian citizens in Israeli politics, however, was full of contradictions. For many Arab political activists, the actual, substantive dismantling of military rule was slow and limited, and their movement was still restricted: they were required to ask for a permit to leave their towns. As late as 1971, members of the Rakah Central Committee from Nazareth missed meetings because the authorities refused to issue a permit for traveling from Nazareth to Haifa.[29] Zayyad missed at least two meetings for that reason (restrictions on his movement were lifted only after his election as a Knesset member in 1974). The ambivalence of the party to state violence created some absurd moments. For example, one party member, Yehuda Unger, was absent from the Central Committee meeting on March 9, 1972, because he was implementing state violence as a soldier in reserve service, while party member Saliba Khamis was absent because he was a victim of state violence in the form of restricted movement.[30]

The disagreements among Rakah leaders were shaped as well by regional developments. The defeat in 1967 led to the collapse of pan-Arabism as an ideology promulgated by revolutionary regimes, which in turn paved the way for the revival of the Palestinian national movement. The Palestine Liberation Organization (PLO), established in 1964 by Nasser to contain Palestinian national aspiration, was taken over in 1968 by the Fatah and gained widespread recognition as the organization representing the Palestinian struggle. The wave of attacks by various PLO-affiliated organizations against Israeli targets in subsequent years required Rakah to take a stand. The consensus among the party leaders was based on two principles: first, that the State of Israel was the expression of the legitimate right of the Israeli-Jewish People to self-determination, while the Palestinian People had a similar right; and second, that the party did not encourage an armed struggle by Palestinian citizens of Israel and should not be perceived as actively encouraging it among other Palestinians, especially if they targeted civilians.[31] Within this consensus, though, there was a wide range of levels of sympathy with the politics and methods implemented by the Palestinian national movement.

On this spectrum, Zayyad was more sympathetic to the PLO than were the senior leaders of the party. He clearly had a genuine interest in bridging the gap between his party and the various factions of the Palestinian national movement. In the Central Committee meeting on May 15, 1969, for example, when Secretary General Vilner commented that the Fatah movement's perspective was chauvinist because it did not recognize the existence of a Jewish national home in the country, Zayyad implored the party "not to throw the baby with the water, not to throw away a national movement because of mistakes." He argued that he could identify a recent change: "The Palestinian liberation movement is moving from empty chauvinist words to political positions that could be debated. The problem with the slogan of the Palestinian state is the will to force the Jewish People to give up on its state [. . .] but there is a great progress among the Arab communist parties. They talk about Israel as a state."[32] Zayyad's attempt to be a bridge between his Israeli party and the PLO, however, led to his poetry being selectively read and edited. The members of his party, and especially the Jews among them, emphasized the pro-peace messages; his Zionist critics emphasized the more combative elements, and Palestinians in the diaspora emphasized the patriotic face of his poetry.

A case in point is Zayyad's ode "The Prisoners of Freedom." In late April 1970, seven hundred administrative detainees in Israeli prisons began a hunger strike to protest detention without trial. Fatah called for a general strike in solidarity with the prisoners in the West Bank and the Gaza Strip and among the Palestinians in Israel. *Al-Ittihad* supported the hunger strike and stated that ten thousand Palestinian prisoners had joined it. Zayyad's personal experience had made him particularly attentive to the predicament of humans behind bars, and he wrote an ode in support of the prisoners. First published on May 8, 1970, in *al-Ittihad* as a series of nine poems, the ode praises the self-sacrifice of the prisoners fighting to ensure that "Arab land would remain Arab" and condemns their oppressors. But the sixth poem, "What I Deny and What I Do Not Deny," adopts a reconciliatory tone:

I do not deny any right
Whatever it would be
Of your Jews, Israel
Because among them
I have comrades in arms.
I would walk with them
Until the last step
To obtain our common bright future.
I do not deny the right of the other People
To be in a state of their own
To build it as they wish.
They could divide it into more than one state
Make it a heaven or hell
Paint it in any color they wish,

Make it a dough, and to bake it into a bread and eat it,
If they so wish.[33]

These lines, which bitterly accept Israel as part of reality, created uneasiness among Palestinian refugees. Later that year, when the PLO-affiliated publisher located in Beirut, Dar al-'Awda, republished the ode in a collection of Zayyad's poetry, *Songs of Revolution and Rage (Ughniyyat al-thawra wa-l-ghadab)*,[34] the editor, Ahmad Muhammadiyya, omitted lines 3 to 5, which might have implied not only a recognition of the State of Israel but even a shared camaraderie with Jewish Israelis. He replaced the missing lyrics with ellipses (see figure 1).[35] From the other side of the border, among the nine poems comprising the ode, only the sixth one, the reconciliatory poem, was translated into Hebrew—and even twice.[36] The controversy was probably noticed in the party. When the ode was republished in a poetry collection in 1973 in Nazareth, the entire sixth poem was excluded.

PRAGUE

While the party made any effort to distance itself from the armed struggle, Zayyad found himself indirectly and nonvoluntarily associated with it. On June 29, 1969, a car bomb exploded in Tel Aviv, injuring twelve people—the first in a series of bombs found or exploded in Israeli cities in the 1969–1970 period. In July 1971, the authorities arrested suspects, including Zayyad's friend and brother-in-law, 'Abd al-Malik Dahamsha. The security services charged Dahamsha with recruiting activists to a Fatah cell,[37] and on May 21, 1971, it sentenced him to seven years in prison plus a three-year suspended sentence. *Davar* reporter Ehud Ya'ari wrote that Zayyad's family connection to the armed struggle was a concern for the Rakah's leadership and speculated that this was the reason Zayyad was sent on a party mission to Prague in 1972–1973,[38] though party officials and Zayyad's family members denied any link.

Regardless of the reason for their journey, on July 16, 1972, Tawfiq Zayyad, his wife, Na'ila, and their children, Wahiba and Amin, arrived in Prague. Zayyad was appointed the editor of the Arabic version of the *Problems of Peace and Socialism*, published by the Information Department of the Communist Party of the Soviet Union as a way to spread the party's views worldwide. The journal's editorial team was also an important hub for sponsorship of international conferences and

٦ — ما انكر وما لا انكر

أنا لا أنكر حقاً

مهما كان

.   .   .   .   .

.   .   .   .   .

.   .   .   .   .

أمشي معهم حتى آخر خطوة

FIGURE 1. The missing lines from Zayyad's poem published
by the PLO.
Source: Tawfīq Zayyad, *Ughniyyat Al-Thawra wa-l-Ghadab*
(Beirut: Dar al-'Awda, 1970), 119.

maintaining contact among representatives of various communist and political
parties worldwide.

Though he was in Prague, Zayyad did not abandon his public presence back
home. He published political commentary in *al-Ittihad*, analyzing international
developments, such as the dynamics of the war in Vietnam and the elections in
France. Away from the constraints on Palestinian political activists in Israel, he
also had the opportunity to meet with leaders from the PLO, and in August 1973,
while he was at the Festival of the Communist Youth in East Berlin, the East
German authorities organized a meeting between him, Yasser Arafat, and the
Jewish Rakah member, Binyamin Gonen. The meeting was attended as well by
Faruq al-Qaddumi, one of the founding leaders of Fatah, and the poet Mahmoud
Darwish, who was already part of the PLO and who translated for Gonen, who
did not speak Arabic. The meeting was held in secret, with the East German
secret services driving Zayyad and Gonen blindfolded so they did not know their
location; Zayyad did not even tell Na'ila, who was with him in Berlin, about the

meeting. For over two decades, none of the participants spoke publicly about the meeting, until in 1994, when Arafat went to the Gaza Strip to establish the Palestinian National Authority he mentioned it in a public event. Gonen described the meeting as friendly, though the communist representatives argued with the PLO and criticized it for adopting armed struggle.[39]

In Prague, the Zayyad family settled first in the modest Koněvova neighborhood and moved later to the more prestigious Dejvice quarter. Zayyad was busy with his work, and had little time to be with his family and for personal development. Nevertheless, after several months in Prague, the family went on a vacation together in Moscow, where Zayyad took his wife and children on a pilgrimage visit to the tomb of Lenin. Back in Prague, Tawfiq and Na'ila both took driving lessons and got their driving license. Tawfiq also adopted the habit of smoking a pipe, which became part of his public image for several years. During his period, the Czechoslovakian security services opened a secret investigation of Zayyad after suspicion was aroused that he was working for the Israeli intelligence.[40] Zayyad, whose code name in the secret files was Pěkna (in Czech, "pretty" in the feminine form), was most likely never aware of this investigation, and the file was closed without any evidence to confirm the suspicion.

In September 1973, Zayyad flew home from Prague to take part in the preparations for the parliamentary elections scheduled for October 30. He clearly positioned himself as an opposition to the established leadership of the party. During the discussion of the list of candidates at a Central Committee meeting, he surprised everyone by suggesting that Meir Vilner and Tawfiq Tubi, the two supreme leaders of the party, who had served as members of the Knesset since 1948 and had led Rakah since the split in 1965, should not be included on the list. This was an exceptional demand in the context of the authoritative style of leadership exercised in the party, and Zayyad was probably the only member of the Central Committee who had the courage to make such a demand. Even in internal discussions, members usually avoided presenting ideas that diametrically opposed the consensus or the leaders' positions. Probably to indicate that he was not trying to promote his own interests, Zayyad declared that he should not be included either: "I do not fit this kind of work. I will keep doing my work in Prague and in the literary field."[41]

It is difficult to see much sincerity in this statement, however, given his inclusion on the list in previous elections and his eventual acceptance of his inclusion toward the top of the party list for the upcoming election. In any case, none of the other committee members supported Zayyad's suggestion. Meir Vilner responded that the result of removing him and Tubi from the list would be "a calamity," and the idea was not discussed further. Zayyad was positioned fourth on the party list, and on January 21, 1974, he pledged allegiance as a member of the Israeli Knesset (MK).

With his election, Zayyad returned to Nazareth with his young daughter, Wahiba, while Na'ila remained with their son, Amin, in Prague until the end of the school year. Because Zayyad was a member of the Communist Party, his MK salary went to the party; he received a much smaller allocation, so his election had little influence on his economic condition. Before leaving for Prague, the income from Na'ila's work as a clerk in a law office enabled them to build their own apartment on the roof of the house of Zayyad's parents. In his new life as a MK, he had to divide his time between Jerusalem and Nazareth, which meant spending a lot of time on the road. In 1974 Tawfiq and Na'ila purchased their first car, a 1969 Volkswagen, which remained with them for the next decade. Zayyad liked driving; he drove fast, and some of his acquaintances described him as a reckless driver. He restrained himself while driving with the solemn senior leaders of the party, but on other occasions, his driving resembled his fiery style of public speaking, with sudden shifts from lane to lane resembling the strategy he had to adopt as a public figure navigating between his status as a Palestinian national icon and a legislator in the Zionist parliament.

FIGHTING ON TWO FRONTS

The first public criticism of Zayyad after he became an MK came from Palestinian poet Mu'in Bsaysu, who on February 14, 1974, published an open letter to Zayyad in the magazine *al-Usbu' al-'Arabi*: "Tawfiq Zayyad—the poet of the occupied land—is now a member of the Israeli Knesset! The poet of resistance is now a member of the Israeli parliament! And believe me that the injury now is bigger than a knife's injury." After further elaborating on how much he was hurt, Bsaysu begged Zayyad to leave the Knesset and asked him to remember what Israel did to other Palestinian authors: "Do you remember with me now how they exploded Ghassan Kanafani and how, for the first time, they separated the author's head from his hand?[42] And remember with me now Kamal Nasir,[43] and how they shot tens of bullets to his mouth! While they killed Kamal Nasir through his mouth, how could you speak from your own mouth under the ceiling of the Israeli parliament, oh Tawfiq Zayyad?" The famous Egyptian composer Shaykh

Imam, who had created his own melodic version of Zayyad's poem "Ashuddu 'ala Ayadikum" while sitting in Egyptian prison, was also baffled. When he met Zayyad in 1984 in France, he told him, "For many years I have been waiting to meet you so I can ask: How could you look at yourself in the mirror while you are a member of the Israeli Knesset?"[44]

The best-known and turbulent controversy during his time as a member of the Knesset, however, unfolded among Zionists angered by his poem about the 1973 war. On October 6, 1973, the Egyptian and Syrian armies surprised Israel with a coordinated attack on the southern and northern fronts. For the first time since 1948, the Arab side achieved decisive tactical victories on the battlefield. Zayyad was highly impressed by the achievement of the Arab armies and saw it as a major turning point. "The world has changed," he stated repeatedly in his political commentary and in his radio speech as part of the 1973 Knesset elections campaign, as well as in his poetry. While in Prague during the war, Zayyad wrote his ode "The Great Crossing" (al-'Ubur al-Kabir) praising the Egyptian army for the successful military operation.[45] The title alluded to the crossing of the Suez Canal by the Egyptian army in the first hours of the war. Al-Ittihad published the ode on December 23, 1973. At the time, the Hebrew media did not express any interest. Three months later, the journalist Danny Rubinstein quoted a few lines from the poem in a report about the euphoria among the Arab citizens of Israel following the war, but he did not highlight the most charged expressions, and his report was published without incident.[46] Toward the first anniversary of the war, though, al-Ittihad republished Zayyad's ode, and this second publication was followed by a public uproar.

It started eleven days after the publication, with a brief report in Davar that translated some selected lines into Hebrew:

> The night was long
> Heavy was the humiliation
> And the wound was deep.
> Even our bread was full of degradation
> But now . . . the joy, watered by blood, sprouted in each entity.
> [. . .]
> The fierce brown faces collapsed the Bar-Lev line,
> The crossing was sacred, and the flags were re-raised in their previous
>   place,
> And tears of joy welled up in the eyes. [47]

There followed an outpouring of angry reactions from across the Zionist political spectrum. In the Hebrew daily *Ma'ariv*, the poet Moshe Dor, after reading a Hebrew translation, condemned Zayyad harshly, stating, "There is no sacredness in death and in the loss of young lives for satisfying the lust for war or for healing an injured pride. There is no beauty in disability, illness, and destruction. This is a hideous lie. And he who lies like that—seemingly for an idea, seemingly for uprightness, seemingly for liberation—does not deserve the right to be a poet."[48]

Publicly, the party gave Zayyad lukewarm backing, and some leaders expressed uneasiness behind closed doors. In the meeting of the Central Committee that took place a day after the publication of Dor's article, there were different opinions. Uzi Burshtein, a prominent Jewish party leader, wondered why the party was not providing more public backing for Zayyad, but another Jewish member, Yoram Gojanski, called for "carefulness" and commented, "Maybe, at that moment, the ode should not have [appeared] in *al-Ittihad*." [49] Arguments against the timing were frequently a subtle way for communists to express opposition to a concrete policy or action.

Zayyad himself noted that the second publication included only parts of the ode, and had he been asked, he would have not agreed to this selective publication. He had nothing to be ashamed of when considering the ode in its entirety, he added, agreeing that the "timing and the selected parts were not the best," but at the same time, "I felt uncomfortable when I saw *al-Ittihad* without any response [to Moshe Dor's criticism]."[50] In his concluding statement, Secretary General Meir Vilner commented that the publication of the ode was "a tactical mistake of the newspaper. I do not criticize the ode itself, but objectively, it did not benefit us."

This very cautious criticism against Zayyad highlights the growing legitimization of the Palestinian national narrative within the party ranks, as well as the decline in the relative share of Jewish voters for the party.[51] Compare Vilner's understated criticism with the harsh rhetoric directed toward the poets Samih al-Qasim and Mahmoud Darwish after they read their poems in the party convention almost six years earlier. Back then, Vilner described al-Qasim's poem as "an awful poem and a noncommunist one. It is not only nationalist but even chauvinist. It must not be ignored. We should argue and convince. This is a poem that contradicts our entire approach."[52] Ramzi Khuri said that he "was shocked" by the poems. I was unable to trace the exact texts the two poets read in the convention, although *Zo ha-Derekh* mentioned that al-Qasim read a poem against the occupation and Darwish read parts from the poem "The New History" (a title that does not appear among Darwish's published poems).[53] At the time, Zayyad alone explicitly contradicted the secretary general, despite it being his first appearance at the Central Committee meeting. He argued that "al-Qasim's poem was not chauvinist. It was a Don Quixote poem, not politically wise but not chauvinist." On Darwish's poem, he said simply that it was a "bad poem."[54]

It seems that in the almost six years that had passed, the revival of the Palestinian national movement and its popularity among Palestinians in Israel had forced Vilner and other communist leaders to adopt a more conciliatory attitude toward Arab Palestinian national sentiments. In addition, not only had the party lost most of its support in the Jewish public following the 1965 split, but it had gradually become the major political force among the Arab public. In the 1973 elections, the party gained 37 percent of the Arab vote, making it the single largest party among Arab citizens for the first time.[55] Trying to "tame" Zayyad, in the same way they treated al-Qasim and Darwish in 1969, would have risked alienating the wide base of the party's support.

The Knesset Committee, a parliamentary committee responsible for internal rules of the Knesset, met on November 5, 1974, to discuss the ode. Zayyad declined the invitation to attend. All the members of the committee except for Avraham Levenbraun, Zayyad's colleague from the party, agreed that the publication of the ode "in its entirety, is a celebration for killing and war, glorification of murder and thirst for the blood of IDF soldiers."[56] The committee's press release concluded that the ode was "incompatible with the pledge of allegiance made by Zayyad as a Knesset member." Some Zionist MKs and other public figures demanded the revocation of Zayyad's parliamentary immunity and urged the authorities to begin a legal process against him. Attorney General Meir Shamgar rejected this demand, and by late December 1974, the party officials became more assertive in defending him, defining the demands to penalize him in the Knessest as "malicious provocation and hypocrisy."[57]

Zayyad did not remain untouched by this widespread condemnation. His uncompromising character and his frequent readiness to confront Israeli authorities might have misled some observers to conclude that he was indifferent to his image among Jewish Israelis. This could not have been further from the truth. As much as he wrote the ode for Palestinian and Arab audiences, the partial regret he expressed in the Central Committee about the circumstances of the second publication of the ode is evidence that he was concerned about the potential implications of the public turmoil on his image among Israeli Jews. Zayyad collected the press reports and reactions, as well as the private letters of protest, and asked his friends among Jewish poets for help.

The Jewish poet Y. B. Y (Yona Ben Yehuda) organized a public talk for him in Tel Aviv. Before leaving Jerusalem to go to Tel Aviv, Zayyad asked his friend, the journalist Ilyas Nasr Allah, to help him by translating certain lines from the ode into Hebrew[58] so he could use them in his speech. About two hundred people attended, and Zayyad defended his position, drawing from a text he wrote for publication in Arabic but adding some messages specifically for his Jewish audience. As usual, Zayyad wrote the notes for his talk in Arabic but delivered his speech in Hebrew. He argued that some of his expressions were taken out of context and were interpreted in a distorted way:

> They are lynching me, inciting murder. This is McCarthyism. Someone took some parts of a poem I wrote a year ago and presented me as if I am thirsty for the blood of IDF soldiers. [...] I am not against the state but against its policy of occupation. I did not pledge allegiance to the occupation. [...] In my poem I described the joy of the Arab People who succeeded, after four hundred years of humiliation, to prove that they are not cowards and to liberate a small part of their occupied lands. Is it forbidden to describe this joy?

Zayyad mentioned that some of his condemnations in the media appeared on the same day and with the exact same wording, arguing that this pattern indicated the involvement of a guiding hand: the security services.[59] In the notes Zayyad prepared for his speech, he described himself as in the "crossfire," and he specifically mentioned Mu'in Bsaysu "and others" who attacked him from a Palestinian perspective for sitting in the Knesset.

While Zayyad only briefly mentioned some politicians who attacked him, he spared no words when rebutting the arguments of writers, especially Moshe Dor and Aharon Megged, two authors who "pretend to be supporters of Arab-Jewish mutual understanding." He recited the Hebrew translation of lines from the ode, quoted their interpretations by Dor and Megged, and explained why they were wrong. He argued that the ode itself contained his clear pacifist orientation, but his critics ignored the relevant lines:

> I hate bloodshed and the sirens of alarm
> I hate the blue color
> On the cars' lights[60]

I hate the cry of a mother or a wife
The killing of a little boy or a girl
I hate a bomb falling on the roads
Or in the yard of a safe house.
I hate all the wars in the world
Except one war
The war for liberation.[61]

In his attempt to avoid the crossfire, Zayyad tried crossing the abyss separating him and most of the Jewish Israeli public. Several weeks after the meeting in Tel Aviv, he asked the poet Moshe Barzilai (known also as A. Nof) to write a Hebrew translation of three of his well-known humanistic universalist poems ("The Singer," "What I Own," and "A Million Suns in My Blood").[62] Zayyad merged these poems under the title "Résumé," as if saying, *This is me; I am not the person the media portrays.* The first poem in the short collection, "The Singer," was written in December 1966 while Na'ila and Tawfiq were expecting their first child, and its first lines read:

I would give half of my life
To anyone who makes a weeping child laugh
And I give my other half to protect a green plant from withering.

In mid-February 1975, Barzilai translated the poems into Hebrew (later published in *Zo ha-Derekh*[63]) and sent them to Zayyad. Coincidently, Zayyad received the translations the same day his third child was born; she was given an uncommon name, 'Ubur, meaning "crossing" in Arabic.

The tension between being an Arab Palestinian national poet and a meaningful actor in Israeli politics was central to Zayyad's public life, and this tension was heightened in the period between 1966 and 1974 as he found sudden international fame as a "poet of resistance" and later became a legislator in the Israeli Knesset. The controversy surrounding his "Great Crossing" poem brought the tension to a head, closing a chapter in his trajectory as a poet. For the next fifteen years he wrote no poetry. Zayyad's own explanation for his silence was lack of time because he needed to focus on his political work. However, the issue was not only one of time allocation; it was related to his duality in his approach to politics. On the one hand, he held a utopian vision of the future of humanity in general and of his own People in particular. This vision was inevitable, its truth was undeniable, and Zayyad articulated it with the enthusiasm and conviction of a revolutionary poet. His messianic-like conviction was a powerful tool in mobilizing followers, and it was an important element in his charismatic public persona. As parliament member and mayor, though, he acted with calculated, realistic, and clear-eyed tactical pragmatism—and the state of mind required for this pragmatism might have been an obstacle for poetry.

At the same time, the combination of fiery poetic charisma with a skill for mundane pragmatism was the source of Zayyad's power in his next challenge: preparing himself to conquer Nazareth city hall to become the first mayor elected against the will of the Israeli government.

Chapter 5

MUNICIPAL STRUGGLES

DURING THE GREAT REVOLT IN THE 1930S, THE YOUNG TAWFIQ Zayyad brought food to his father when he was detained by the British authorities in the local jail. Almost four decades after the revolt, Zayyad entered that same building, now transformed into the house of the Nazareth Municipality, as the city's new mayor. His way to the mayoralty had been an uphill battle against a hostile government that considered communist rule in Nazareth a major threat. The battle had many twists and turns, culminating in a memorable victory on a December night in 1975. That victory was much more than a personal one. Because Palestinian citizens had limited access to the political centers of power at the state level, municipalities became by default a sphere of direct political influence. The antiestablishment victory in Nazareth was the first in a series of successes at the local level that cumulatively extended the political power of Palestinian citizens.

AN UPHILL BATTLE

In March 1968, Fu'ad Khuri, who had led the communist list in the elections for the Nazareth Municipal Council since its establishment in 1954, died from cancer at the age of forty-nine. Although Zayyad was not the most senior activist in the Nazareth branch, he was well positioned to inherit his mentor's position as the party leader in the city. Together with his long-time guide and ally, Mun'im Jarjura, Zayyad took on Khuri's responsibilities in the Nazareth party branch.

Khuri's death also coincided with Zayyad's emergence as a recognized Palestinian national poet, a development that boosted his local prestige. The party leadership understood Zayyad's electoral appeal, and in addition to including him in the Central Committee and in fifth place on the party list for the 1969 Knesset election (which was not high enough to make him a Knesset member that year), he became the party's mayoral candidate in the December 1970 local elections .

Since 1948, Nazareth had been a major political battleground between communists and Israeli governments, which consistently supported and encouraged other parties in order to keep the communists out of power. Because Nazareth was the largest Palestinian urban center inside Israel and its religious importance made it a focus of international attention, both sides invested great effort in gaining control over the city's municipal council. The 1970 municipal elections, the first to be held after the 1967 war, coincided with a new momentum within the Palestinian national movement. Therefore, both the Israeli government and Rakah considered them a major power test. As Emile Habibi wrote during the 1970 municipal election campaigns, "The battle is local, but the beams of Nazareth are far reaching."[1]

In June 1970, Israel's General Security Service (Shabak) reported that "there is a real concern that the municipal elections will enable Rakah to gain the mayorship" and speculated that "maybe if we immediately put a concentrated effort into improving the situation in the city, in the time left before the elections, we will be able to prevent the election of a mayor representing Rakah."[2] Therefore, the government, after years of neglecting Nazareth's infrastructure, suddenly found significant funding for paving roads and installing lights, as well as building and renovating schools, in the month before the elections, and it made sure residents would see the projects.[3]

During the election campaign, the party and Zayyad himself capitalized on his fame as a poet. In the party list, which identified candidates by their profession (a common communist custom), Zayyad was described as a poet, and in reports about party events from that period, any mention of Zayyad almost always linked him to a poem he publicly recited. The day before the municipal elections, *al-Ittihad* republished the first part of Zayyad's famous poem "I Clasp Your Hands" ("Ashuddu 'Ala Ayadikum"), but this time under the title "I Call on You All" ("Unadikum"), with explicit framing: "For the people of Nazareth, tomorrow—I CALL ON YOU ALL—by Tawfiq Zayyad, the first candidate in the communist list."[4] Below the excerpt from the poem, *al-Ittihad* reminded readers of Zayyad's global fame. In the elections, the communists gained 39 percent of the votes, but after 161 days of a convoluted process, with intensive involvement of the Israeli government behind the scenes, they remained again in the opposition. The new coalition elected the government's candidate, Sayf al-Din al-Zu'bi, as mayor.

In a Central Committee meeting in summer 1972, Zayyad reflected on the future of his municipal service: "I will not grow in the direction of municipal work. I have served nineteen years in the Nazareth Municipal Council. [There] they accepted my position—that I will stop leading the party in the city hall. I want to be released completely. [. . .] I would like to develop in the direction that will serve best the party."[5] While what party members said in public about their personal aspirations should be taken with a grain of salt—denials of personal interest were frequently a smoke screen or a form of compliance with communist norms—it is possible that after the years of futile attempts to lead his party into power in city hall, Zayyad got tired and considered focusing on becoming a Knesset member or pursuing his literary interests. His travel to Prague in 1972 might have been related to this fatigue as well.

When Zayyad resigned from the municipal council and left for Prague, Mun'im Jarjura resigned with him, creating a vacuum in the leadership of the Nazareth branch. At the same time, Emile Habibi resigned from the Knesset and, according to reports in the Hebrew press, intended to take control of the Nazareth branch and run for mayor.[6] Publicly, Habibi denied the reports. Another prominent activist, Ghassan Habib, became a dominant public figure in Nazareth and began forming alliances with other local forces in order to conquer city hall in the next elections. For this purpose, he joined efforts with the Association of Academics, a group of university graduates and professionals established in 1971 to influence local politics in opposition to the government that was independent from Rakah.[7]

In August 1973, while the different forces prepared for the municipal elections scheduled for October 30 (at the time, parliamentary and municipal elections took place on the same day), the Interior Ministry announced that the elections in Nazareth and eleven other Arab localities would be postponed until the next year (December 1974). Communist protests and legal appeals failed to change the verdict.[8] Because of the October war, parliamentary and municipal elections in the country were postponed until December 31, 1973, but Nazareth municipal elections were still excluded. The results for the Knesset elections, though, confirmed the national government's fears: in Nazareth, 60 percent of the voters preferred Rakah, an unprecedented success that demonstrated its ability to take control of the local council should local elections take place.

The city administration elected in 1970, meanwhile, had proved to be dysfunctional, and it suffered from an ongoing financial crisis stemming from extreme underfunding and discrimination of Nazareth, as an Arab city, in government grants.[9] In April 1974, the financial crisis in Nazareth led to the resignation of Mayor Zu'bi, who left behind a corrupt and wasteful municipal apparatus and a failing tax-collection system.[10] Rather than allowing the communists to establish a coalition under their leadership, the interior minister dismissed the local council, reappointed an external committee to run the city, and postponed elections to an unknown date. In an April 1974 interview with *Zo ha-Derekh*, Zayyad blamed the crisis primarily on the Israeli government, which underfunded his city, he argued, and he provided data to substantiate his claim. He stated that under his leadership, the communists had repeatedly sought to join the coalition in order to share the burden, but the government forced its supporters in the municipality to avoid any collaboration.[11]

Zayyad, who had been sworn in as a member of the Knesset in January that same year, addressed the Knesset assembly, demanding an investigation of the minister's decision. He argued that the dire condition of the city—its corruption, negligence, and chaos—had been known for a while and that the state of affairs actually served the state's interests. Zayyad took full advantage of the opportunity to highlight the predicament of his city. He outlined the discrimination in planning and land confiscation. He reminded the assembly that there was no single worthy factory in the city, that the transportation infrastructure was wretched and the streets were in horrible condition, and that there were no parks, no public library, no intellectual life, and no appropriate buildings for schools. He pointed out that the governmental annual funding per capita for the city was only one-sixth of the amount given to a Jewish city of a similar size. The government prevented the communists from governing the city, but the people of Nazareth, said Zayyad, knew how to respond to the minister's decision: by forming a national unification.[12]

In invoking national unification, Zayyad was referring to a process that had begun to unfold in Nazareth since August 1973 as the government's refusal to allow municipal elections galvanized opposition and mobilized wide circles of activism. In late June 1974, a group of 117 religious leaders, lawyers, doctors, pharmacists, engineers, accountants, high school teachers, and other college graduates from the city sent a letter of protest to Prime Minister Yitzhak Rabin and his interior minister, urging them to conduct elections in Nazareth.[13] Similar public letters of protest were signed in July by 177 merchants and craftsmen, as well as by Nazarene university students.[14] The political dynamics at the time were influenced by the Arab achievement in the 1973 war and the growing international recognition of the PLO, including a UN Assembly resolution from October that recognized it as the representative of the Palestinians.[15] Furthermore, the Arab League decided later that month to define the PLO as "the sole legitimate representative of the Palestinian People" in order to confront Israeli attempts to bypass the PLO by negotiation with other parties. These parties included the king of Jordan and the local Israel-friendly "leadership" that the military occupation in the West Bank and the Gaza Strip tried to nurture.

Among Palestinians in Israel, the communists faced the growing power of noncommunist nationalist voices. Under these circumstances, the collaboration between communists and academics blossomed into an official united front aimed at challenging the pro-establishment actors in Nazareth. The newly established alliance, the Nazareth Democratic Front, also included the Committee of Merchants and Craftsmen and the Association of University Students of Nazareth. The idea of a "front" of communists and noncommunists has deep roots in communist political philosophy and practice, particularly in the writing of the Italian scholar and political leader Antonio Gramsci and the Bulgarian leader Georgi Dimitrov, both of whom party publications referenced on occasion.[16]

The establishment of the front was based on the hope that despite the state's pattern of canceling Nazareth's municipal elections, the elections on December 9, 1974, would take place as planned. The Israeli government watched with alarm as the front grew in popularity, such that by fall 1974, common wisdom predicted a victory for the front, while the lists affiliated with the Zionist parties seemed unready for the elections.[17] Once more, the interior minister used his authority to postpone the elections for another year.[18] On October 30, 1974, Zayyad stood again on the Knesset assembly podium and scolded the minister, calling his decision "a gross blow to democracy" and demanding that he reconsider his decision. The minister insisted, however, and elections were scheduled for December 9, 1975.

THE 1975 ELECTIONS

In summer 1975, the government announced a plan to confiscate lands in the Galilee, provoking large-scale, carefully organized protest initiatives that crossed party lines. Political tensions were high, and the government feared that

public frustration among Arab citizens could strengthen the power of other political elements that the government considered even less legitimate than the
communists or inclined to cross the line of legality. Israeli policymakers were
divided between the "accommodationists," whose prominent voice was Shmuel
Toledano, the adviser on Arab affairs, who believed that allowing some autonomy among the Arab citizens would encourage so-called moderate elements,
and the "hardliners," who refused to release the grip of the authorities. The decision in December 1974 to delay the elections yet again until December of the
next year, made despite the objection of the minister of justice and the attorney
general, already had been a controversial issue that divided these camps even
more.[19] After that second delay, Prime Minister Rabin stated in a closed discussion that "it will not be possible to postpone the elections again." The interior
minister, Yosef Burg, suggested that the government should start preparing for
the elections by "providing two or three spectacular things, either a playground,
or a garden, and later water to the neighborhoods. We should do what is needed
as much as possible, and also what creates an impression—even if it is spectacular and is not 100 percent necessary."[20] In early August, Burg finally announced
that the elections would take place as planned, on December 9, 1975.

The 1975 elections in Nazareth were the first after the Knesset approved, earlier
that same year, the introduction of a new nationwide system, in which the mayor
would be directly elected by voters rather than by the elected local council. Too
late, the Labor Party realized that the new direct election would pave the way for
an opposition candidate to become the mayor of Nazareth and tried in the last
minute to postpone the implementation of the direct election of mayor until 1977.
Their attempts were thwarted by other parties, especially the right-wing Likud
Party, which made its own partisan calculations and concluded that the new law
served their interests as well.[21] In another attempt to prevent a communist victory,
the government tried to break the front by co-opting the Association of Academics.
Leaders of the association were invited to meet the adviser on Arab affairs in a
fancy restaurant in Jerusalem. The activists enjoyed the food but rejected the
request to leave the front.[22]

The front was ready for the challenge, but Zayyad himself was not yet in charge.
One indication of the commitment of the party's leadership in Nazareth to the idea
of a suprapartisan front was their intention to offer the leadership of the combined
list and the mayoral candidacy to the candidate suggested by the Association of
Academics, Anis Kardush, even though he was not a party member.[23] That same

fall, however, Kardush was diagnosed with a terminal disease and had to step down. The only communist member who was acceptable to the noncommunist elements of the front was Tawfiq Zayyad, but inside Rakah, there was a struggle over leadership. Ghassan Habib, the secretary of the Nazareth branch and the main architect of the Nazareth Democratic Front, saw himself as the default alternative, especially since Zayyad, the 1970 communist candidate for mayor, was now a member of the Knesset. Emil Habibi, though, nominated Tawfiq Zayyad and threw all his weight behind him. The Nazareth branch convened to discuss the two candidates and held a vote by secret ballot in which Zayyad gained one vote more than Habib.[24] He was announced as the party candidate only a month before the elections; Kardush died on December 3, just a few days before the election was held.

Although the official party line denies any consideration related to the confessional affiliation of its candidates, it is apparent that the replacement of Kardush with Zayyad was not smooth. The Christians, who once were the absolute majority in the city, were in a demographic retreat, and by 1975, they constituted only slightly more than half of the population and were rapidly becoming a minority. As in the case of Zayyad's cross-confessional marriage, the anxiety of Christians in the city was considered illegitimate in a Marxist context, but nevertheless affected the party. In a meeting of the Central Committee, Ghassan Habib gave voice to this anxiety and accused Emile Habibi of strategically replacing a Christian candidate with a Muslim one. This accusation led to a confrontation between Habib and Zayyad, who took offense at being considered a "Muslim candidate."[25]

The anxiety of Israeli decision makers over the inevitable communist victory in Nazareth was evident, and the PLO's public declaration of support of the front added another cause for worry.[26] As a last resort, the government created three separate confessional local parties, which they hoped would mobilize voters along confessional lines and thereby prevent the front from winning a majority of the seats in the council, which would render the council dysfunctional and provide the government with an excuse to dismantle it and appoint an external mayor.[27] Another desperate move, three weeks before election day, was the announced decision to return four acres of private land expropriated in 1954 to their Arab owners in Nazareth.[28]

The government accompanied this carrot of land return with several sticks. With election day approaching, government officials began to publicly threaten the residents of Nazareth, implying that the government would punish the city if residents elected Zayyad as mayor. On December 1, Moshe Bar'am, the minister of labor, visited Nazareth to support the lists affiliated with Labor Party and declared that his government would "react severely" if the front were to win. He added that the government "could not be expected to show consideration for a city headed by a man who may be an agent of Arafat or of murderous gangs."[29] The minister of housing, Avraham Ofer, threatened to deprive Nazareth of public funds if the communists won.[30] In its election campaign, the front itself kept a low profile. Optimistic about their chance to win, its activists were careful not to rock the boat or give the authorities any excuse to postpone the elections again. The campaign therefore focused on small-scale in-house meetings and avoided large public rallies.[31]

Election day, December 9, 1975, was cold and rainy in Nazareth. Because no other municipal elections took place that day, Rakah could mobilize its resources throughout the country to support its Nazareth branch. Suhayl Diab, the chair of the party cell at the Hebrew University of Jerusalem, organized two buses that brought students from the university to encourage and assist supporters to reach the ballots or help supervise the election process at each polling place. Diab described a collective sentiment of a historical moment. He was assigned to coordinate the party's activity in the Arab Workers Neighborhood, known for its pro-establishment orientation. Throughout the day, he said, his team faced harassment that was not far from physical violence.[32]

Until 3:00 p.m., the voting turnout was only 22 percent, a reason for concern for the front. Only in the early evening, when employees returned from work, did the city wake up.[33] At 11:00 p.m., when the voting was over, Diab and representatives of the other parties opened the ballot box to count the votes. At that moment, an armed man entered the polling place, pointed a pistol at Diab's head, and ordered him to discard all votes. The man was persuaded to back away, but the atmosphere remained tense. The rumors about the incident spread quickly, and Zayyad himself rushed to that polling place. He sat on a chair with his pipe between his lips without saying a word and quietly watched the counting of the votes until it was complete, shortly after 1:00 a.m. In that polling station, the front won 72 percent of the votes, and Zayyad won a similar percentage of the votes in elections for mayor. Within minutes, the news came that similar results were registered in other polling places across the city.[34] More than two-thirds of voters—9,510 out of 14,777—had voted for Tawfiq Zayyad as mayor, and the front won eleven out of seventeen seats in the municipal council.

Soon convoys of cars filled the streets honking in joy. Front supporters gathered in the House of Friendship, the communist headquarters in Nazareth, not far from Mary's Well, to celebrate the victory. They were joined by communist activists from across the Galilee who wanted to share the moment, and the crowd overflowed the building and filled the adjacent square. Front leaders were carried on the shoulders of their supporters, and together they celebrated for hours with singing, dancing, and drinking. Zayyad himself described that moment with a blatant atheist metaphor (when coming from a nominal Muslim), referring to an alcoholic beverage for the collective sentiment of a political climax: "The elections to the Nazareth Municipality were like removing the cork from the champagne bottle, the champagne that had begun to ferment in struggle and sacrifice."[35] Early in the morning Zayyad arrived at the House of Friendship, exhausted and emotional. In a hoarse voice, he delivered his victory speech, which captured the spirit of the front as a coalition that encompassed various interest groups: "Oh people of Nazareth, intellectuals, educated, merchants, craftsmen, students and graduates, youths, citizens, men, and women! In the name of the elected municipal council and in the name of the democratic majority in it, I announce that from now on the city hall of Nazareth is in the hands of the people of Nazareth, in your own hands! The old dream has materialized today." To signify the revolutionary nature of the moment, Zayyad attempted to leave his footprint on the collective calendar and make the victory day another secular holiday: "'Eid al-Adha is in few days, and few days later Christmas and the New Year. These holidays have become popular holidays of all the communities [. . .] and today the people of Nazareth added a new holiday, and its name is the Ninth of December." Zayyad declared his willingness to work hand in hand with the various government ministries, "but at the same time," he qualified, "we warn against conspiring or placing artificial obstacles in our way. We are not alone. Standing with us is our entire People in this country, as well as all the good forces in the Jewish People and throughout the world. The voices of Nazareth and its people, of joy or pain, will echo in every corner of the world."[36]

REACTIONS

For the first time in Zayyad's life, international media were paying serious attention to him. Reports about the front's victory in Nazareth appeared in major news outlets, including *Newsweek, Time,* and *Der Spiegel.* US media were fascinated by the symbolism of a communist triumph in the city of Jesus just before

Christmas, and reports associated Zayyad with Christ, as *al-Ittihad* had done in its reference to Zayyad's "crucifixion" in jail in 1955. For example, in an interview with CBS that aired on Christmas Day, Zayyad was asked about this association. Cigarette in hand, he replied with poise: "I think that Jesus Christ, like all prophets, stood for the poor, all the time, and struggled with them. So, there is a certain point that we meet, but of course with big differences, especially ideological differences."

Soon enthusiastic reactions came from Palestinians everywhere. The PLO welcomed the victory, and the January–February 1976 issue of its quarterly magazine, *Shu'un Filastiniyya*, published an article on Zayyad's poetry: "Tawfiq Zayyad, the Poet of Fighting Realism." The author, Faysal Darraj, declared Tawfiq Zayyad's poetry to be "the voice of reality and tool for changing it."[37] In the same issue, the journalist 'Isa al-Shu'aybi analyzed the elections and stated, "Those who voted for the Nazareth Democratic Front knew that the vote is for the city's Arabness and a protest against Israeli rule, not only in Nazareth and in the Galilee, but in the Triangle and the Naqab as well."[38] The mayors of Ramallah and Gaza in the occupied Palestinian territories also sent their greetings.

Equally evident was the Israeli authorities' intention to punish the voters in Nazareth for their choice. Appearing on Israel's only television channel at the time, the adviser on Arab affairs, Shmuel Toledano, stated that he had made an effort to prevent land expropriation in the Nazareth area, but "this goodwill has vanished now."[39] Ra'anan Cohen, head of the Arab Department in the Labor Party, called for using a "tough hand" when dealing with Nazareth.[40] The Ministry of Tourism and the Ministry of Information announced that they would not be involved in organizing that year's traditional Christmas celebrations in Nazareth, as they had in previous years.[41] The interior minister, Yosef Burg, adopted a pragmatic position and immediately declared his readiness to work together with the city's elected leadership. He met with Zayyad a week after the elections and reaffirmed his commitment. But Zayyad's first meeting with the Northern District commissioner of the Interior Ministry, Yisrael Koenig (who was not appointed by Burg), was tense. Koenig told Zayyad that he decided to appoint a special district construction superintendent to supervise construction in the municipality. Zayyad questioned the director's authority to do so, and the meeting almost exploded after several minutes.[42]

On January 13, Zayyad convened the first meeting of the new council. He promised that most of the council meetings would be open to the public, a demand he had been making since he first became a council member in 1954. In that meeting, the council approved the appointment of three deputies: Mun'im Jarjura and two noncommunist members of the front, Kamil al-Zahir and Ra'iq Jarjura. The front inherited a tough legacy: the Nazareth Municipality suffered from unreliable public services, deteriorated infrastructure, and an inefficient municipal apparatus, reflecting years of corruption and nepotism, as well as discrimination by the government. A huge debt required the municipality to pay high interest from its meager budget.[43] This legacy was aggravated by the Israeli government's hostile attitude toward Nazareth, and the first seven years after the front's victory were characterized by frequent financial crises, repetitive protest strikes (including one that lasted for thirty-six days in 1981), and legal battles between the municipal council and the government as government officials prevented resources from reaching Nazareth by dragging their feet whenever possible. For example, the municipal budgets were approved only after long delays. The 1977/78 budget was submitted for approval in March 1977 and was not approved until the municipality appealed to the Supreme Court in late July; the court ordered the Interior Ministry to justify the delay, and a reduced budget was finally approved only in late August.[44] Zayyad was still a member of the Knesset—at the time, Israeli law allowed politicians to hold the position of mayor and MK simultaneously—and in this capacity, he frequently brought the issue of discrimination against Nazareth to the Knesset assembly and the Interior Committee and would compare the government funding it received with funding given to Acre, a city similar in size but with a Jewish majority.[45] In 1978, the government also decided to move its regional government offices from Nazareth to nearby Upper Nazareth, a Jewish town the state developed on confiscated land, resulting in a significant loss of tax revenue and jobs for Nazareth.

The person who oversaw much of the national government's policy on Nazareth was District Commissioner Koenig. In the centralist Israeli political system, the district commissioner is an immensely powerful position, and local authorities are dependent on him in many crucial spheres, including budget approval and construction authorization. As mayor, Zayyad regularly demanded Koenig's dismissal, and in a discussion at the party's Central Committee meeting in March 1976, he referred to Koenig as a "mentally ill baby" and blamed him for the Interior Ministry's discriminatory policies.[46] In his endless populist optimism and deeply rooted belief in the moral compass and power of the masses, Zayyad dismissed the lasting significance of bureaucrats like Koenig and pinned his hope on the masses.

After outlining the financial predicament of Nazareth and Koenig's hostility, he stated, "What we're missing is a way to reach the public! We had a mass rally, open meetings of the city council—but they [the government] disseminate lies about us. The main problem is how to reach the general public [beyond the local public in Nazareth]. We cannot afford to fail here. We have to raise the public awareness abroad as well."[47]

An opportunity for the party to reach the general public presented itself on September 7, 1976, when a confidential internal memorandum Koenig had signed on March 1 and sent to Prime Minister Yitzhak Rabin was leaked to the press. Its content confirmed much of what Zayyad had said about the Interior Ministry being guided by a racist, discriminatory worldview. The memorandum put forward a number of steps aimed at reducing the number of Arabs in the Galilee region and limiting their political empowerment.[48] It had been drafted in early 1974 by three Jewish mayors from the Galilee,[49] but the repeated references to the front victory in Nazareth is evidence that it was updated and that this victory was seen as supporting the memorandum's original arguments. Criticizing the current policymakers for "not taking into account the Levantine and shallow Arab character, in which imagination overarches rationality," the memorandum, endorsed by Koenig, an official at the Interior Ministry, exposed the prejudice that shaped the ministry's policy. Koenig proposed a policy of "reward and punishment (within the realm of legality) of leaders and localities who express any form of hostility to the state and Zionism; [. . .] to appoint a special team in the Shabak to investigate the personal habits of Rakah leaders and other negative figures and to bring these findings to their constituencies," and "to take personal measures against every negative figure at any level." The document revealed a high level of anxiety about the empowerment of Rakah, especially its success in Nazareth. The historian Gadi Algazi found that the document was leaked earlier that year and had served as the basis for a July 23 article in *Yedi'ot Aharonot* in which the content of the Koenig memorandum was ascribed to "internal reports submitted to the authorized institutions." Its text focuses on the parts of the memorandum that demonize Rakah rather than on the discriminative policy recommendations. In that earlier article, though, the government's fear about Zayyad himself was expressed explicitly.[50]

After the memo leaked, Koenig, the Interior Ministry, and other state representatives argued in public that they implemented universal standards and that Nazareth's dire condition derived from overemployment in public offices and a low tax rate. The Koenig memorandum, however, is not the only internal document that tells a different story from the official public narrative. A secret letter from Toledano to Rabin in July 1976, for example, states: "The Nazareth Municipality: it was decided to continue the same policy decided upon in the past for the next three months, and after this period to have comprehensive discussion, with the participation of the Interior Ministry."[51] The document does not mention what this policy was, but in all cases, this document is evidence that the government did have a separate policy toward Nazareth. This special policy relied on the broader reward-and-punishment strategy, and it aimed at punishing Nazareth for electing Zayyad and the front. Clearly, it had a direct effect on budget allocation. For example, in 1979, when Koenig wanted to justify his decision to halt the transfer of government funds to Nazareth, he sent the attorney general a poster designed by the municipality and, claiming the poster was "expressing hostility toward state authorities," demanded the government take legal measure against municipal authorities.[52] Furthermore, a policy paper authored by an interministerial committee on policy in the Arab sector recommended allocating regular budgets according to universal criteria but proposed that "development budgets for infrastructure and other special budgets should be approved after consultation with the Committee for Coordination of Policy in the Arab Sector."[53] This policy paper, like the Koenig memorandum before it, is evidence of the determination of Israeli policymakers, as well as of functionaries in the deep state, to preserve the state's ethnic power structure. These documents highlight the rigidity of the structured mechanism of discrimination Zayyad faced as a mayor of Nazareth.

SPIRIT OF MOBILIZATION

The Interior Ministry attempted to punish the residents of Nazareth to dissuade them from supporting the front, but popular support for the front-led municipality flourished. After Zayyad issued a call for Nazarenes to pay all their municipal taxes, they lined up to do so.[54] Nazarenes also volunteered to serve on neighborhood committees that organized local activities and mediated between the residents and the municipal council. People enthusiastically volunteered to repair and renovate infrastructure, as well as clean the streets, all without compensation, which significantly lowered the municipality's expenses. With palpable disappointment, the Koenig memorandum admitted the authorities' failure to foresee this development: "The exceptional and unpredictable mobilization of the residents of Nazareth helped the municipality to flow cash into the municipal treasury, a development that helps Rakah, at the moment, to run the city." According to Zayyad himself, income from taxes in the first quarter of 1976 was 55 percent higher than in the first quarter of 1975, an indication of residents' increased motivation to pay taxes.[55] In one year, the municipal council doubled the total length of the sewage lines in the city.[56] Zayyad's ability to inspire a spirit of volunteerism was enabled partly by the personal example he provided. He declined his right to purchase a new car with municipal funding and instead transferred the budget allocated for this purpose toward purchasing a car for the Electricity Department.[57]

The jewel in the crown of public mobilization was the yearly working camps the municipal council organized starting in 1976. With the help of fourteen youths, women, and student organizations, the municipality initiated a summer work camp under the slogan "for a beautiful and clean Nazareth." For Zayyad, the camp not only served immediate municipal needs, but also cultivated a broader ideological awareness, and in his speech at the opening ceremony, Zayyad described the camp as "the wedding of work and dignity." Over four days, 450 volunteers from the Galilee and the Triangle, who came to express solidarity with Nazareth took part in cleaning streets, paving new roads, installing new sewage pipes, fixing equipment in schools, and planting trees. At the end of every workday, they listened to lectures about social and political issues and participated in cultural activities, such as dancing, singing, and sports competitions.

Aware of its historical significance, the organizers started to name the camp "the first volunteer camp," implying that it was only the beginning of a new tradition. Indeed, the 1976 camp was the start of an annual tradition that lasted fourteen years. In his opening speech at the 1977 camp, Zayyad was explicit about the camp's pedagogic goals: "We will come out from this camp more united and organized, not only in the battle for development and construction but also for knowledge and culture. Let our camp be a festival of work and dignity in the morning and a festival of culture in the evening."[58] Subsequent camps included volunteers from the Triangle, the Naqab, the West Bank, and the Gaza Strip, as well as Jewish Israeli participants and delegations from several European countries. By the mid-1980s, the number of volunteers reached the thousands and the number of participants in the opening ceremonies numbered in the tens of thousands, according to the reports in al-Ittihad. The opening ceremonies became a major stage for displaying national pride, and in the 1980s, they opened with the singing of one of Palestine's unofficial anthem, "Biladi, Biladi," with modified lyrics glorifying the Nazareth Democratic Front, authored by Samih al-Qasim.

EDUCATION

The pedagogical orientation of the volunteer camps was part of the broader importance Zayyad ascribed to education. Even after the end of the military rule in 1966, Israeli state institutions continued to closely monitor Arab formal education, the official curriculum still ignored the Palestinian national narrative, and security services were still directly involved in hiring and firing teachers and school directors. As a result, pedagogic and managerial skills were not the main criteria for appointments at public schools. The poor material infrastructure and the low quality of the schools were among the major issues on the front's campaign agenda. Because high school teachers are employed by municipal councils, the front victory opened new, though limited, opportunities for the communists to change the municipal education system.

Shortly after taking control over the municipal council, the new leadership in the city made a first attempt in this direction by dismissing the director of the only public high school for boys, his deputy, and a teacher, all known for their affiliation with the Labor Party. The three appealed to the Labor Court, which ruled to reinstate the director and deputy.[59] During the first day of school on September 1, 1976, Zayyad and council member Ghassan Habib showed up at that school and confronted the reinstated deputy, Samih Abu Sa'id. The controversy deteriorated into physical violence, and the deputy filed a complaint with the police, accusing Zayyad and Habib of assaulting him.[60]

The municipal leadership was unable to replace the existing school management, but it did have more power in deciding on new appointments in high schools, which created a new challenge for the national government. The adviser for Arab affairs at the time, Moshe Sharon, sent a letter to the attorney general, Aharon Barak, regretting that "the ability of the Ministry of Education to intervene in order to prevent the appointment of teachers or directors known for their activity against the state does not exist, practically," and asking if there was any legal way to allow the Ministry of Education to intervene to prevent "unwanted" appointments.[61] Although Nazareth was not mentioned in the letter, there is no doubt that Nazareth was the most serious, if not the only, challenge to the authority of the ministry at the time. The letter was forwarded to the Arab Department of the Ministry of Education, and its director argued that the ministry still had the power to veto the hiring of certain teachers and directors, although it could not force the local authorities to hire a new teacher or director they did not want to hire.[62] One long-term effect of the municipality's control over secondary education was that Nazareth became an incubator for relatively daring teaching staff, as the municipal council's oppositional orientation gave Nazareth's teachers flexibility to diverge from the government political line in the classroom.[63]

The front's aspirations, though, went beyond secondary education. In September 1980, the Nazareth Municipal Council adopted the initiative of the Association for the Development of Culture and Education (ADCE), a group of local nationalist activists, to establish an Arab university in Nazareth. The ADCE even managed to raise funds abroad for the project.[64] The ADCE and the council were motivated more by cultural-political considerations of identity and belonging than by economic concerns, as reflected in the intention to prioritize the creation of departments for Arabic and Middle Eastern history and the explicit demand that Arabic be the language of instruction. The council even started consulting with local Arab intellectuals regarding the curriculum and technical arrangements and hoped that the university would attract many of the seventeen hundred Arab students who at the time studied in Hebrew universities. Municipal councils, however, are not authorized to establish and accredit universities, and if they want to open a university, they have to submit a request to the Council for Higher Education (CHE). *Davar* quoted unidentified governmental sources who raised concerns that an Arab university would encourage nationalist sentiments.[65] Accordingly, the CHE reaction was prompt and negative. Zayyad sent a letter to the CHE secretary asking him to reconsider his position,[66] but the plan to establish Nazareth University never materialized.

OPPOSITION

Many people who worked with Zayyad closely during his time as mayor emphasized his courage, assertiveness, integrity, incorruptibility, adherence to principles, and leadership. More critical observers referred to his impulsiveness, stubbornness, and rude language. His followers admired him. His adversaries are still bitter, and many refused to talk with me about him. Although the role of interpersonal rivalries should not be underestimated, criticism of Zayyad and his party was frequently based on power struggles between different political orientations, and over the course of his mayoralty, he faced challenges from a variety of political forces.

The initial challenge came from the allies of the Labor Party, which had ruled the city for many years. They criticized Zayyad from his very first days in office, when he nominated three deputies, one at full salary and the other two at half salary—a move, they argued, that violated the Interior Ministry's criteria that only cities with at least 250,000 residents could have three deputies (Nazareth at the time had only 40,000 residents).[67] Former mayor Sayf al-Din al-Zu'bi was still an MK and used his public visibility to emphasize any shortcoming of the municipality. By the mid-1980s, though, the Labor Party's power in the city had almost vanished. More important, although discrimination against Arab municipalities and frequent financial crises did not end, the authorities abandoned their obsession with overthrowing Zayyad after their repeated failures to achieve this goal. In February 1983 for the first time, a government minister (Minister of Welfare Aharon Uzan) visited Nazareth city hall, indicating a crack in the revenge policy, while a formal visit to the city by the president, Chaim Herzog, on September 14, 1984, signaled the final abandonment of the "special treatment" approach.

Zayyad was also defied, however, by elements from his own political camp. Ghassan Habib, a long-time rival, challenged him days after his election in a Central Committee meeting, where he demanded that Zayyad resign from the Knesset so his time could be devoted entirely to municipal issues. Later Habib criticized Zayyad for his frequent absences from the city and argued that Zayyad should decide between being a mayor and being an MK. He also complained that in both 1975 and 1978, the front list did not include any women in a position with a realistic chance to be elected.[68]

Habib found allies among the Association of Academics, the main noncommunist element in the front, many of whose members felt that the front marginalized them and did not treat them as equal partners. The party leadership worried that the conflict between Zayyad and Habib, and between the various elements in the Nazareth Democratic Front, would hinder their attempts to replicate the front model in other contexts, and the issue was discussed at a 1977 meeting of the Politburo (neither Zayyad nor Habib was yet a member). Secretary General Vilner warned, "The issue of the Nazareth Municipality is so important, so I am talking to the conscience of our comrades: you are playing with fire. It is not even an issue of Nazareth. This is the showcase of progressive forces, of the party. A failure in Nazareth is a failure in all the fronts."[69] Days before the submission of the candidate lists for the 1978 municipal elections, Zayyad's deputy, Kamil al-Zahir, demanded that he be named the mayoral candidate, arguing that Zayyad spent too much time in the Knesset. When the candidacy was given again to Zayyad, al-Zahir announced in a dramatic meeting of the front leadership that he was stepping down from the front's list of council candidates.

Although the front won the 1978 elections and Zayyad was reelected as mayor, the relations among the different elements of the front continued to deteriorate. In November 1981, al-Zahir led a group of seventy-seven academics who broke away from the Association of Academics, as well as the front, to found the Progressive Movement in Nazareth, which ran in the 1983 municipal elections and won 23 percent of the votes.[70] Although personal conflicts could explain much of these dynamics, this opposition reflected that significant circles of Palestinians in Israel were feeling alienated by communist ideology and rhetoric, which was perceived as rigid. They were also frustrated by the underrepresentation of Arabs in the leadership of a party whose constituency was more than 90 percent Arab. The Progressive Movement presented itself as an alternative to the local lists affiliated with the Zionist parties but without the baggage of communism. The founding leaders of the movement expressed the hope that similar movements would be established in other localities and did not exclude the possibility of developing their movement into a political party. Indeed, before the 1984 elections, the Progressive Movement joined a Jewish leftist group, Alternative, to establish the Progressive List for Peace (PLP). For the next eight years, the Progressive Movement in Nazareth and PLP countrywide posed a major challenge to the communists, and their rivalry would be a source of turbulence, especially in Nazareth (see chapter 7).

One instance where local politics and national considerations merged was President Herzog's official visit to Nazareth and Zayyad's decision to grant him honorary citizenship of the city. The decision was compatible with Rakah's emphasis on the legitimacy and necessity of Israeli citizenship for the Palestinians who lived in Israel, as well as with Zayyad's pragmatic orientation toward optimizing the resources the city could get from the central authority. The Progressive Movement protested, arguing that Zayyad should have brought the issue to the council meeting for a vote, and they presented the decision as unpatriotic: "The mayor of Nazareth grants an honorary citizenship to the President of the State Herzog . . . and Herzog in his turn grants the Jews the right to settle in the occupied territories."[71] A similar scenario took place in April 1986, when Prime Minister Shimon Peres became the first prime minister to conduct an official visit of Nazareth. The Progressive Movement boycotted the reception ceremony.[72]

A related development that Zayyad and his party had to deal with was the diversification of Arabic-language media in Israel. Until the early 1980s, all Arabic media in Israel were sponsored by either the state or political parties. Under these circumstances, the communist press enjoyed the highest level of credibility among Palestinians in Israel. In 1983, the journalist Lutfi Mash'ur, who owned an advertising agency in Nazareth, established the first private for-profit Arabic newspaper, *al-Sinara*. Mash'ur and Rakah had been in conflict since the party withdrew from an agreement to provide Mash'ur exclusivity in advertising in *al-Ittihad*. *Al-Sinara* became quickly the voice of the opposition in Nazareth, supporting the Progressive Movement in the local elections and frequently attacking Zayyad personally, in particular for holding simultaneously a seat in the Knesset and the position of mayor. Kamil al-Zahir, the leader of the Progressive Movement in the municipal council, had free access to publish in *al-Sinara*, and he used it. In February 1988, for example, he accused the Nazareth Municipality of exploiting Palestinian workers from the West Bank and withholding their wages.[73] Zayyad's deputy, Ramiz Jaraysi, spent almost an entire council meeting refuting the allegations. Zayyad fought back against the newspaper in his own way. When *al-Sinara* and the soccer club Akha' al-Nasira reached a sponsorship agreement, Zayyad threatened the team managers and demanded the removal of *al-Sinara* commercial signs from the municipal stadium. According to *al-Watan*, the Progressive Movement's bulletin, the threats led to a tension between Zayyad and the club's fans, most of them concentrated in Zayyad's Eastern Neighborhood.[74] The level of hostility expressed in *al-Sinara* against the Communist Party in general and Zayyad in particular led many in the party to the conclusion that *al-Sinara* was secretly supported by the government.

In the 1989 elections, the Progressive List for Peace was defeated (shrinking from four to two seats in the council), and a new oppositional actor, the Islamic Movement, gained six seats. In the following years, the city would witness charged confrontations between Zayyad and the Islamist activists—clashes that reflected the broader political conflicts over the role of Islam in politics among the Palestinian citizens of Israel (chapter 8).

THE LOCAL AND THE NATIONAL

One common thread in Zayyad's municipal leadership was his consistent reluctance to separate the local needs of Nazareth from the collective national goals of Palestinians. This merging of the local and the national might be one of the reasons he chose to maintain his Knesset membership after his election as mayor. The volunteer camp, the attempt to establish an Arab university in Nazareth, and the contextualization of the struggle for municipal resources as part of a struggle against national discrimination were related to a framework that saw the local and the national struggles as interconnected. Under Zayyad's leadership, the municipal council consistently discussed national issues and never limited itself to purely local issues. Frequently, Zayyad opened the council meeting with a reference to recent developments in the military-occupied West Bank and the Gaza Strip, sometimes asking the council members to stand for a moment of silence to honor Palestinian victims of the occupation, especially during the intifada (uprising) from 1987 to 1993. On some occasions, his opening announcements referred to the anniversary of a historical event (for example, the beginning of the 1967 war) that coincided with the date of the meeting. The municipality took decisions that expressed solidarity with Palestinian universities under occupation, Palestinian prisoners, and more.

In 1990, Zayyad broke his years-long hiatus from writing poetry. One of the best-known of his poems from that period is "I Am from This City," which opens with the following lines:

> I am from this city, from its sad alleys,
> From the arteries of houses of poverty, from the heart of the fortified
> buildings.
> I am from Land Day Street and the First of May Plaza
> And from the Sabra and Shatila Square and those alleys where the po-
> lice do not dare
> To enter when people start to get angry.[75]

The poem links Zayyd's local patriotism with broader themes related to the Palestinian national struggle, and it invokes as well the role of Nazareth in these historical events. It refers, for example, to the massacre of Palestinians in camps near Beirut during the Israeli invasion in 1982, which was followed by a mass protest in Nazareth that the police harshly suppressed (see chapter 7). Even more central to the local-national memory and identity is the reference to Land Day. Zayyad's election as mayor of Nazareth in 1975 increased his visibility and legitimized his claim for national leadership. Nowhere else was this as evident as in the events surrounding Land Day, the day of strike and protest on March 30, 1976, discussed in the next chapter.

Chapter 6

NATIONAL LEADERSHIP

ADDRESSING THE PARTY'S CENTRAL COMMITTEE IN A MEETING JUST
a few days after the 1975 municipal elections in which he was elected mayor,
Zayyad said, "I would like to emphasize that the main meaning of the elections
in Nazareth is that the Arab residents no longer agree to live according to the old
criteria. The elections platform conveyed the message that it would be wrong to
limit our work to issues of streets and sewage. It has a more important meaning, and the elections' next stage is the cooperation between the different local
communities in the battle against land expropriation."[1] The land expropriation
Zayyad referred to was the state's expropriation of large tracts of private Arab
lands as part of a large-scale project by the government and the Jewish Agency
aimed primarily at changing the demographic balance in the Galilee in favor of
the Jewish population. In November 1974, the chair of the Settlement Department
in the Jewish Agency presented the plan to the Labor Committee and the Knesset,
triggering protest among Palestinians in Israel that gained momentum over the
course of the next year and culminated on March 30, 1976.[2]

A series of meetings in summer 1975 led to a large-scale convention on October 18, in which activists from all over the country and from diverse political
orientations gathered in Nazareth. The convention decided to establish the Follow-Up Committee for the Protection of Arab Land (hereafter Land Committee)
for coordinating and leading protest, working together with various local land

committees in villages in the Galilee and the Triangle.[3] Zayyad's role in this organizing was modest, partly because Rakah in general preferred that the struggle not be perceived as a partisan issue and therefore intentionally diminished its representation on the Land Committee.[4] His main contribution until early 1976 was to raise concerns in the Knesset whenever possible. The Knesset presidency rejected his demands to bring the confiscation of Arab lands to a discussion in the assembly,[5] but when the Knesset discussed a piece of legislation about compensation for expropriated land, Zayyad took the opportunity to talk about the larger plan and argued that the issue was not a simple matter of real estate and property rights: "You have to understand the meaning of the land for the Arab residents. The land for them is not only a source of living. It is a homeland. It is the People's future." Hinting at the Zionist ideology embraced by his audience in the Knesset, he added, "Isn't it strange that you cannot understand this issue and recognize it?"[6]

When in early February 1976 the Ministry of Defense prohibited access to private lands belonging to residents of three Arab villages (Sakhnin, 'Arraba, and Dayr Hanna), the protests gained momentum, and a large-scale rally was held in Sakhnin on February 14. In his speech at the rally, Zayyad emphasized that the local struggle had a national dimension: "We totally reject the racist Judaization of the Galilee program, aiming at building the future of one People on the ruins of another People [...] The land is homeland and not only a source of livelihood."[7] On February 21, Saliba Khamis, a leading member of the Land Committee, called for a general strike on March 30, which he declared Land Day. This call might not have been so effective had the government not confirmed on February 29 that it would be implementing its plan for confiscating twenty thousand dunums of land in the Galilee. On March 6, the Land Committee and nineteen Arab mayors convened in Nazareth and officially endorsed the call for a general strike on March 30. Zayyad's position in that discussion was even blunter: he suggested declaring as well a general hunger strike and mass demonstrations that same day, but he was satisfied with the decision to hold a general labor strike.[8]

Some of the Rakah leaders were concerned about what they saw as a direct confrontation with the authorities. When the Central Committee met on March 20, the strike was not on the agenda, and although four members, including Zayyad and Khamis, addressed the issue, Secretary General Vilner chose to ignore it in his concluding remarks. It is likely that Vilner was aware of the controversial nature of the topic and preferred to discuss it in a more exclusive forum, the Politburo.

The minutes of the Politburo from the first half of 1976, though, are mysteriously missing from the Communist Party Archive. Meanwhile, the government, determined to prevent the strike, increased the pressure on Arab mayors, whose job performance was highly dependent on their ability to obtain resources from the central government. It pinned its hope on the Committee of Arab Mayors, a body that the government itself established two years earlier in order to contain Arab protest. Despite the heavy pressure on them, the committee members who met on March 21 did not decide to cancel the strike and decided instead to convene a general conference of all Arab mayors four days later, on March 25.

Before the meeting, which was to take place at Shafa'amr's city hall, the adviser on Arab affairs, Shmuel Toledano, met personally with most of the forty-six mayors and used threats to pressure them to oppose the strike. Thirty-three mayors did sign a document Toledano had prepared committing themselves to oppose the strike. During the meeting, Toledano was waiting at the Shafa'amr police station, while police officers and Shabak senior agents were inside the municipality building. A police force surrounded the building, while beyond the police, a crowd of thousands gathered, loudly expressing their support for the strike. The hall was closed to the press, and even mayor deputies were not allowed in.[9]

The discussion began at 3:30 p.m. In the coverage of that event in 1976, *al-Ittihad* gave little attention to the personal role that various leaders played, focusing more on the outcome of that meeting. The Hebrew media, though, emphasized Zayyad's central role, an emphasis that both reflected his perception as a threat, as well as a way to avoid discussing the broader political reality of discrimination that led to the protest. Nevertheless, it is evident that as the mayor of the largest Arab locality, recently elected in an act of collective defiance, Zayyad's voice was especially prominent. The journalist and orientalist Uri Standel reported that strike supporters gathered near the building when the meeting took place. The crowd responded to Zayyad's emotional preaching in favor of the strike, chanting, "With our spirit, with our blood, we will protect you, Zayyad," an emblematic slogan of Palestinian political protest (which was probably what concerned Standel).[10] Those who opposed the strike understood that in the existing political climate, their position was highly unpopular among Palestinians, and they demanded a secret ballot. In response, the strike supporters at the meeting leaned out of the windows and informed the crowd outside of the names of those who spoke against the strike. The discussion became turbulent, and according to Jamal Tarabiyya, mayor of Sakhnin at the time, it bordered on physical violence.[11] In the vote, thirty-five mayors supported the cancellation of the strike, two abstained, and one voted against the cancellation.[12] Six mayors, including Zayyad, refused to participate in the vote.[13] They argued that the mayors were not authorized to vote on the issue, since they could not cancel a decision made by the Land Committee.[14] Zayyad was determined to not even let the process be completed. After three hours of discussion and voting, he left the hall with the other strike supporters, stood in front of the cheering crowd, and declared, "The People have decided—a strike!" Zayyad had a talent for creating drama and making full use of its potential for political mobilization, and this was a defining moment in his political life. The pro-strike mayors were carried on the shoulders of their supporters. While the government officials announced to the press that the strike was cancelled, the Land Committee announced that the strike would take place as planned.

The Rakah leadership set up an emergency meeting in Haifa (on the following day, according to Vilner; that same night, according to Tubi) to discuss the mayors' decision.[15] It was the party's heyday among Israel's Palestinian citizens, and it was evident that regardless of the position of other political forces, the strike would not take place without its blessing. What we know about what transpired at that meeting comes from the testimony of Secretary General Meir Vilner, published in 1996,[16] and a 2006 interview that the researcher Nabih Bashir conducted with 'Umar Sa'di, then the secretary of the Communist Youth in Nazareth, who reportedly met with Tawfiq Zayyad shortly after the meeting.[17] Both accounts emphasize the key role that Zayyad had on the final party's stand, although with different nuances. According to Sa'di, after that meeting, he and several other young party members met Zayyad, who was highly agitated. He told them that he and Saliba Khamis were late to the meeting, and in their absence, the party's leaders almost took a stand against the strike. Zayyad and Khamis struggled to change the minds of their fellow party members and were finally successful, but not before they had to raise their voices. According to Vilner's memoirs, the party leaders were divided, but they ascribed particular importance to Zayyad's opinion because they saw him as best placed to evaluate whether a sufficient number of people could be mobilized and to predict the implications of the strike among Arab citizens. Zayyad, wrote Vilner, was determined; he insisted that the strike should take place and predicted that it would be successful. He asserted that the mayors who opposed the strike did not represent popular sentiment. The decisions in Rakah were not made by voting, and discussions always ended by the secretary general, who was assumed to be able to identify the consensus among the discussants. Therefore,

Vilner's conclusion in favor of the strike and his testimony about Zayyad's pivotal influence on his decision partly confirms Sa'di's version and illustrates once more how crucial Zayyad's role in enabling the 1976 strike was.

The Hebrew press made its own contribution to Zayyad's status by identifying him as the strike leader and making ad hominem attacks on him. Almost every report about the upcoming strike described him as a personification of emerging defiant tendencies among the Arab citizens of Israel. At the same time, Zayyad, like other leaders of his party, did not want the strike to turn violent. In the meeting of the Central Committee on March 20, Saliba Khamis stated that the strike should be "respectable" and called on the party to prevent the distribution of "extremist flyers." A major protest rally that was scheduled to take place in Nazareth on Land Day had been canceled a day earlier, and so was the plan to conduct "strike vigils" in the city to verify compliance with the strike. Commissioner Koenig argued that Zayyad promised him that the municipal offices would remain open on the day of the strike,[18] although it is unclear whether Koenig's declaration was not part of the psychological warfare that preceded the strike.

In any case, it seems that Rakah and the Land Committee were unable to contain the events. The historian Elie Rekhess estimates that on the evening before the strike, the dynamics of the protest were dictated by small but more radical and militant groups that aspired to confront the police and the army. That evening, a military truck leading soldiers from their training in the region faced a road blocked by rocks and burning tires near 'Arraba. According to the authorities' version, the truck was attacked with rocks and burning gasoline cans. These soldiers were not part of the forces that were supposed to deal with the demonstrations. In fact, they were not aware of the previous understanding between the local police and the Arab local councils to avoid confrontation, and they were not equipped or trained to deal with violent civil demonstrations. The forces used live ammunition and critically wounded one resident, who later died.[19] The anger and frustration that spread quickly in the region was beyond control.

In the light of these developments, on March 30 at 4:30 a.m., Zayyad got a phone call from Koenig, urging him to cancel the strike.[20] Zayyad and Koenig had been meeting weekly, but given the tense relations between the two, Koenig was the last person able to persuade Zayyad to change his mind. Zayyad answered that his conscience would not allow him to make such a decision.

Most schools were open that morning, and Zayyad went to at least one high school and spoke to the students about the importance of the strike.[21] Later he went home for lunch. Around 1:00 p.m., hundreds of demonstrators confronted the police in the Eastern Neighborhood, not far from Zayyad's home. Soon after, a group of twenty-five to thirty Border Patrol troops approached Zayyad's house, claiming that rocks were thrown toward them from the house's window (a claim that was denied by half a dozen journalists who witnessed the scene).[22] *Davar* reporter Yoel Dar, who usually relied on official sources, said that some of the rock throwers tried to hide in Zayyad's house.[23] According to Rakah accounts, the police specifically targeted Zayyad, and the police were heard calling, "Where is Tawfiq Zayyad?" and "We will kill Tawfiq Zayyad."[24] The common assumption in the party was that the police followed Zayyad as the strike leader and attempted to provoke him in order to find a pretext to hurt him.[25] Tawfiq Zayyad, though, had left the house minutes earlier through the back door. His wife, Na'ila, was on the second floor, and when she heard the troops approach, she went downstairs to the front entrance and spread her arms to block their entry. The scene was captured by the cameras of a Belgian television station, as well as CBS, and the films show the soldiers dragging Na'ila out from the main entrance to the balcony, but without getting inside, then kicking and smashing the front door, side door, windows, and flowerpots with their bats. Tawfiq Zayyad's mother is seen leaving from the side entrance, yelling at the troops, who several minutes later suddenly departed, leaving behind them a path of destruction.

While the Land Committee and Rakah estimated that the Palestinians in Israel were fully mobilized for striking, government sources estimated the rate of participation as no more than 40 percent.[26] Politically, however, the importance of the figure is marginal because public attention quickly shifted from the strike itself to the violence and casualties. Five young Palestinians had been killed by police in various locations (in addition to the one who was shot the previous evening). The public immediately regarded the six victims as martyrs who sacrificed their lives to protect Arab land, and March 30, Land Day, became an annual memorial day during which political leaders and public intellectuals highlight themes of courage, sacrifice, and steadfastness. In the party's internal narrative, Land Day was a natural continuation of their municipal victory in Nazareth. Zayyad himself actively contributed to connecting the dots between the events: "The ninth of December and the thirtieth of March are organically connected, being the two most important events in the history of our Arab People in the country. They signified a new, higher, and more progressive stage in the struggles against land expropriation and national oppression."[27]

Zayyad was highly affected by Land Day events. The following day in the Knesset assembly, he could not sit still in his seat and interrupted some of the speakers at the podium. When Prime Minister Rabin climbed to the podium, Zayyad erupted: "This is a policy of murder," while MK Shulamit Aloni from Ratz and MK Tawfiq Tubi from his own party tried to calm him down. Later, MK Tubi himself interrupted Rabin, and when the Knesset deputy speaker, Moshe Shahal, told Tubi, "In accordance with article 67 I am telling you . . . ," Zayyad stood again and called out, "According to which article were six Arab citizens murdered yesterday?" Shahal asked Zayyad to sit down, and Zayyad responded, "According to which article were six innocent people shot?" When Shahal asked Zayyad once more to sit down, he shouted, "According to which article do you dispossess a people from their land?"

Following Land Day, Zayyad's popularity among Palestinians in Israel skyrocketed. While on the West Bank, his fame in the late 1970s continued to be based on his poetry,[28] it was his public political activity that was of great importance for Palestinians inside Israel. His speeches attracted audiences all over the country, as his rhetorical skills were far beyond the standard set by the heavy, calculated, and colorless style of most of the party's top leaders at the time. He was a fiery and charismatic speaker who connected with the audience, who in turn frequently responded with cheering, chanting, laughing, and whistling. He moved with ease between poetic language and unrefined colloquial Arabic, gesticulating theatrically and changing his cadence frequently and dramatically—slow and drawn out at times, short and punctuated at others. When speaking outside in front of a large audience, especially on Land Day anniversaries, he stood at a distance from the microphone, which enabled him to shout without microphone feedback.

Nevertheless, the rigid structure of the party and the Bolshevik-like tradition of not replacing living leaders, as well as senior leaders' concern that the Jewish public saw Zayyad as belligerent, delayed his rise to the top ranks of the party leadership. His popularity was translated into an almost guaranteed position as a member of the Knesset in the 1977 elections (he was ranked fourth in the candidates' list) but did not make him a decision maker in the party. The journalist Ehud Ya'ari, who covered the party's Eighteenth Congress in December 1976, had the following impression of Zayyad's status: "As much as the party is successful among the Arab national circles, the leadership is in the hands of pedantic, pious, seasoned communists. On the stage, therefore, we saw the familiar faces. Even the Nazareth mayor, MK Tawfiq Zayyad, was sitting only in the third row. He is not a member of the party secretariat or even its Politburo. Vilner is the 'boss,' and there is no room for mistakes about it."[29] About the Arab leaders of the party, Ya'ari wrote, "Tawfiq Tubi—comfortable and smiling; Imil Tuma—the elegant theorist; Emile Habibi, in a bad mood—but silent. Tawfiq Zayyad, a star of popular rallies, belongs only to the second rank."

Only in 1981 was Zayyad's mass appeal translated into membership in the Politburo. According to the journalist Samih Ghanadri (who is Emile Habibi's son-in-law), Habibi threatened Vilner and Tubi that if they did not appoint Zayyad to the Politburo, he would no longer serve as a member.[30] Zayyad's inclusion in this body created for the first time an Arab majority in the Politburo, a change that was necessary for better reflecting the party's constituency. Secretary General Vilner probably recognized that Zayyad was an electoral asset, but at the same time, as his subtly expressed reservations in the Central Committee protocols reveal, he was concerned that Zayyad's emphasis on Arab Palestinian nationalism might further undermine the party's ability to attract Jewish supporters. It would take eleven more years, the collapse of the Soviet Union, and the withdrawal of the two elder leaders (Vilner and Tubi) from the Knesset before Zayyad would become the leader of the party in the Knesset. Because Zayyad's status among Jews is crucial for understanding this delay, it is important to elaborate on his image in the Jewish media and public following Land Day.

ZAYYAD AND THE HEBREW MEDIA AFTER LAND DAY

Despite his anger and frustration following Land Day, Zayyad did not give up on his universalist rhetoric. In his first public speech after Land Day, at a rally in Jaffa on April 9, he stated, "Despite what happened on 30 March, our People regard the Jewish workers, the Jewish democratic forces, and every person of conscience, with an unspeakable love. Protecting the rights of another nation is also a defense of the rights of the protecting nation. In other words, we are proud of our Jewish friends, and the forces of progress and democracy, and this pride will continue to flourish in the future."[31] While Rakah highlighted this message in its Hebrew publication, *Zo ha-Derekh*, I could not find any reference to this speech in the mainstream Hebrew media. There, Zayyad continued to be demonized as a dangerous, hypernationalist, hate-filled zealot. The author (and former deputy for the adviser on Arab affairs for the prime minister) Uri Standel gave him the colorful title, "the venomous poet,"[32] and poet Haim Guri referred to him as "an unbearable mixture of Jesus, Stalin, and Arafat."[33] The journalist

Yehushu'a Bitsur added, "His eyes sparkle with the fire of hate."[34] This collective fear of Zayyad reflected deep-seated Zionist anxieties, unrelated to Zayyad's words and actions. At the same time, Zayyad elicited these anxious reactions more than any other member of his party.

This fear of Zayyad is puzzling, given that he consistently presented himself as a citizen of a state who demanded reform and as a leader of a national minority who demanded rights within the framework of citizenship—not as a separatist politician who questioned the state's sovereignty. The coverage in the mainstream Hebrew media following Land Day consistently underplayed the integrative element while highlighting selective quotes that apparently proved the opposite. One notable case is the coverage given to his speech at the First of May demonstration, only a month after Land Day, when Zayyad spoke in front of thousands in a rally in the square of the Church of the Annunciation (in an act of defiant secularization, renamed the First of May Square by the communists) in Nazareth. It was his first public speech in Nazareth since Land Day, and according to *al-Ittihad*, the crowd in the square was ecstatic: "When the emcee, comrade Salim al-Qasim invited Mayor Tawfiq Zayyad to deliver his speech, the sky of the First of May Square thundered from the call of the crowd: 'With spirit, with blood, we will protect you, Zayyad!'"[35] In his speech, Zayyad expressed his hope that there would be a real integration of the Arab citizens in the state and insisted that the Arabs wanted to be full citizens but the state ignored their rights. Because the Arabs were 15 percent of the citizenry, they should be represented by three ministers and eighteen MKs, general directors in the government ministries, and ambassadors. He demanded that all the Arab departments in the ministries be abolished and that Arabs be appointed as directors of public radio and television in Arabic. "This is in order to allow the Arab citizens to take part in general decisions," he explained, "and not only in issues related to them." He demanded national and cultural rights for the Arabs in Israel "in order to dance dabka[36] and not only hora,[37] and to learn Arabic poetry and not only Bialik."[38]

In this speech, Zayyad went beyond the traditional communist demands for integration when he asked for Arab citizens to be part of the government, a demand that no communist leader had ever made before. Since 1948, Israeli governments and the communists had implemented a consistent mutual boycott. What caught the attention of the Hebrew media, though, was one sentence implying that Arab citizens had other options. Zayyad warned that if the government did not grant full equality to Arab citizens, they "will post announcements in the market and in the press in order to look for another state that might want them and their lands."[39] The last words implied the hypothetical possibility of eliminating Israeli sovereignty over areas with a large Arab population and therefore indirectly questioned the permanent status of the 1948 armistice line as Israel's border. By that, Zayyad contradicted the party line. Since the mid-1950s, the party accepted the armistice line as the new international borders of Israel and did not suggest changing the borders to match the 1947 UN partition plan. This caution was adopted partly because such a demand would have put a question mark on the already shaky citizenship of Arab citizens in the disputed territories. *Al-Ittihad*'s editor, Emile Habibi, was probably aware of the explosive potential of the statement, and it was omitted from the report about Zayyad's speech in the newspaper. The Hebrew media, though, did not ignore the statement, though it was only an aside, and they even used paraphrased versions of it in headlines. The "separatist threat" became the focus of public attention while the integrative message was ignored. The Movement for Greater Israel,[40] for example, published a media release condemning Zayyad's words as treason and calling on the government to press charges against him.[41]

The public uproar might explain a seemingly bizarre event that took place the following day, which happened to be Israel's Independence Day. Zayyad and his two municipal deputies, Ra'iq Jarjura and Kamil al-Zahir, attended the Independence Day reception organized in Nazareth by Yisrael Koenig and Shmuel Toledano. The three approached Koenig and Toledano, as well as the commander of Northern District police, and surprised them with a "happy holidays" greeting.[42] This congratulation might not seem so bizarre if we remember that Zayyad and his party always made a distinction between Zionism and an inclusive non-Zionist Israeli national identity. Zayyad's short visit at the Independence Day reception probably aimed at highlighting this aspect of his political ideology as a response to public criticism.

THE OCCUPATION SPEECH SCANDAL

Another frontline in the relations between Zayyad and the Hebrew media was his solidarity with Palestinians living under Israeli military occupation in the West Bank and Gaza Strip. In summer 1980, Zayyad's identification with Arabs fighting against Israeli occupying forces provoked public uproar, echoing the scandal that erupted in fall 1974 following the republication of his "Great Crossing" poem. On June 2, 1980, Jewish terrorists attempted to assassinate three Palestinian mayors in the West Bank and severely injured two of them. Following the event, Palestinian mayors inside Israel convened in Nazareth to express their solidarity with the West Bank mayors. Zayyad was the main speaker, and according to a report in the Hebrew newspaper *Ma'ariv*, he said that "those who do not want to be killed in Hebron should not impose themselves on the people of Hebron," and explained, "Every People living under occupation has the right to resist, and the occupied People chooses the methods. We are part of the Palestinian People and part of the State of Israel and we care about both of them. What happened there could happen here as well."[43] If the implicit support for armed resistance was not enough to elicit furious reactions, a reference to the Holocaust and the comparison of Israel to Nazi Germany ensured that the speech would be the focus of public attention for a while: "There is a policy of physical extermination of the Palestinian People. The master planners of this policy are beasts who forgot that in the place of every victim ten thousand new lives sprout up. Hitler attempted to exterminate the Jews and failed. In our days, there is no place for the annihilation of a People, and therefore there is no possibility for annihilating their rights."[44]

That Friday night, Zayyad's speech was broadcast on Israel's single television channel, and the public turmoil begun. Prime Minister Menachem Begin said that Zayyad's words were "very severe," and his minister of justice, Shmuel Tamir, said that Zayyad used inciting language and that the state should uproot such expressions of incitement for rebellion at their sprouting stage.[45] *Davar* reporter Israel Landers wrote of Zayyad, "His words provoked a turmoil of protest not only because of their content but also because of their tone and the facial expression of the speaker on the television screen. Whoever saw him could not be mistaken in evaluating the emotions stirring in his heart."[46]

Zayyad was not the only cause of the government's concern. In the late 1970s, Rakah's status as the leading party among Palestinians in Israel was being challenged by more radical forces that did not recognize the legitimacy of the State of Israel (and therefore the legitimacy of a two-state solution) or the distinction between Palestinians who were Israeli citizens and those who were not, and emphasized their loyalty to the armed struggle.[47] In keeping with the emerging zeitgeist that legitimized Palestinian identification and also seeking to protect their popularity, the Arab members of Rakah radicalized their own discourse. Following Zayyad's speech, the government took advantage of the public protest against it and issued restriction orders for four Arab communist activists. It later extended the order to include Arab activists of other movements and parties under the pretext of "fighting incitement." After the restriction orders were issued, unnamed government sources were quoted in the media stating, "We very much doubt that they [the activists] dare now to say things that a week ago were acceptable to say in Israel."[48]

Because Zayyad was a member of the Knesset, he was protected from a restriction order, although after his speech, the phone line at his house was mysteriously disconnected for several days.[49] When the Knesset assembly met three days later, the discussion was turbulent and included a lot of heckling and name-calling between Zayyad and his opponents. Several MKs demanded that his immunity be revoked so he could stand trial. One, MK Geula Cohen of the Far Right Tehiya Party, said: "I refuse to sit in one parliament with someone who calls for a military rebellion against the State of Israel." Zayyad, Tubi, and Vilner interrupted her, saying that she was lying and distorting Zayyad's words. "If MK Zayyad has the courage" Cohen added, "he should stand behind his words and should stand trial. This is a Zionist Knesset, until further notice."[50]

The party itself supported Zayyad in both public and private meetings. Still, in the Central Committee meeting, Secretary General Vilner, always careful and calculated, commented, "We will oppose vehemently the incitement and threats against comrade Tawfiq Zayyad. Along with our public display, which is correct in principle, we should be very tactical in order not to provide our enemies the possibility of picking on things that we say or do not say." Zayyad answered that he did not say anything in the conference that he had not said before in the Knesset and other places, but that the government was taking advantage of the current psychological condition of the public. He added that the published quotation was provided to the press by the adviser on Arab affairs, Binyamin Gur-Aryeh, who distorted his original words.[51]

After Attorney General Yitshak Zamir clarified that Zayyad's speech could not justify the revocation of his immunity (he based his evaluation on the broadcast text, not the printed quotations),[52] the minister of justice introduced legislation that would extend the definition of support for a terrorist organization to any person who "does any act manifesting identification or sympathy with a terrorist organization in a public place or in such manner that persons in a public place can see or hear such manifestation of identification or sympathy, either by flying a flag or displaying a symbol or slogan or by causing an anthem or slogan to be heard or any other similar overt act clearly manifesting such identification or sympathy."[53]

Zayyad, the intended target of this legislation, protested on the Knesset podium, "According to the law our entire People would be sitting on the trial bench. [. . .] If you respect the flag of your People, the Palestinian flag, it means that you identify with a terrorist organization [. . .] The aim of this law is the elimination of our national identity, because we are part of the Arab Palestinian People." The discussion in the assembly soon deteriorated again into name-calling, with author and playwright MK Moshe Shamir calling Zayyad "a student of Hitler" and Zayyad retaliating by calling Shamir "a small Hitler" and "a fascist of the seventh division."[54] Zayyad concluded the exchange with "tuzz," an interjection that in colloquial Arabic could be translated, depending on context, as "I don't give a damn," or "screw it," but when embedded in a Hebrew conversation usually sounds more profane than in Arabic.[55] Zayyad's objections went unheeded, and the assembly approved the Amendment for the Prevention of Terror Ordinance.

This kind of confrontation fit well with the image nurtured by journalists in the Hebrew media of Zayyad as stormy, aggressive, and hypernationalistic. During the same period, Zayyad's poetry finally gained a first review in Hebrew—one that did not deviate from this characterization: "The code of his poetry is not difficult to decipher. His means are direct and blatant. Even though sometimes he imposes on himself partial silence, it is not difficult to 'complete' his silence. *His* truth is clear to *him* and he has no doubts. He rarely expresses himself in half-tones. [. . .] I would dare to say that more than one of the Palestinian National Charter's paragraphs could have been 'translated' into Tawfiq Zayyad's poetry and vice versa."[56]

This almost singular negative depiction of Zayyad and the growing fascination with him among Jewish audiences prompted the elitist and innovative Hebrew monthly *Monitin* to initiate a detailed report about Zayyad. The journalist David Halevi met with him for several long meetings and produced the most detailed and nuanced journalistic profile of Zayyad ever written.[57] The image of Zayyad in the report, published in February 1981, was far from the menacing one that characterized previous coverage:

> Tawfiq Zayyad: A folk man, average height, a small belly dropping the pants down. A melancholic-like look, disgruntled, a hearty smile, as if innocent. Even a little shy. A low voice that becomes husky as he tries to raise it. Certainly not an image of a politician. It is nice talking with him. Often he uses parables and juicy images. Citing ceaselessly from Marx, Lenin, Engels. He has mastered four languages: Arabic, Hebrew, English, and Russian.

Halevi also met Sayf al-Din al-Zu'bi, Zayyad's establishment-backed predecessor in city hall and compared the impressive splendor of his house with Zayyad's unassuming lifestyle:

> In his house in the Eastern Neighborhood, considered the poor neighborhood of Nazareth, Zayyad looks like the complete opposite of Zu'bi. Seemingly, as an Israeli, I am going from the "good" Arab to the "bad" Arab. Only seemingly. A humble house, modestly furnished ("I give my salary from the Knesset to the party. From the city hall I do not get anything. The party salary is way below the poverty line. I have a '69 Volkswagen. I want to replace it. I can't"). A simple dress, even sloppy.

Helavi's report also quoted from people who worked with Zayyad at the time, further emphasizing his humanity. MK Charlie Bitton, for example, highlighted how engaged and accessible Zayyad was: "He is a little bit different from the other communists. He knows how to eat, drink, and tell off-color jokes in serious events. He understands the layman in the street." Halevi also emphasized Zayyad's pragmatism and universalist orientation. "I identify with progressive national sentiments, but I oppose reactionary Arab nationalism," he quoted Zayyad as stating. "A Jewish worker or democrat is closer to me than the king of Morocco or this spoiled child, [King] Hussein, or another Arab fascist."

Monitin's editor, Adam Baruch, had a clear agenda of challenging the existing image of Zayyad among Israeli Jews. He added his own paragraph to the interview. With its text in red and surrounded with a red frame, he satirized the common Jewish Israeli perception of Zayyad:

> Tawfiq Zayyad threatens me. His mere existence threatens me. I, in this context, am the neurotic Jewish Israeli. I am sure that he aspires to humiliate me, that he strives for revenge. [...] I do not know him but my own fears, and he is the stereotype derived from these fears. I feel Zayyad without seeing him. He is in my house, without being in it. His penis is full with vengeance. [...] I do not know Zayyad, not personally. He is a symbol, and our psychology is made out of symbols. I would have preferred that his portrait be of a cunning careerist. I would prefer that he would compare me to Hitler and promise us a blood bath. That it would be possible to buy him by money and honors [...] that he would be an aggressive and primitive nationalist. [...] But the image portrayed in

this report is more complicated, a different image of a potential partner for a dialogue. Blessed is the believer. I do not believe.

Baruch's text would remain a valid parody of the Hebrew media's representation of Zayyad for years to come, although with the relative liberalization of the Hebrew public sphere and diversification of media outlets in the early 1990s, more journalists discovered the gap between Zayyad's stereotypical caricature and his actual personality and political worldview.

THE CREATION OF THE DEMOCRATIC FRONT FOR PEACE AND EQUALITY

The phenomenal success of the Nazareth Democratic Front prompted Rakah to implement the concept in other localities and in national politics as well, and this effort gained momentum after Land Day as the party's self-confidence grew. Zayyad encouraged the creation of alliances in many other Arab localities and also advocated for the creation of a front for the Knesset election. Although most party leaders, including Meir Vilner and Tawfiq Tubi,[58] initially rejected the idea of a parliamentary front, they eventually shifted their position, and in December 1976, the Eighteenth Congress of the party decided to create a front for the Knesset elections, scheduled for May 17, 1977.

Over the next months, the party leadership negotiated with several potential allies. One was a faction of the Black Panthers, a protest movement giving voice to ethnoclass frustration of second-generation Jewish immigrants from North Africa and Middle Eastern countries (at the time, they were generally referred to as Sephardi Jews. In contemporary vocabulary; the common term is *Mizrahi* Jews). The movement shook the country in a series of turbulent demonstrations in early 1971 but failed to gain representation in the Knesset in the 1973 elections.[59] Other potential allies were a group of noncommunist Arab mayors through whom the party hoped to gain influence in localities that were not their traditional base of support, and a group of Jewish activists organized under the name Israeli Socialist Left. In addition, the party negotiated with former leaders of the Arab nationalist al-'Ard movement, Muhammad Mi'ari and Mansur Kardush.

The tension between including the Black Panthers, which adopted what was in effect an agnostic position toward Zionism, and the Mi'ari group, which was explicitly and actively anti-Zionist, was evident. Zayyad preferred the exclusion of Arab elements he considered extremist, which in his view included Mi'ari: "I oppose the inclusion of extremists like Mi'ari and partners of his kind. We will not be able to bear responsibility for this partnership."[60] Nevertheless, Zayyad was a member the negotiation team appointed by the Politburo to meet Mi'ari and his group—negotiation that did not bear fruit. Although some scholars have argued that Arab leaders of the party were skeptical of the alliance with the Panthers from the very beginning,[61] Zayyad saw this alliance as a first step toward a large-scale Arab-Jewish partnership, which he consistently emphasized as a priority in the party's internal discussions about the front. "We need a Jewish-Arab list, namely more Jewish forces," he urged at a Central Committee meeting. For him, such a partnership was part of a long-term strategy that went beyond the immediate elections: "We need at least one noncommunist figure, democratic, representative—even if this figure has no direct electoral power." Zayyad's support for the alliance with the Panthers also reflected his deep commitment to class-based struggle as well as his emotional identification with Mizrahi Jews as victims of racial discrimination. In the meeting of the Central Committee during the negotiations with the Panthers, he stated, "I support the Black Panthers issue not only as an electoral asset [. . .] this is a huge thing. And the reason is because we are also panthers. We are THE panthers—but not members of this organization. [Some members] talk about a benefit, as if it is a commodity in the market. The real essence of our benefit is our allies."[62]

It is noteworthy that this stand was compatible with Zayyad's broader interest in racially based oppression. His daughter, Wahiba, an elementary school student at the time, remembers that her parents were strict about their children's bedtime, but her father made an exception—he allowed them to stay awake for the weekly broadcast of the US miniseries *Roots* about African American enslavement when it aired in Israel in 1978. Zayyad was even explicit about the color dimension of his solidarity with the Panthers. After the agreement was signed and the Democratic Front for Peace and Equality (DFPE) was established, Zayyad said (in Hebrew) in the opening rally of the election campaign: "The Black Panthers are not only our brothers in color [*ahim le-tseva*], but also brothers in the aspiration to liberate from exploitation. The place of our Jewish brothers who are here is not only in the front, but in the heart of every one of us."[63] (Interestingly, this sentence appeared only in the Hebrew bulletin of the party, not in *al-Ittihad*'s report about the rally.)

On different occasions, Zayyad repeated his claim that short-term instrumental considerations should be put aside: "Quantitatively, the front is still small, but it is very wide in its perspective. It represents very diverse forces. How to use our potential—this is our big responsibility."[64] When the DFPE was officially declared on March 8, 1977, it included the Black Panthers, the noncommunist Arab mayors, and the Israeli Socialist Left. Mi'ari's group was left out. A Black Panther, Charlie Bitton, was ranked third in the election list. Zayyad's enthusiasm about the emerging Arab-Jewish partnership might explain his opposition to declaring a general strike on the first anniversary of Land Day. In a joint meeting of the Committee of Arab Mayors and the Land Committee that discussed the plans for that day, he said, "We should know how to manage our struggle and at what level. Today we must unify all the residents and all the democratic forces in the Jewish public to protect Arab lands, and from this perspective we should consider every step in our struggle."[65]

Zayyad and the rest of the communist leaders had expected that the alliance with the Panthers would bridge the divide between the party and Jewish voters, but the election results reflected the harsh reality of ethnic segregation and the hegemony of Zionist ideology among Jewish Israelis. Bitton was elected as MK, but no more than a few thousand Jews voted for the DFPE, far below the fifteen thousand votes that would have mathematically justified a seat for a Jewish representative. Before the 1981 elections, Zayyad asked another leader of the Panthers, Kochavi Shemesh, to take Bitton's place on the list, but Shemesh rejected the idea.[66] After the 1981 election results replicated the front's 1977 failure, protests against the alliance among party members became vocal.[67] Zayyad, however, remained silent in public. He also continued to believe in the potential of an alliance between Palestinian citizens and Jews from Arab countries. When in February 1983, Aharon Uzan, the minister of welfare from the Sephardi party Tami, visited Nazareth, breaking the government boycott of Nazareth, Zayyad raised the Israeli flag over city hall. When a journalist asked him to explain the good chemistry in his meeting with Uzan, he answered: "Sephardi Jews understand us Arabs better."[68] When Zayyad finally joined the critics of the inclusion of Bitton in the mid-1980s, he said that he was personally disappointed in Bitton, who failed to mobilize Jewish voters, but he did not publicly criticize the political alliance. The party leaders rejected the criticism, and Bitton remained in a secured high ranking on the DFPE list for the 1984 and 1988 elections; he left the front only in 1990. By then, his movement which he supposedly represented, the Black Panthers, had vanished.

ASSASSINATION ATTEMPT

On the evening of May 12, 1977, five days before the election, Zayyad returned home from an election rally in Tamra accompanied by party members from the town, who joined him for coffee. The four children, including two-month-old Faris, were asleep. When the guests left, Zayyad went to read newspapers in the bedroom. Shortly after 1:00 a.m., he went to put the newspapers back in the guest room.[69] This was the first moment in the entire evening Zayyad was alone in a lighted room facing the street. Two seconds after he left the room, he heard a burst of gunfire. When he and Na'ila inspected the room, they found four bullets and later counted twenty bullet marks on the house's exterior. Zayyad filed a complaint with the police, who opened an investigation, and the following day they found an abandoned stolen car with bullet casings that matched the Uzi submachine gun bullets found at Zayyad's house.[70] This was the last report about the investigation in the press. Nazareth, however, is a small town with dense social networks. Zayyad found out who was responsible for the shooting and even met with the perpetrators. When a reporter asked why he did not pass their names to the police, he answered, "I can't, there are political considerations, I can't."[71]

PALESTINIAN UNITY

Since the creation of the State of Israel, its authorities have implemented a consistent policy of divide and rule toward Arab-Palestinian citizens. This policy has aimed to prevent the emergence of Arab or Palestinian national consciousness by emphasizing alternative identities, such as local, ethnic, and, above all, religious identities. As a result, while the state does not recognize the Palestinian citizens as a national minority, it nurtured religious affiliations as meaningful political categories and institutionalized them.[72] After his election as mayor in 1975, and even more so since Land Day, Zayyad growingly defied this policy in his rhetoric and practice. On September 6, 1980, he chaired a conference of 150 mayors, political leaders, and educators who convened in Shafa'amr to build an institutional framework that would express Palestinian identification inside Israel and mobilize Israel's Palestinian citizens for political action. Conference attendees approved a plan to convene the "Congress of the Arab Masses" in November and approved a political platform for the congress. The platform called for the establishment of a Palestinian state next to Israel; it declared that the Arabs in Israel were an inseparable part of the Palestinian People and that the Palestine Liberation Organization was the only representative of the Palestinian People. Unlike previous supralocal initiatives, such as the Committee of Arab Mayors, that promoted collective interests under the guise of aggregated local issues, the Congress of the Arab Masses intended to explicitly promote collective national rights. To the alarmed Hebrew press, Zayyad explained, "We are a minority with national rights. We want to be recognized as a People, as a nation. We do not want to be referred to as religious minorities anymore."[73]

The adviser on Arab affairs, Binyamin Gur-Aryeh, was determined that the congress, which he saw as opening the floodgates of separatist initiatives, would fail.[74] And when Zayyad went to the US in mid-September 1980, the Hebrew media, most likely fed by official sources, watched with concern as he took part in the Conference for the Protection of the Palestinian Person, a gathering of 940 delegates, including senior leaders of the PLO. At the conference, Zayyad lectured about the planned congress, and some observers saw his lecture as a sign that the congress was coordinated with the PLO.[75] At the same time, the police investigated Zayyad, arguably for hiding fund transfers from abroad to the municipal account.[76] The investigation relied on information that had been published nine months earlier, in the Report of the State Comptroller, but it never led to an indictment. The timing of the interrogation and its quick ending suggest it was an attempt to fish for an indictment, and it had much to do with the policy of personal harassment of Rakah leaders recommended by the Koenig memorandum.

The congress was scheduled for December 6, 1980, but on December 1, Prime Minister Menachem Begin, who served also as minister of defense at the time, used his authority under emergency regulations to sign an order banning the congress. Minister of Justice Moshe Nissim met with the editors of Israel's major newspapers to explain the decision and stated that the government saw in the congress a "clear irredentist tendency." The minister argued that the PLO supported the congress financially and was embedded in the organization's long-term plan to dismantle the State of Israel.[77] Zayyad protested the ban, describing the decision as "an anti-Arab, anti-democratic, racist move." Some observers, however, noted that he appeared quite satisfied and seemed to have found a positive side to this development. Following a television news report about the cancellation, for example, the Jewish Israeli poet Dahlia Ravikovitch wrote that "whoever saw Tawfiq Zayyad laughing joyfully, saw a wise person whose work was done by others. Instead of the canceled congress, the government prepared an international festival for Rakah, with police cars driving in the streets and many cameras and microphones documenting the event."[78] The journalist David Halevi mentioned that Zayyad "did not look sad" following the cancellation, and later Zayyad explained, "The government entered the net like a shark. The important thing is that the net will not break. Most of the goals of the congress were achieved, people heard what we have to say."[79]

If in the late 1960s Zayyad established himself as a national poet, in the late 1970s, he became a national leader. As an antiestablishment mayor of Nazareth, he accumulated countrywide popularity and political capital, which he used to push his party toward supporting a nationwide general strike on Land Day. He played an important role in transforming the blood spilled on Land Day into a mobilizing narrative of sacrifice, heroism, and the struggle for equality. He insisted on considering Palestinians in Israel as a national minority rather than an aggregation of religious groups, and he expressed explicit and unapologetic solidarity with the struggle of Palestinians in the West Bank and the Gaza Strip against the occupation. In that period, these stands, as well as his directness and temperament, increased his popularity among Palestinians while at the same time led to his frequent vilification by mainstream Hebrew media. The next chapter discusses how these two diametrically opposed images of Zayyad were further solidified when he mobilized protest against the Israeli invasion of Lebanon and the harsh suppression of the first intifada.

Chapter 7

CHILDREN IN THE BATTLEFIELD

IN THE 1980 WORK CAMP IN NAZARETH, VOLUNTEERS FROM NABLUS and Ramallah brought Palestinian flags with them that they wanted to raise; in addition, they demanded that Israeli flags, commonly raised by the Communist Youth and the Arab Scouts, not be raised. In the opening ceremony, three volunteers from the West Bank waved a Palestinian flag, outlawed that same year by the Israeli government, in front of a visible contingent of Israeli police. The Israeli journalist David Halevi, who attended the event, described what followed:

> Zayyad leaves the stage, runs between the seats, jumps above the people standing in his way, and disappears inside the gathering around the flag. After a minute, following a loud argument, he leaves with the flag. With much gentleness and respect, he folds the flag and hands it to an usher who takes it away. Around the rebelling group, people from the Birzeit College, the argument continues. Zayyad returns to his place on the stage.[1]

Zayyad's response satisfied neither the police nor the West Bank activists. Following the flag incident, the police opened an investigation.[2] On the following day a police force arrived at the camp and detained fifteen activists for not carrying identity cards, though following Zayyad's intervention, they were released after a short while.[3] That same day, 150 volunteers from Nablus returned home in protest, and Zayyad was later condemned by Palestinian organizations in the West Bank.[4]

Zayyad's double move of removing the flag and respecting it by folding it gently conveyed his pragmatic political approach of recognizing the importance of the Palestinian solidarity and valuing its symbols, while also declaring that there is a time and place for every symbolic statement, and one should consider the practical implications of every move. Once more, Zayyad faced the challenges of fighting Israel's colonial policy with the pragmatism required in order to manage this fight from within Israeli politics. The major events of the 1980s only sharpened this tension, as Palestinian resistance in Lebanon, the West Bank, and the Gaza Strip and harsh Israeli measures to oppress this resistance resulted in the most violent and deadly decade in the Zionist-Palestinian conflict since 1948 to that point. These developments repeatedly tested the limits of his ability to reconcile his commitment to Palestinian rights with being an Israeli legislator. This chapter follows his efforts to navigate between the two as the war in Lebanon (1982–1985) progressed and was followed by growing unrest in the West Bank and the Gaza Strip that led to the first intifada (1987–1993).

PROTESTING THE WAR IN LEBANON

"This war is a war initiated by the government of Israel," said Tawfiq Zayyad in addressing the Knesset assembly on May 19, 1982, eighteen days before Israel launched its invasion of Lebanon. He continued,

> We see it in the daily provocations, we see it in the bombardments in Lebanon, we see actions of oppression in the occupied territories, in the daily flights of Israeli planes above Lebanon that cost us billions. Beyond all this the chief of staff announced the cancellation of the ceasefire agreement with the PLO. This is evidence that something is being cooked in the war kitchen of the government.[5]

Although it was widely known during the first months of 1982 that the Israeli government was preparing for war, no significant public protest was registered, and Zayyad's public warning remained an isolated case, certainly inside the Knesset.

Indeed, on June 6, Israel invaded Lebanon in order to uproot the PLO infrastructure in the country and establish an Israel-friendly puppet regime led by Christian Maronite forces. In the first days of the war, the Democratic Front for Peace and Equality (DFPE) was the only political party protesting the war, and its MKs even submitted a no-confidence motion in the assembly. Within a week of the invasion, the Israeli forces reached Beirut and, seeking to push PLO forces out, imposed a siege on the city. Failing to achieve that goal in the short term, on August 10, Defense Minister Ariel Sharon ordered a saturation bombing of Beirut, killing at least three hundred people. When the Knesset speaker refused to allow MK Meir Vilner to put the issue on the agenda, both Vilner and Zayyad interrupted the discussion. Zayyad yelled, "Shame on you! Murderers of children, murderers of women!" and ignored the speaker's request to stop until he was ordered to leave the assembly hall and was dragged out by the Knesset ushers.

Zayyad continued to protest the war. It is evident, however, that in his speeches, he carefully measured the doses of Palestinian national pride, messages of peace, and emphasis on Arab-Jewish cooperation in order to avoid the public scandals that followed his protests in the past. In his traditional speech at the opening ceremony of the Nazareth volunteering camp in late August 1982, he said:

> Our People firmly chose the way of steadfastness and struggle. It is our People who are holding on after seventy-five days against unprecedented evil aggression. The Israeli forces launched in one day, 12 August, 240,000 shells on West Beirut alone, and encircled the city with 120,000 soldiers. Despite the forest of blood and fire they imposed on Lebanon, our People have been holding on with legendary heroism and advanced their cause several years ahead. [...] We are congratulating the military officer Eli Geva, who refused to break through West Beirut, and the soldier Eli Gojanski, who refused to serve in Lebanon. The opposition we see in Israel is natural because the Israeli People are also bleeding. We have always aspired and worked for living with this People in peace. With this People, but with another leadership.[6]

Protest against the war intensified in the following month. Then, between September 16 and 18, the Lebanese Phalange forces, sent by Israel to the Sabra and Shatila refugee camps in Beirut to capture Palestinian fighters, massacred hundreds of Palestinians and Lebanese citizens. Warnings by Israeli officials in internal discussions before the operation that it might lead to a massacre were ignored. The Israeli army received reports of some of the Phalanges' atrocities in the camps but failed to stop them.[7] The Committee of Arab Mayors announced a countrywide day of general strike on September 22 to protest the massacre. In the most turbulent confrontations in Nazareth since 1958, demonstrators clashed with the police, who injured thirty-nine civilians (twelve of them shot) and arrested twenty (including Zayyad's two deputies). Amin Zayyad, Tawfiq's thirteen-year-old son, was injured in his arm from a rubber bullet. As on Land Day, police surrounded Zayyad's house and, according to *al-Ittihad*, even shot at it.[8]

That day Zayyad was in Jerusalem, taking part in the special Knesset assembly about the massacre. When the news about the violence in Nazareth started to reach Jerusalem, Zayyad's protest about the massacre was mixed with his protest about the more recent aggression in his city. Zayyad was especially agitated, frequently interrupting Defense Minister Sharon, and significant parts of the text of his interruption were omitted from the official minutes. A month later, the Knesset assembly rejected Zayyad's demand to appoint a commission of inquiry headed by a judge to investigate police behavior in Nazareth.[9]

Meanwhile, the war continued with no end in sight. In Jerusalem on February 10, 1983, a hand grenade was thrown into an antiwar demonstration organized by Peace Now, and a demonstrator, Emil Grunzweig, was killed. The discussion in the Knesset assembly was an opportunity for Zayyad to criticize the war in the harshest terms while arguing that protesting it was a joint Arab-Jewish struggle:

> The war of annihilation against Lebanon that entered its ninth month exposed the depth of the bloody abyss into which this government could push the state and the region. [. .]. The truth is that this government does not want to end the war in Lebanon, does not want to withdraw from Lebanon. It wants only one solution: the complete surrender of the Arab Palestinian People, the complete concession of their legitimate national rights, recognized by the entire word. This will never happen. [. . .] Members of the Knesset, the fascist hand grenade that murdered Emil Grunzweig and injured others is a crime showing where we have arrived and to where we might go in the future. There is a constant increase in the power of fascist organizations and circles, nurtured by the government, which encourages violence and fascist crimes. [. . .] The struggle for peace, for complete withdrawal from all the occupied territories, is a struggle for democracy inside Israel, it is a struggle to stop the increased fascist phenomenon. Nobody should have the illusion that it is possible to separate these two things. The fascists who attacked the Peace Now demonstration yelled at the demonstrators, "We will make for you Sabra and Shatila here!"

THE CONFLICT WITH THE PROGRESSIVE LIST FOR PEACE

In late August 1982, under Israeli military pressure, the PLO was forced to evacuate its Beirut headquarters, and after several stopovers, the organization reestablished itself in Tunisia. The PLO's continued resistance despite the lack of support from Arab countries, as well as the violence in Lebanon, including the massacre in Sabra and Shatila, intensified sentiments of Palestinian patriotism, as well as the popularity of the PLO among Arab citizens of Israel.[10] For Arab politicians, public identification with the PLO as the only legitimate representative of the Palestinian People turned from an option into a necessity.

One of the indirect results of the intensification of Palestinian patriotic sentiments was the emergence of the Progressive List for Peace (PLP), an ad hoc combination of an Arab list and a Jewish list, as an alternative to the DFPE. While the practical policy regarding the Palestinian-Israeli conflict supported by both the DFPE and the PLP was very similar, the DFPE was officially a supranational body with a universalist message, whereas the PLP emphasized a binational worldview, and its message among the Arabs was unambiguously Palestinian nationalist.[11] In addition, unlike the DFPE, the PLP was not suspected of prioritizing Soviet interests over Palestinian aspirations.

As the Knesset elections scheduled for July 23, 1984, drew near, the DFPE and the PLP competed over Arafat's blessing. As part of this competition, Meir Vilner, Tawfiq Zayyad, and two other members of the Central Committee went to Geneva to meet Arafat on July 10 and 11, twelve days before the elections. The meeting was attended as well by Faruq al-Qaddumi, the head of the PLO Political Department, and Zuhdi Tarazi, the PLO's representative at the UN. The DFPE attempted to maximize the political gains from this meeting by convening a press conference with the delegation at the airport immediately upon its return and reporting on it in a sensational manner in *al-Ittihad*. Four days later, *al-Ittihad* published an interview with Zayyad about the meeting in which he conveyed a twofold message—one geared toward influencing Arab public opinion and the other the general Israeli public (Zayyad was aware that Hebrew media were attentive to his words and might translate and reproduce them). The former aimed to marginalize the PLP and elevate the patriotic image of the DFPE, with Zayyad stating that Arafat "wholeheartedly wished the DFPE success in the elections," and arguing that the Hebrew-language media conspired to present the PLP as an ally of the PLO in order to weaken the DFPE.[12] The latter focused on portraying the PLO as a legitimate political partner, and Zayyad emphasized that Arafat expressed his support for establishing an international conference for solving the Palestinian issue under the auspices of the UN and with the participation of all the relevant actors, including the PLO, Israel, the Soviet Union, and the US.[13] Zayyad interpreted Arafat's position as a support of a two-state solution, and MK Vilner made similar statements in the Hebrew media.[14]

That both the DFPE and the PLP sought Arafat's blessing provoked angry—as Zayyad put it, "hysterical"[15]—reactions in the mainstream Hebrew media and among politicians from across the entire Zionist spectrum. For example, the poet Moshe Dor, who had launched a fierce attack against Zayyad a decade earlier following the publication of his "Great Crossing" poem, described the desire for Arafat's approval as "dangerous, catastrophic," and "shameful."[16] The journalist Matti Golan used similar rhetoric to describe the meeting.[17] Given the demonic image of Arafat among Jewish Israelis, even some members inside Rakah raised concerns about the wisdom of organizing the meeting with Arafat. Vilner had to defend the decision in a meeting of the Central Committee.[18]

In that same interview, Zayyad was explicit about what he thought of the PLP. The common wisdom among communist leaders was that the PLP was created by the Israeli authorities and supported by pro-American elements inside the PLO as a tool against the communists. Like many others in his party, Zayyad believed that the creation of the PLP was part of a large-scale conspiracy to undermine the Communist Party. In a column he published in *al-Ittihad* a week before election day, he wrote:

> After the failure of official Israeli politics to subjugate our Arab masses and force them to surrender, they decided to change the tactics. In the past they addressed us through their direct collaborators, who called on us to surrender to the official policy, and this tactic continued until the early 1970s. The new tactic is based on the construction of a new party that attacks the DFPE and what it represents, including the unity of our masses and progressive orientations (including the friendship with the Soviet Union). It is based on composing a temporary structure (not a party) promoting a solution [for the Palestinian Israeli conflict] that fits the parameters of American policy, while giving this party the "liberty" to raise "patriotic" slogans and providing it with all the necessary media coverage. What is required from them is only not to deviate from the American-Israeli strategic line. For this purpose, the PLP was built on a "patriotic" base, but this is an artificial plastic patriotism.[19]

While many communist leaders shared the concern about the popularity of the PLP because Nazareth was the site of origin for the PLP and its major base, the conflict with the party affected Zayyad more than other leaders. Frequently it was difficult to distinguish between the macropolitical, local, and personal dimensions of the intense conflict. Days before the elections, the tension in Nazareth even reached the point of physical violence between activists of both parties, resulting in police intervention.[20] It is likely also that Zayyad's tendency to directly express his feelings toward people, frequently ignoring the socially accepted rules of politeness, had intensified the tension. For the PLP, Zayyad became the main target of criticism. On election night at 2:00 a.m., the statistician at the Israeli Broadcast Authority announced that Zayyad might not be reelected to the Knesset. A *Haaretz* reporter who attended the PLP headquarters wrote that he witnessed hundreds of activists roaring with joy. A teenage boy started dancing and singing, "Our horses will run over the communists," and hundreds of activists joined him.[21]

The relative success of the PLP in the 1984 elections—winning approximately 18 percent of the Arab votes and gaining two seats in the Knesset—worried the communists even more, and in the subsequent months, PLP empowerment was discussed in almost every meeting of the Politburo. Vilner stated after the elections that "our strategic goal is to hit them, and our tactic is to dismantle them." At the same meeting, the Politburo assigned the journalist Nazir Majali the task of preparing a "black book" (namely, to "dig up dirt") on PLP members.[22] Vilner was especially concerned about the close ties between some PLP leaders and Arafat and the potential political capital they might accumulate through those ties. Publicly the party leaders expressed confidence that Arafat supported them, but behind closed doors, they expressed disappointment about Arafat's sympathy toward the PLP.[23]

INTIFADA

In 1985 the Israel Defense Forces (IDF) evacuated most of its forces in occupied Lebanon, while still holding a narrow strip in the south. The fighting was not over, but its intensity and frequency significantly decreased. Public attention gradually moved to the West Bank and the Gaza Strip, where resistance was growing. On September 9, 1987, exactly three months before the eruption of the first intifada, Zayyad addressed the International Conference of Nongovernmental Organizations in Geneva and described the life of Palestinians under occupation:

This is the twentieth year of the Israeli occupation. [. . .] Five thousand prisoners in the occupation prisons has been a constant for years. But the number of those who passed through these prisons over twenty years is above 250,000—more than 25 percent of the population and more than 50 percent of the adults. House demolitions, administrative detentions, and expulsion of leaders continue, and so does the shutdown of universities and other institutions of higher education. Attacks against the refugee camps, cities, and villages by the occupation army and the fascist settler gangs have become part of daily life—and so have the killing of demonstrators, among them children between ten and twenty years old. The colonizing and taking over of land and water sources, and the destruction of livelihood continue as well. [. . .] The bottom line: an entire People is on the cross, inside and outside its homeland. This [Israeli] policy, however, leads to the absolute opposite consequences. The [Palestinian] People is driven more toward confrontation and resistance."[24]

On December 9, Palestinians in the West Bank and the Gaza Strip rebelled. They held general strikes and tax strikes, boycotted Israeli institutions, and threw stones and Molotov cocktails. The occupying forces harshly repressed the uprising, in the first week killing twenty-two Palestinians, including children. Palestinians inside the Green Line demonstrated in protest throughout the country.

In the Nazareth Municipal Council meeting on December 16, 1987, Zayyad asked the council members to stand for a moment of silence to honor the martyrs who died in the West Bank and the Gaza Strip, and then made a long announcement, analyzing the intifada in its local and global contexts. As usual, Zayyad was optimistic, identifying "a movement in the depth of the Israeli public opinion."[25] It is worth mentioning that future academic studies confirmed Zayyad's intuitive observation. Although the shift was not immediate, the rate of support among Jewish Israelis for establishing a Palestinian state increased from 21 percent to 34 percent two years into the intifada.[26]

Zayyad's projection of endless optimism was certainly a political tool for mobilization, but sometimes it appeared to have the qualities of messianic faith. His belief in the inevitability of the liberation of the People currently "on the cross," as well as the establishment of a Palestinian state through the uprising, is a case in point. Messianic thinking tends to interpret every hardship as a sign of the imminent coming of the Messiah, a bringing forth akin to labor pain. In his speech to the DFPE cadre on December 19, Zayyad said, "It seems that these bloody days open wide the gate for the beginning of the end of the tragedy of this People. We are just before Christmas and we recognize that these days are pregnant, before another birth, which our entire People and the friendly Peoples are expecting. This is the day of birth of the Palestinian state."[27] Whether this rhetoric exposed latent religiosity in Zayyad's worldview or was a calculated mobilizing tool, it seemed to be effective. On January 23, 1988, Nazareth witnessed a mass rally in support of the intifada, which *al-Ittihad* described as "the largest in the history of Nazareth and the largest in the history of the Arab masses in Israel."[28] Addressing the crowd, Zayyad emphasized that the support the Arabs in Israel provided to their brothers and sisters did not stem from merely humanitarian motivation, but "our solidarity with them is a political solidarity, because we are part of this battle."[29]

In February 1988, the PLO planned to ferry 135 Palestinian deportees and hundreds of journalists from the Cypriot port of Limassol to the port city of Haifa for a "journey of return" as a symbolic protest. Zayyad went to Cyprus with a group of Arab and Jewish politicians and activists who intended to join the journey. In a press conference in Nicosia, highlighted in *al-Ittihad*, he praised the "Ship of Return" initiative, the PLO, the intifada, Palestinian unity, and the role of the Arab masses in Israel in the battle to end the occupation.[30] It is noteworthy that Zayyad did not include the PLP within this Palestinian unity, and a few days later, when he and MK Mia'ri from the PLP met on the stage at a demonstration in Greece, Zayyad refused to shake his hand.[31]

The ship's journey was canceled after a limpet mine attached to the hull exploded and put a hole in its fuel tank. However, the shortened distance between Israel's Palestinian citizens and other Palestinians, and the enthusiastic support of the intifada by the communists and their organ *al-Ittihad*, had become a major concern for the state authorities. It touched on a deep anxiety they had been harboring since 1967 about the spread of political consciousness and method of struggle from Palestinians in the West Bank, the Gaza Strip, and the diaspora to Palestinians inside the Green Line. This pan-Palestinian solidarity was not only a security concern, but was also a reminder that in the long term, the post-1967 Israeli occupation of the West Bank and Gaza Strip might make Jews the demographic minority in the territory under Israeli rule.

As a result, the state reverted to its military rule practices and shut down *al-Ittihad* from March 25 to 31 to prevent "incitement" around Land Day events. To justify the government's decision, the adviser on Arab affairs, Amos Gilbo'a, presented to the press a translation of Tawfiq Zayyad's words, allegedly translated from *al-Ittihad*: "The Palestinian flag is our flag and this is undebatable. Whether it should be raised on certain occasions is a tactical question, and not a question of principle. When we decide to raise it we will do so in such a way that it will never go down."[32] Although I could not find this quote in *al-Ittihad*, this position is compatible with Zayyad's position at the time (Gilbo'a probably based his claim on another source). During the first intifada, the banned Palestinian flag was a major symbol of defiance, and Zayyad highlighted his identification with the flag and its defiant message but without crossing the line of legality by actually waving it or explicitly calling on his followers to do so.

The intifada was also a challenge to Arab-Jewish partnership, a cornerstone in the DFPE ideology. Although the PLP was de facto a Jewish-Arab list, its Arabic-language rhetoric rarely mentioned this element, and among Jews, the party was even less popular than the DFPE. The emerging trend of Arab independent politics in Israel continued in early 1988 with the founding of the Arab Democratic Party by MK Muhammad Darawsha, who previously had been a member of the Labor Party. Although Zayyad's identification as an Arab and a Palestinian was unquestionable, he firmly rejected the emerging emphasis on identity politics and even suggested that the motivation of those who did adopt identity politics was not genuinely patriotic: "The basic division in our society is political and social. Are the Jews united in one party? Every serious struggle has to be Jewish-Arab, and we learned from experience that what characterized whoever called for an Arab party or Arab lists was their being agents of the ruling party. Every call to establish a party of this kind is suspicious."[33] Zayyad sought to bridge the gap between Arabs and Jews on many occasions. On April 7, 1988, he spoke in front of the Arab Club in London and urged his audience to not underestimate the Israeli peace camp, "which has significantly expanded over the past years, and especially in the past few months because of the intifada."[34]

In November 1988 at the Nineteenth Session of the Palestine National Council, the PLO accepted the two-state solution and practically adopted the political plan of the DFPE. Zayyad and other party leaders considered it a victory. Attacking the Progressive List in early 1989, Zayyad said, "Before the nineteenth National Council in Algiers, maybe their problem was with us [. . .] They criticized the communists, the communist way, and the DFPE—but today, after the Nineteenth Council and its decisions, they have a problem with the Palestine Liberation Organization and the intifada."[35] The PLO's adoption of the two-state solution had turned the communists' abstract views into a concrete and relevant political plan, thereby exposing them to criticism. The author Muhammad 'Ali Taha re-members attending a lecture by Zayyad at the University of Haifa in which one of the students attacked him for accepting the two-state solution, demanding, "Who authorized you to make these concessions?" Zayyad slammed the table and responded, "Who told you to give up on Haifa and Acre? Why don't you liberate Haifa? Are you trying to liberate Palestine and I'm the one who prevents you from doing it, bastard?" Unlike his rhetoric in the party's Central Committee, where he justified the two-state solution in legalistic terms and international legitimacy, here Zayyad presented the two-state solution as pragmatic compromise, painful but necessary, given the power equation between Palestinians and Zionism. The two justifications do not necessarily contradict one another.

Still, compared with other party leaders, Zayyad's position was considered more in line with the Palestinian national movement, and his rhetoric repeatedly emphasized Arab Palestinian belonging and deep solidarity with Palestinians beyond the Green Line. This was especially pronounced during the First Gulf War, which threw the party into a controversy. While the Iraqi invasion of Kuwait on August 2, 1990, met mostly with international condemnation, for most Pales-tinians, Iraq's invasion of Kuwait represented Iraq's defiance of US hegemony in the region and therefore hope for upsetting the status quo. When the US began its military attack on Iraq in January 1991, Moscow's response was confused and contradictory, as were the positions of party leaders in Israel. Zayyad himself, though, was outspoken. In a long article published in *al-Ittihad* in five install-ments, he reflected on the popular Palestinian consensus: the goals of the US-led war were taking control over the oil fields, destroying Iraqi military and political power, and doing away with Palestinian demands (in Palestine). A defeat of US aggression would be a defeat of the Israeli occupation.[36]

HAUNTING MEMORIES FROM BEHIND BARS

As a Knesset member, Zayyad made the conditions and rights of Palestinian prisoners a high priority. He submitted many queries and motions on the issue and visited inmates in prison to learn about their conditions and listen to their complaints. Zayyad also continued to refer to his own imprisonment whenever he was asked to describe himself. In March 1978, for example, when the Knesset published a notebook in which MKs defined their public service in a few sen-tences, Zayyad submitted the following profile: "Arrested and sentenced several times between the years 1949–1967 for his political activity. Until his election as Knesset member in 1973 was not allowed to leave his city without a military permit."[37] Similarly, three days before his death in 1994, Zayyad was asked by the French Palestinian director Samir 'Abdallah to describe his identity in few words. He answered: "Tawfiq Zayyad, born in Nazareth in 1929, in the political life since the 1940s, arrested and imprisoned many times, married with four children, published several collections of poems and several books, some of them on Palestinian folklore."[38]

The war in Lebanon and the first intifada made clear how central Zayyad's experience as a prisoner was to his self-image and how deeply the torture he experienced in the Tiberias jail in 1955 shaped him. For example, during the first intifada, Israel detained thousands of Palestinians, most of them without trial ("administrative detention"), in a detention camp in the desert. Reports about the tough conditions at Ktsi'ot Prison, known as Ansar 3 among Palestinians, led Zayyad and MK Tawfiq Tubi to visit the facility on July 4, 1988, after which they published in al-Ittihad a call to the Israeli and international public to protest against it. In their report, they described in detail the camp's substandard sanitary conditions and failure to provide adequate nutrition, and they added a desperate call for the government to shut down the facility: "Our words are helpless in face of reality. Detention camp Ansar 3 is hell itself. It is the worst symbol of the occupation and the barbaric oppression which has no bounds. [. . .] We cry out from the depth of our hearts: shut down this camp immediately, and release all its detainees, as well as the other detainees of the intifada."[39]

During the Israeli invasion of Lebanon, Zayyad was alarmed when he learned that Israeli forces had captured thousands of Palestinians and Lebanese and was holding them in abusive conditions and torturing many of them. On January 4, 1983, he submitted a motion concerning prisoners captured in Lebanon. His speech in the Knesset alluded to the continuity in Israel's treatment of Arab prisoners throughout history by connecting the current affairs with memories from 1948:

> Honorable Knesset, the prisoners issue is one of the darkest facets of the aggressive war against Lebanon. One aspect of this issue is the cruel treatment [of prisoners], based on physical and mental torture. As a result of this torture many were killed. [. . .] The Israeli authorities refuse to publish any fact related to these prisoners, their numbers, names, where they are being held, and under what conditions, and they also ban visits by their families, as well as by international and humanitarian entities. [. . .] The vast majority of them

are regular people, who were arguably related to the PLO or could have been PLO members. It reminds me of 1948. In Nazareth and in various villages, hundreds of people, whom I know personally and know that they never touched a weapon, were jailed. They were detained for many months, sometimes even a year or more, in order to scare them and humiliate them. What happens today reminds me of 1948.

Zayyad continued, outlining individual cases of detainees and their suffering. He ended his speech:

We are crying from this stage the cry of humanity. Stop this cruelty, stop the torture. [. . .] The entire world is shocked and asking: how is it possible that a government representing the State of Israel, the state of the Jewish People, who suffered immensely under the Nazis, allows this kind of thing?[40]

In this speech, Zayyad's connected the dots of Palestinian imprisonment from 1948 to the war in Lebanon, presenting a historical continuum of Palestinian suffering. In an interview by the poet Shakib Jahshan the following month, he spoke at length about the place of prison bars in his own life. "My issue with prisons begins under British rule, while I was a fourth grader," he recounted. "I was arrested with some of my classmates, all of us were ten or eleven years old, while watching a tennis game of the British army. They lost the ball, so [they blamed us], they beat us and detained us." Zayyad then outlined the subsequent times he was detained and added, "I do not know whether it [detention] ended or might start again"[41]—perhaps an unintentional admission of a certain personal sense of existential vulnerability belying his political optimism.

Tellingly, in this interview Zayyad mentioned his detentions in 1949, 1951, 1958, and 1967, but he skipped the most painful episode, his arrest and torture in 1955. (Jahshan, who edited the interview, added a comment to bridge the gap.) Zayyad's daughter 'Ubur has vivid memories of her father's pained reaction to prison and torture, confirming that he was uncomfortable dealing with that episode. Until a certain point in his life, she said, he refused to travel to Tiberias and refused without explanation his children's requests to go there. After finally agreeing, while traveling with his family and passing near the prison, he would say, "Here I was tortured, here I was crucified." 'Ubur explained, "We knew that he was tortured, but as children I do not think we understood the level of pain and sadness that curled up inside him."[42]

'UBUR'S INJURY AND THE RETURN TO POETRY

Zayyad was especially close to 'Ubur. When she was in elementary school, she used to spend her Fridays off from school at city hall with her father while he worked. She said:

> My father taught me the importance of a dialogue and the legitimacy of the argument. When I was sixteen years old I wanted to go to a party, and he refused to allow me to go. I did not argue with him, and then he told me: "Why don't you ask me for the reasons of my refusal? Why don't you try to convince me of your point of view? Do not accept my refusal as it is. Do not just obey me. Argue with me, try to change my mind."

'Ubur shared her most intimate secrets only with her father, talking with him about boys and love. "As a teenager, I loved a boy. I asked my father why should the girl always wait for the boy to come and say 'I love you'—what's wrong with being the one initiating? He told me: 'Don't be afraid—if you love a boy, go and tell him this.'"

The bond between 'Ubur and her father became even closer under painful circumstances. On May 20, 1990, at the peak of the first intifada, a Jewish Israeli citizen named 'Ami Poper shot a group of Palestinian workers from the Gaza Strip, killing seven and injuring seventeen. The murder was followed by riots on both sides of the Green Line. The Follow-Up Committee declared three days of strike, and in some towns and villages young Palestinians confronted the police.[43] The house of Tawfiq Zayyad's brother Musbah, which was part of the same compound as Tawfiq and Na'ila's house, served as an improvised shelter for people who were fleeing the tear gas and other forms of police violence. On the morning of the first day of the strike, Na'ila Zayyad was arrested, allegedly for inciting violence. 'Ubur, then fifteen years old, was at her uncle's house that morning. While she was looking through the kitchen window to the street, some troops gathered below the window, and one of them directed his gun to the window and shot a tear-gas grenade. The grenade shattered the glass, injuring 'Ubur in her eye, and she was rushed to the 'Afula hospital, where doctors operated on her for six hours.

When her father, who was taking care of organizing the countrywide protest, was informed about his daughter's injury, he rushed to the hospital. After the operation, the doctors had bad news: 'Ubur's cornea was severely damaged, the nature of her injury did not allow a cornea transplant, and she had lost her sight in one eye. According to 'Ubur, her father felt guilty because her injury was indirectly related to his own activism, and he refused to accept the verdict. He investigated the medical options and told 'Ubur that medical science is constantly improving and that a cure for her would be found. "He ceaselessly implanted the hope in me," 'Ubur remembers, "he always told me: be optimistic and patient. Nothing comes easy."

His daughter's eye injury deeply affected Zayyad. Following the incident, he began to express himself visually through drawing. Especially during long political meetings, he would make sketches. Many of his drawings are abstract, but in the abstract background, Zayyad embedded human faces, animals, and objects, with a single wide-open eye a regular motif.

'Ubur's injury and treatment coincided with another development: Zayyad return to writing poetry. Although in January 1990, Arafat had awarded Zayyad the Palestine Prize for Palestinian Authors and Poets in a ceremony in Cairo, this was after sixteen years of poetic drought as Zayyad focused on politics. His temporary absence from the Knesset between February 1990 and July 1992 (see chapter 9) surely contributed to this creative renaissance. Most of the poems in this wave were written in spring 1991, in the months that followed the Iraq war. Many relate to the intifada, and especially to the role of children in the uprising. Like many other Palestinians, Zayyad was greatly affected by the children who wrote graffiti, raised Palestinian flags, and even threw stones at the soldiers. Approximately 18 percent of the Palestinians killed during that uprising were below the age of seventeen,[44] and their deaths echoed in Zayyad's poems. One prominent example is the poem "New 'Adnan," which tells the story of a seven-year-old boy named 'Adnan who was killed by a bullet between his eyes. "New 'Adnan" ends with a determined resistance and a refusal to let tragedy mean defeat. It glorifies the mother, who "kept cheering like a lioness / in the face of the soldiers: /'in my womb / there is a new 'Adnan / in my womb / Occupier / There is a new 'Adnan.'"[45]

Another new poem reflected the sense of urgency that Zayyad shared with other communists regarding direct negotiations between Israel and the PLO, especially after the PLO's acceptance of the two-state solution. However, in 1986, the Knesset had banned any contact between Israeli citizens and the PLO. The Jewish peace activist Abie Nathan violated the ban, and in September 1989, he was sentenced to six months in prison. In late April 1991, Nathan begun a hunger strike in protest of the law. On May 28, Zayyad led a group of DFPE members of the Nazareth Municipal Council on a one-day hunger strike, in solidarity with Nathan.[46] During the same period, he wrote "The Abie Nathan Ode," with the

FIGURE 2. Tawfıq Zayyad's illustration, June 15, 1994.
Source: Tawfıq Zayyad Institute.

opening line: "To Abie Nathan, a Nazarian bottle of champagne." The ode itself is a long antiwar statement:

> Has not the time come
>> For us to meet and talk like the rest of humanity?
> We will greet and shake each other's hand
> We will call each other by our names
> We will beat our swords into ploughshares
> We will plant a flower in the ground
> And collect the moonlight.
> […]
> Do not give the tank of death
> And the tip of the vengeful dagger
> The right to speak.
> Do not give the dungeon of torture
> And the dark prison
> The right to speak
> […]
> Give the children
> The right to speak.
> Give the one who protest until death
> The right to speak.
> Give Abie, the People's conscience,
> The right to speak.[47]

It is possible that 'Ubur's injury, an incident in which national politics affected Zayyd's personal life in the most disturbing way, is what explains his brief return to personal poems, in which politics was at least not explicit. The most remarkable among these poems was written a year after the injury, a year during which Zayyad regularly accompanied his daughter to doctors' appointments. In this poem, "The Death of My Young Friend 'Umar," the speaker is mourning a two-year-old child who died from sickness. He visits the child's grave and repeatedly apologizes for not being able to attend his funeral.

> And on the grave that looks like a flower
> I went for reading 'Umar
> A story … and another one … and another one,

And I call upon all the heroes of the children stories
And he is hearing me, for the last time
He is listening, and listening, and his face shines
From underneath the soil.
[...]
Farewell, 'Umar's grave
And farewell, 'Umar
And farewell, children, above the ground and below it,
In the cradle and the tomb, alive or dead
From every country and every People,
Every time and every place.[48]

In the 1950s, Zayyad was denied freedom and subjected to torture because of his political protest, and this experience is reflected in a shift in his poetry toward Arab and Palestinian national themes. In the protests of the 1980s, two of his own children were injured, 'Ubur permanently so. For Zayyad, her injury was interwoven with the growing violence against Palestinian children during the intifada, inspiring poetry that was still political and patriotic but also conveyed vulnerability. It might be this side of Zayyad that led the poet Mahmoud Darwish to write that Zayyad "married silk with iron."[49]

The 1980s also witnessed a decline in the dominance of Zayyad's party among the Palestinians in Israel, and in his struggle to preserve the party's standing, Zayyad was deeply involved in a bitter conflict with the major challenging force, the PLP. Toward the end of the decade, the PLP was defeated, but a new challenge emerged. The conflict this time had a much deeper ideological rift and a much more fundamental question at stake: What is the place of religion in politics? I discuss Zayyad's confrontation with the Islamic Movement in the next chapter.

Chapter 8

A SECULAR HOLY WARRIOR

AFTER ZAYYAD WAS ELECTED MAYOR IN 1975, A JOURNALIST FROM THE EN-glish-language Israeli newspaper *Jerusalem Post* asked him whether he observed any Islamic customs. Zayyad, the article reports, "shook his head and with a pained, forbearing look and tone of a sorely-tried teacher said: 'No. You see: I'm a communist.'" In other words, for Zayyad, not observing religious rules was more than a personal preference; it was part of his broader worldview and the ideology he subscribed to, with his own quasi-religious faith. During the 1950s and 1960s, this blunt secularism was compatible with the dominance of secular forces in the Arab world, including within the Palestinian national movement and among Palestinian citizens of Israel. After the 1970s, however, new forces had been gaining power in these spheres—forces for whom religious observance was not only a personal choice but a declaration aiming at political and social change.

While conflicts in neighboring Arab countries between secular regimes and an Islamist opposition sometimes have been imported and embedded in local partisan struggles among Palestinians in Israel, it never could have reached the level of violence experienced in those countries. Unlike the situation in Egypt, Syria, and Algeria, supporters in Israel of both political Islam and secular Arab movements share a similar experience of dispossession and discrimination on an ethnonational basis. This structural condition makes their cooperation more durable and stable, and Islamic opposition to the Israeli regime is frequently articulated in a Palestinian nationalist vocabulary.

Still, Tawfiq Zayyad's disdain of political Islam was remarkable, and he consistently rejected its displays of Palestinian and Arab patriotism as inauthentic and instrumental. For the Islamist activists, Zayyad's political vision was only part of the problem. He also became the personification of everything they considered wrong in contemporary Muslim society. Zayyad lived modestly, but he was far from a religious ascetic. Mahmoud Darwish wrote that Zayyad "merged [political] enthusiasm with fun" and that he embodied "the urge to live and to love life."[2] He enjoyed partying, laughing, and drinking with friends, and he refused to wait patiently for the afterlife. His frank secularist lifestyle, his civil marriage to a Christian woman who did not convert to Islam, and his decision not to raise his children to be religious would make him vulnerable to criticism from the Islamic Movement when it became a major political force in the late 1980s.

Indeed, eighteen years after that interview with the *Jerusalem Post*, Zayyad's confident secularism faced a much less tolerant public sphere. In a January 1994 interview with a Hebrew-language newspaper, Zayyad attacked the Islamists and took pride in his secular lifestyle. The deputy chair of the movement, Kamal Khatib, responded with a venomous ad hominem attack peppered with rumors about Zayyad's drinking habits, which Khatib contextualized in a broader abrogation of Muslim tradition:[3]

> Not because he left the hotel drunk wobbling to the right and left . . . not because he drove his car under this condition and hit two cars in the parking lot[4] . . . not because he forgot his bag with documents and files concerning his People in the parking lot and an explosives expert was called to explode it . . . not because he drinks wine, vodka, whiskey and cognac . . . not because he displays his colorful picture in the newspapers with a glass of wine as if it were natural . . . not because he is proud to have a golden dictionary of insults and curses he uses whenever he gets angry . . . not because he is proud that he married his wife Na'ila in a civil marriage in Cyprus, with no religious legitimacy . . . and not because he says that he has no objection to see his daughter marrying a Jewish man if she so chooses . . . not because he is proud that his daughter would date her boyfriend for many years before she married him, and that he never asked her where she is coming from or where she is going because she is free. We are not asking and wondering about all these issues because they

might be personal matters of a man, who does them after he takes off the dress of virility and dignity and then the allowed becomes forbidden while the forbidden becomes allowed.[5]

Khatib's harsh attack was the culmination of five years of an overt and intense ideological conflict that had personal dimensions. Most of the wrongdoings Khatib accused Zayyad of, especially those related to his family, reflect aspects of his life that Zayyad himself was proud of and never tried to hide. Khatib's condemnation thus illustrates the vastly different social values idealized by communists and Islamists.

THE ISLAMIC MOVEMENT

Unlike inside Israel, where the Muslim Brotherhood's activity vanished following the Nakba, and the Gaza Strip where it was repressed by the Egyptian authorities, the movement was permitted to pursue its activities openly in the West Bank.[6] The movement provided Islamic seminars that following the 1967 war attracted lower-middle-class Muslims from the Triangle. In the early 1970s, graduates of these seminars were the main force behind the gradual establishment of a loose network of organizations, collectively known as the Muslim Youth, throughout the Triangle and the Galilee.[7] These organizations set up welfare and educational institutions, including libraries, institutes for Islamic studies, and charity committees and, in locations where they had a strong base, even medical centers and rehabilitation centers for drug addicts.[8] Following the model established by the communists several years earlier in Nazareth, they organized volunteer working camps for the maintenance and renovation of local infrastructure. A special emphasis was placed on the da'wa, the call to Islam and the dissemination of its values.

During the 1970s, the influence of these activists had more cultural than direct or explicit political implications. Committees were formed that organized social activities, such as art exhibits and festivals, with an Islamic slant.[9] They also organized weddings and more generally called for weddings to adhere to a conservative interpretation of Islam in which men and women would be separated, there would be no alcohol or dancing, and religious leaders would deliver sermons. These developments were especially pronounced in the Triangle area, where the population is Muslim with well-established ties with the adjacent West Bank and was less visible in the Muslim-Christian Galilee. Nevertheless, by 1980, Muslims in the Galilee had slowly joined the trend, and in Nazareth, an Islamic library was established where students could borrow previously inaccessible religious Islamic literature, some of it imported from the West Bank.[10]

Tawfiq Zayyad followed the cultural change with concern. His brother-in-law and close friend 'Abd al-Malik Dahamsha became religious while in Israeli prison from 1972 to 1975, and after his release, he greatly influenced other members of his family. In 1980, he invited Zayyad to the wedding of his younger brother in Kafr Kanna. The wedding, however, was to be an "Islamic wedding," which by that time served as a political display of power by the emerging Islamic Movement. Zayyad had to decide between rejecting an invitation from a family member and lending public legitimacy to political Islam, and he chose the former. Dahamsha recounted their exchange: "I told him, 'You and I are like people wandering together in the desert, very thirsty. I found a source of water and tried it and the water was good. Come and try this water with me.' Zayyad answered, 'I tasted this water and I found it bitter. I do not want to drink it.'"[11]

Toward the mid-1980s, inspired by the Iranian Revolution and adjacent regional trends, the various local organizations became more coordinated and a central leadership was gradually institutionalized, claiming the name "the Islamic Movement." It became clear that for this movement, culture had never been separate from politics. The movement not only presented itself as an alternative to communism in terms of style and sources of inspiration, but also questioned the basic idea of a secular politics. Its first countrywide leader, 'Abdallah Nimr Darwish, from Kafr Qasim, explicitly criticized the PLO's goal to establish a "secular democratic state" in Palestine.[12]

The Islamist Movement offered an alternative vision of hope from the one that Zayyad was advocating for. Adherents adopted the slogan of their mother movement, the Muslim Brotherhood, "Islam is the solution," implying that a society whose institutions are based on Islamic religious law would be the answer to any social or political predicament. However, this long-term vision coexisted with concrete activity dealing with the welfare of the movement's potential constituency. While the communists aspired to divert public funding to welfare through the central political system, the Islamic Movement provided these services directly and in doing so strengthened its political base.[13] In addition, the movement adopted the Marxist tradition of popular grassroots activism but extended it and entered fields neglected by the Communist Party. While the communists invested great effort in organizing college students, academics, and professionals, the Islamic

Movement started its recruitment and socialization efforts at kindergarten age and targeted the nuclear family as a cultural-political unit.[14]

In 1983, representatives of the Islamic Movement competed for the first time in municipal races in several localities, and one of its candidates was elected mayor. The Islamic Movement did not take part in the 1984 Knesset elections, but some of its activists supported the Progressive List for Peace (PLP), support that partly explains its success in gaining 18 percent of Arab votes in its first election campaign. Preoccupied with the PLP threat, the DFPE leaders were slow to react to the challenge posed by the Islamic Movement in the early 1980s.[15] Gradually, however, the communist leadership started to consider the Islamists a threat as well. From 1984, we can find sporadic references to the "Islamic Brotherhood" or "Muslim circles" in the notes from Politburo and the Central Committee discussions, but usually it is in the context of their being allies of the PLP.[16] In 1985, Vilner commented, "The Islamic Brotherhood: some of them are political enemies and others take religion seriously. This is why it is important to take the matter seriously. We are not against religion and religious people. We are atheists [but] a person who believes in God can be a party member."[17]

Publicly, though, DFPE leaders did not express any concern about this emerging danger to their hegemony until 1988. Zayyad's first documented public criticism of the Islamic Movement appeared in that year's First of May speech. He referred to it as "Shaykh 'Abdallah Nimr Darwish's movement" and was careful to distinguish it from "the various religious groups in Nazareth." He reminded his audience that Darwish's group and the PLP did not play any role in Land Day in 1976, and now they joined the commemorative events not to promote unity but to undermine it. He argued that the Palestinian issue had two major allies, the Soviet Union and the Jewish democratic forces, while both the PLP and "Darwish's movement" targeted these allies, as well as Palestinians who were connected to them. He referred to an interview published in al-Sinara in which Darwish emphasized the importance of three circles: the Islamic, the Arab, and the Palestinian. "What circles is he talking about?" he asked, "What Islam? The Islam of the rulers of Pakistan or the one of Saudi Arabia's king? [. . .] There are only two circles."[18] Then in the run-up to the February 1989 municipal elections in Nazareth, Zayyad attacked the Islamists for the first time in the context of a local election campaign, calling them "a list of jahiliyya[19] in the name of Islam"[20] and portraying them as corrupt. In one speech, he sarcastically asked whether the vote should be given to "those who claim to promote religion in their publications but do not have a single letter against the criminal practices of the Israeli occupation against al-Aqsa, Islam, and the Muslims?"[21]

These efforts to block the growing popularity of the Islamists were not very successful. In the municipal elections that took place ten days after that speech, the Islamic Movement gained five mayoral positions throughout the country, as well as weighty representation in all twelve Arab local councils and the two mixed cities in which the movement competed. In Nazareth, the movement participated in the elections as the Islamic List and won six of nineteen seats in the City Council. Its activists celebrated their achievements in the streets with their green flags, and Zayyad blamed the Israeli authorities for the Islamic Movement's increasing power: "[For] forty years you do not solve the problem. People lose hope, there is despair. If we do not have this world, they say, let's earn the afterlife. They adopt metaphysics and mysticism."[22] He was also concerned about the increase in religious extremism among Jewish Israelis and worldwide, which he considered a frightening wave of irrationality: "We have to protect the world from the mystic vertigo," he said.[23]

The extreme tension between the communists and the Islamic Movement from 1988 to 1994 was partly a result of the accelerated but inverse trajectories the two political currents experienced in terms of their local and global power. Encouraged by their 1989 municipal victories, Islamist activists were self-confident and imagined the sky as the limit. Further regional trends such as the electoral success of Islamists in Algeria in 1990 and 1991, as well as the proclamation of Islamist regimes in Mauritania in 1991 and Afghanistan in 1992, created a sense of an Islamist momentum. On their side, the communists were not only anxious about the Islamist tide, but they were also on the defense following the collapse of the socialist regimes in Eastern Europe in late 1989, as well as the rapid crumbling and finally the collapse of the Soviet Union in 1991 (see chapter 9). These global developments coincided with the decline in the hegemonic status of the communists in the local political sphere.

LOCAL STRUGGLES OVER RELIGION

Encouraged by their success in the 1989 municipal elections, supporters of the Islamic List turned the first council meeting after the elections into a spectacle of power. Thanks to Zayyad's policy that council meetings were open to the public, many of them came to the meeting itself, and the many others who could not enter gathered in the adjacent square, where they chanted in support of their movement and also attacked Zayyad: "Oh Zayyad, out, out—Nazareth is free from you!"[24] Zayyad attempted to appease the Islamic List by including them in the ruling coalition of the council and offered their representative the office of deputy mayor, but they refused.[25] This first council meeting set the tone for future meetings, which were frequently tense and several times deteriorated into threats of lawsuits and even physical violence. In May 1990, flyers distributed in Nazareth accused Zayyad of saying in the council meeting that "Islam is darkness." Zayyad, in turn, accused the six members of the Islamic List for distributing the flyers and filed a compensation claim for libel.[26] On December 13, 1990, the meeting ended in a brawl after Zayyad refused to answer some queries submitted by Mazin Makhzumi, a council member from the Islamic List. Afterward, Makhzumi and another council member filed a complaint against Zayyad at the local police station, and the police detained Zayyad that same night for several hours.[27]

From 1988 to 1994, the Islamists and the communists shared the Nazareth council, and as mayor, Zayyad regularly rejected their demands. While his supporters considered his decisions ideologically consistent, the Islamists considered them petty. For example, the Islamic Movement established a separate soccer league, where athletes played in long trousers and the games opened with a prayer.[28] Like the Islamic wedding, the Islamic teams became a symbol of political prowess that challenged communist hegemony. When the local Islamic team in Nazareth, al-Huda al-Islami, was founded in 1986, it requested permission to practice and play on the municipal soccer field, as well as financial support from the city, just as other soccer teams in the city did. Zayyad rejected the request and argued that only teams officially belonging to the Israeli Football Association were allowed access to the municipal stadium and municipal funding, and the field was already overloaded.[29]

Another source of frustration for the Islamist activists in Nazareth was what they saw as the municipality's preferential treatment of Christians in the city. This frustration found its focal point in the generous attention Zayyad gave to Christmas celebrations and the city's involvement in organizing and sponsoring these celebrations. Zayyad made Christmas ceremonies into political spectacles, sometimes borrowing from Christian religious vocabulary to make his point. For example, in 1985, at the traditional municipality-sponsored Christmas party, he ended his speech in this way: "We will rise above our cross and our pains, and we will fight for our natural and legitimate right for living in dignity in the land of our fathers and grandfathers and for a just peace and equality."[30] After the Islamists gained seats in city hall, they officially demanded that the municipality sponsor the celebration of Mawlid al-Nabi, the prophet's birthday, just as it sponsored the celebration of Christmas.[31] Interestingly, in the early days of the Arab national movement in Palestine, national intellectuals, including Christians, adopted this holiday as a secular national holiday.[32] By the late 1980s, however, it became identified with the agenda of the Islamic Movement, which Zayyad was determined to undermine, and he denied the Islamic List's request.

Another demand that Zayyad repeatedly rejected was the inclusion of religion in the curriculum of the municipal high school. Because all Arab private schools in Israel belong to Christian communities, Christians have the option to provide regular and formal religious education for their children. Muslims, however, have to rely on extracurricular activities or on what public schools provide. Islam was taught in elementary schools in Nazareth because those are under the direct control of the Ministry of Education. In high schools, though, municipal authorities have much more power, and Zayyad used this power to block religious studies (even though since 1990, Islam has been an optional topic for the high school matriculation exams in Israel, and many Jewish and Arab schools opted for this option). Responding to the complaints of the Islamic List members, Zayyad argued that the high school curriculum was supposed to prepare students for academic studies and professionalization, and "those who want to specialize in religion can go to institutes specializing in the field."[33] On another occasion he said, "The Ministry of Education does not fund religious studies, unless they are being taught at the expense of another topic. We do not intend to diminish the study of chemistry, math or any other topic."[34]

In these cases, Zayyad rejected the demands of the Islamic List using dry, bureaucratic language, seemingly devoid of moral judgment. On the issue of gender segregation, however, he departed from this style more than once. At the council meeting on June 12, 1991, for example, when the Islamic List demanded some classes at the municipal high school be segregated by gender, Zayyad refused to include the topic in the agenda, stating, "The proposal is uncivilized." He added, "This will develop a lack of self-confidence among the female students, and it neither protects them nor defends them from anything."[35] By using the term *uncivilized*, Zayyad presented the Islamic activists as backward, touching directly on their anxiety of being perceived as insufficiently modern. Both issues—women's presence in the public sphere and the Islamists' concern about their own image as modern—would shape Zayyad's relations with the movement.

ZAYYAD'S RHETORIC AGAINST THE ISLAMIC MOVEMENT

Of all the communist leaders, Zayyad was the most outspoken against the Islamic Movement and the one its leaders most frequently targeted. In their rhetorical battle, Zayyad relied on three lines of attack. First, he cast doubt on their patriotic commitment, emphasizing their late appearance on the political stage, which he contrasted to the much longer history of the communists. Second, he discussed the impracticality of their political plan. Third—and the trope he seemed to enjoy above all—he presented them as backward actors who would take Palestinian society toward the wrong pole of the modernity spectrum.

Each year, tensions between the communists and the Islamic Movement came to a head during the Land Day commemoration. From 1976, the day had been a major site of political struggle between various parties and movements, each fighting for its own visibility and over the content and symbols of the commemoration.[36] While in the first decade of Land Day commemoration the communists struggled against state authorities and their Arab satellites, as well as against the "nationalists," more and more green flags began to appear at the rallies starting in the mid-1980s. The visible presence of the new rival provoked several low-key confrontations in 1987 and 1988, but the tension was usually contained. After their significant achievement in the February 1989 municipal elections, however, the Islamic Movement now demanded more assertively its share of representation in the Follow-Up Committee, the Land Committee, and the roster of speakers at major Land Day events. The communists were determined to minimize this representation. The tension could no longer be contained.

In the central 1989 Land Day event in Dayr Hanna, a group of a hundred Islamic Movement activists showed up with green flags. At the time, the Palestinian flag was illegal, and the other parties had agreed not to bring their own partisan flags. The arrival of the Islamists and their flags provoked high tension, and other participants began to shout slogans in support of Christian-Muslin unity. Later, Zayyad attacked the Islamists from the podium, portraying them as separatists who were undermining the national unity between Muslims and Christians. He quoted the famous liberal-secular slogan from the Egyptian Revolution of 1919: "Religion is for God, the homeland is for all." His supporters echoed him with the slogan "National unity—Christian—Muslim." The Islamist activists, concentrated in one corner of the square with their green flags, answered with "Allahu akbar" (God is great).[37] The organizers rejected the request of Kamal Khatib, one of the movement's leaders, to speak at the rally, and the controversy deteriorated into a fistfight in which ten people were injured.

Zayyad's concern about the Islamic Movement's excluding Christians was based on more than his view of good political strategy. His charge of separatism reflected his view, as a modernist with linear understanding of history, that national solidarity was a more advanced form of political organization than religious solidarity. This is why his reference to the exclusion of Christians was embedded in a broader discussion about the maladjustment of Islamist ideology to modern life:

> This is religious demagogy. Take for example their slogan [Zayyad slammed the table, then held his head with his two hands to signal disbelief, and then lifted his arm high in the air and raised his voice in protest] "Islam is the solution." Islam is a religion, it is between humans and their God. Islam is the solution? What solution do you come to talk about! Whoever says "Islam is the solution" means that he wants an Islamic state. Please, go ahead: Saudi Arabia is Islamic, and Kuwait is Islamic, as well as the Emirates, Qatar, Bahrain, and more [. . .] all these are Islamic states, so where is the solution? Let's assume we do what they want—Israel, Palestine—is all Islamic. What is the solution? Where is the solution? [. . .] So what do we do with the Christians? [He smiled sarcastically.] The US is a religious country. Most of its residents are Christians. If the solution is in religion, all the problems of the world would have been resolved long time ago. The Islamic rulers in Islamic history and Arab history destroyed the house of Islam and they have continued for five hundred years to say "the solution is Islam." [. . .] The solution is in national unity. Everyone should be blessed in his own religion. Muslims, Christians, Jews, Buddhists, and others— they should all be blessed in their faith. No one should use the slogan [Islam is the solution], which has a religious meaning, for the purpose of political ruling. One should confront real life, and suggest solutions to problems, and not hide in a locked circle called "Islam is the solution."[38]

The speech took place in the midst of the Gulf crisis, after Saddam Hussein had invaded Kuwait and challenged the US, thereby becoming a hero among Palestinians, many of whom considered Saudi Arabia and the Gulf countries as corrupt regimes that served Western interests in the region and opposed social progress. By associating the Islamic Movement with these regimes and presenting these regimes as the end goal of the utopian vision of the Islamic Movement,

Zayyad could only win points among his constituency.

Following the Iraqi defeat in the war, Zayyad published an article in which he presented his argument more systematically. Both Western leaders like President George H. W. Bush and corrupt pro-Western Muslim rulers like King Faruq of Egypt or King Fahd of Saudi Arabia, he asserted, had used religion to justify their politics. Recently, religious rhetoric was used to justify the aggression of Christian countries against the Muslim People of Iraq. The Peoples of the East and the Third World were religious, and they saw religion as a source of justice and equality, but the Gulf War was a reminder that it was necessary to distinguish between religion and religious quackery, "which can legitimize the strongest prohibitions in the name of any religion." The war, he concluded, "reaffirm[ed] the truth of our popular maxim: religion for God, the homeland for everyone."[39]

GENDER SEGREGATION IN LAND DAY RALLIES

As much as Zayyad ascribed importance to national unity and Muslim-Christian fraternity, he was espcially eager to attack the Islamic Movement on the issue of gender segregation. There was a reason for that. As Leila Ahmed has indicated, laws imposing restrictions on women are typically among the first "Islamic" measures introduced by Islamist groups upon coming to power.[40] During the first intifada, the assertiveness of Islamist Palestinians in the West Bank and the Gaza Strip on demands related to public visibility of a woman's body increased.[41] In the relatively secular Palestinian society in the Galilee, emphasizing the demand for gender segregation was a political risk for the Islamic Movement activists, as it would have marked them as "not-modern" among their wider potential constituency, limiting their ability to expand their ranks. Islamist activists therefore mostly avoided publicly admitting their concerns about mixed-gender spaces. And they claimed that they supported "women's rights," although they usually added a disclaimer that these rights should be defined by Islamic rather than Western terms. In private discussions, however, they were more open about their moral objection to mixed crowds. The communists, and particularly Zayyad, were well aware of this Achilles' heel in Islamist politics and backed them into the corner on the issue whenever possible. Therefore, gender was an explicit subject in the communists' rhetoric but rarely articulated by Islamist leaders. Nevertheless, it was always in the background in debates on other issues.

After Land Day in 1990, *al-Ittihad* reported that representatives of the Islamic Movement demanded that women be excluded from the Land Day rallies. The report reproduced photographs from rallies under the caption, "Our women reject submission—and thousands of them participate in Land Day parades."[42] In July that year, Zayyad spoke at the closing ceremony of a summer camp for mothers of large families in Nazareth and took the opportunity to make a jab at the Islamists without mentioning them explicitly: "We are proud of all of our women and we will fight relentlessly against all those who say that the woman is no more than a rib[43] and that women have no say in society and its problems. We see the woman as an active and principal part in all our popular activities and the daily life of our city and our People."[44] In a Follow-Up Committee meeting before Land Day in 1991, a tense discussion almost deteriorated into a fistfight. Shaykh Ra'id Salah, the mayor of Umm al-Fahm and a rising star of the Islamic Movement, demanded more Islamic Movement representation among the speakers. According to al-Sinara, Zayyad told him, "What you want is to ride on our shoulders, and we won't let you do that. You want to destroy the Land Committee. You do not like its decisions—establish your own institutions and organize the ceremonies by yourselves." Indeed, that year the Islamic Movement commemorated Land Day separately. Al-Ittihad reported again that one of the demands the Islamists made and the communists rejected was the exclusion of women from Land Day activities.[45]

The conflict reached its peak in 1993, again a year of municipal elections. In the weeks before Land Day, tension mounted as the communists and Islamists exchanged accusations in the press about the Land Day ceremonies. Seemingly unrelated to that, both sides took part in an intellectual debate about women's rights, occasioned by the celebration of International Women's Day on March 8. While the communist rhetoric was full of modernist pathos, the Islamists were more careful and implicit, repeatedly arguing that they supported women's rights, although the nature of these rights remained ambiguous. Kamal Khatib wrote, "The woman should know her right and demand it, but within the realm of Islam and not through the worldview provided us by the West."[46]

At the central Land Day rally in Shafa'amr, Zayyad's speech was interrupted. According to al-Ittihad (a report that was echoed unanimously in the Hebrew media), the Islamic Movement had consistently been pressing for the rally to be gender segregated. Instead, Zayyad welcomed the women who came to demonstrate and explicitly denounced those who wanted the women "to dress in black clothes and step in a separate bloc." The crowd echoed Zayyad's enthusiastic words, chanting, "National unity—the boy beside the girl" (Wahda wataniyya—al-shab *bi-had al-sabiyya*)! At that moment, in a scene recorded by the Israel Broadcast Authority (IBA), Kamal Khatib stormed onto the stage toward Zayyad in protest. The camera captured Zayyad giving Khatib a sneering look as he contemptuously exclaimed, "Off with you!" Then other Islamist activists followed Khatib onto the stage waving wooden sticks, and soon a large brawl erupted.[47] The police intervened, bringing the event to a premature end. The Islamist press denied that gender controversy triggered the fight and blamed Zayyad, whose speech they considered full of provocations against them. The movement's leaders, it was argued, were only trying to distance the angry crowd from the stage.[48] In a television interview with IBA Arabic news, Zayyad argued that the attack against him was planned. "They consider a woman's place to be in the kitchen and in the bed," he states. "We consider women to have the same rights as men to participate in all the battles. [. . .] Every society that separates men from women in the way they call for is a backward society. The civilized society is a society based on the joint action for men and women."[49]

The event prompted a series of articles and public declarations by the leaders of the Islamic Movement. All of them emphasized that women were welcome in political activism, but consistently avoided a direct reference to the issue of gender segregation. Ra'id Salah, the charismatic mayor of Umm al-Fahm, argued against the communists: "The woman issue is the nails you put on in order to stab the Islamic Movement."[50] Only the founder of the movement, 'Abdallah Nimr Darwish, was less apologetic, stating, "If you think that the Islamic Movement is ashamed of calling to follow the rule of God, who orders women to dress in the religiously sanctioned dress, you are more than hallucinating."[51] Even Darwish, however, did not refer publicly to gender segregation.

On First of May that year, Zayyad gave an emotional and fierce speech in Nazareth in which he attacked the Islamic Movement in the harshest words of his ever recorded on tape. He likened their treatment of women to "someone who takes a cucumber, a tomato, or an eggplant and puts them in a jar." With a heavy dose of sarcasm, he attacked them exactly at their vulnerable point: their anxiety about being perceived as antimodern. Referring directly to the movement's leaders, he declared, "Shame on them. At the end of the twentieth century, they invite us to backwardness. Each one of them grows a beard and becomes a shaykh.[52] What shaykh?" He compared their beards to the fake military ranks that soldiers of the Salvation Army used in 1948—a reference to the volunteer soldiers who were sent by neighboring Arab countries and are remembered for their poor treatment of the local population.[53] The 1993 First of May speech signaled a rapid escalation in the conflict between Zayyad and the leaders of the Islamist Movement, which became more personal and more emotional than ever before.

The harsh reaction of Zayyad and other communist activists to the Islamist momentum should be considered within the context of another major event that took place in the same years: the immense reforms in the Soviet Union and the collapse of the socialist regimes in Eastern Europe. These developments threatened to falsify the utopic Marxist vision of the loyal members of the Communist Party and made them alert to local threats to their power. The next chapter discusses how Zayyad reacted to the biggest challenge to his own system of beliefs.

Chapter 9

A SPOKE IN THE WHEEL OF HISTORY

AS A MEMBER OF THE KNESSET, ZAYYAD PREFERRED TO HAVE HIS meal in the self-service general dining hall rather than in the more prestigious dining hall designated for Knesset members. This choice stemmed from his class consciousness, embedded in his deeply seated Marxist conviction. Since the late 1980s, though, Zayyad's Marxist faith was challenged by perestroika, the reforms in the Soviet Union. The threat intensified with the collapse of the socialist regimes in Eastern Europe in 1989, as well as the ultimate demise of the Soviet Union itself. His desperate attempts to protect his Marxist utopian vision and belief that the Soviet Union was the realization of this vision were in the background of a bitter conflict that emerged between him and his close friend Emile Habibi.

Zayyad and Habibi shared a long history, going back to the mid-1940s when Habibi published Zayyad's first poems in the literary bulletin *al-Mihmaz*, which Habibi coedited. Seven years older than Zayyad, Habibi migrated from Haifa to Nazareth in 1956 and settled in the Eastern Neighborhood, not far from Zayyad's home. Family members of both leaders describe a close friendship and political partnership that developed between them. Many of the party veterans are convinced that Zayyad's public appearance and style of public speaking were largely inspired by his older comrade Habibi. In major internal party controversies, the two shared the same positions. External observers considered both to be on the

Arab "nationalist" edge of the party's political spectrum, a position that frequently troubled other leaders who were concerned about the public image of the party among Jewish Israelis. Therefore, the two trusted and supported each other. Before Zayyad left for Prague in 1971, he was concerned that in his absence, it would be easier for Habibi's rivals to undermine his status. In a farewell party with communist friends before he left, Zayyad reportedly said, "Keep an eye on Emile Habibi, do not let anyone hurt him."[1] Although according to some reports in the Hebrew press, a tension emerged between the two in early 1974 when Habibi considered seeking to be the party's candidate for mayor in Nazareth,[2] the minutes of the Central Committee show that at least from summer 1975, Habibi supported Zayyad in the internal party struggles over the candidacy. In 1981 Habibi demanded that Zayyad be included in the Politburo and reportedly even threatened to leave the Politburo if Zayyad was not.[3]

There was, however, a fundamental difference between them, which was probably related more to their personalities than to their politics. Whereas Habibi's political convictions were qualified by a certain distance and skepticism, Zayyad held a messianic-like deterministic utopian vision. Consider, for example, Zayyad's speech at the Eighteenth Congress of the Communist Party in December 1976. Zayyad arrived at the congress after winning the mayorship in Nazareth a year earlier and leading the strike on Land Day, and his words carried more weight than his official position in the party. He concluded his speech with the following lines:

> We are today in the middle of a battle for peace and democracy, in the middle of a battle for our land and the national rights of our People. We are today in the period following the victory in Nazareth and after Land Day. Our People is no longer the People of 1948 and 1956, but the People of 1973, with the Democratic Front of Nazareth and Land Day—and there is no power that can reverse the wheel of history."[4]

These lines encapsulate Zayyad's teleological understanding of history, shaped by his Marxist socialization and revolutionary spirit. Human history is going in only one direction—toward progress, equality, freedom, and peace.

Compared with Zayyad's optimism, Habibi's political convictions were always moderated by some distance and even a grain of cynicism, epitomized by the title of his most famous book, *The Pessoptimist*.[5] Published in 1974, when Zayyad had just become a Knesset member, the book tells the story of a Palestinian who after

1948 finds himself living in the newly founded State of Israel. Habibi's protagonist is a comic antihero, whose simplicity leads him to a series of tragicomic episodes that illustrate the paradoxes of being a Palestinian citizen of Israel. Reconciling this contradiction requires the adoption of a seemingly impossible combination of pessimism and optimism: "I don't differentiate between optimism and pessimism and am quite at a loss as to which of the two characterizes me. When I awake each morning I thank the Lord he did not take my soul during the night. If harm befalls me during the day, I thank him that it was no worse. So which am I, a pessimist or an optimist?"[6]

Zayyad's way of reconciling the paradoxes of being a Palestinian citizen of Israel was incompatible with Habibi's irony and self-reflection. This was especially evident in Zayyad's relation to the Soviet Union. Since his adolescence, he had unequivocally identified the Soviet Union with progress and justice. His book *A Nazarian in the Red Square* is a long song of praise for what Zayyad believed to be a socialist utopia. His admiration of the Soviet Union was fueled as well by the general Soviet support of Third World anticolonial movements since the 1950s and its backing of the PLO from the late 1960s until the late 1980s. For example, in his 1961 poem "To the Workers of Moscow," he thanked the Soviet workers for "sending us weapon / from machine guns to cannon / so we can defend the sacred homeland."[7] In 1973 he ended his famous "Great Crossing" ode by thanking Moscow for its contribution to the Arab achievements in the war:

Where are you, Moscow
The capital of the world
And the heart of this era?
Weaving my life
Above Lenin's tomb
And I shall raise my voice in the face of the world:
As long as the red star
Is above your domes,
The world is well
The world is well![8]

Similarly, Zayyad trusted Moscow when in June 1982 Israel invaded Lebanon in order to destroy the PLO infrastructure in the country and impose a regime friendly to Israel (chapter 7). In a discussion in the Knesset in December 1983, Zayyad said:

The position of the Soviet Union is known—Israel has the right to exist. However, it is against Israel's plan to annihilate the Arab Palestinian People, who fight for their national rights, under the auspice[s] of the Arab national liberation movement. You should know this—the Soviet Union will not stand by. Especially not this time. It is possible that because of Israeli aggression the Soviet Union would not only avoid standing by but would provide direct assistance, even military, to Syria and to the patriotic forces in Lebanon.

In other words, when Zayyad felt that his own People faced the risk of annihilation, the Soviet Union was the savior, the deus ex machina, both a moral authority and a mighty power to whom he looked in dire times. At a private event in the 1980s, a math teacher from Nazareth, Habib Khuri, challenged Zayyad with the following question: "What would you do if tomorrow, *Pravda* [the official newspaper of the party in the Soviet Union] would adopt a stand opposing a Palestinian state and Palestinian rights?" Zayyad objected that Khuri posed an impossible scenario, but after further pressure, he answered: "I am an internationalist [*umami*]."[9] Zayyad's commitment to the struggle for Palestinian rights is unquestionable, but so was his commitment to universal justice embodied by the communist vision. His trust in the wisdom and the goodwill of the most authorized interpreter of communism, the Soviet Union, was absolute. This absolute loyalty had driven even a close friend of Zayyad, the poet Muhammad Ali Taha, to describe him as a "Stalinist."[10]

Zayyad's hard ideological line might have had extreme expressions, but he was not unique among his party members. Seemingly, Marxist ideological rigidity and absolute reliance on the Soviet Union might be in tension with Arab and Palestinian nationalism. However, there is a good reason that among communist parties worldwide, the ICP before 1965 and Rakah after the split were considered among the most loyal to Moscow and that this loyalty was especially pronounced among its Arab members. Under Zionist hegemony in the Jewish society, the potential for Jewish Zionist communism was always in the air. Arab national communism, similar to the pre-1948 NLL, could not survive in the State of Israel because the state considered any form of Arab nationalism as subversive (for example, when al-'Ard was disqualified from participating in the election). For Zayyad and many other Arab communists, orthodox Marxism and loyalty to the Soviet Union guaranteed that the party would not develop a Jewish nationalist deviation.

In summer 1986, however, the Soviet Union undertook an accelerated process of political and economic change known as perestroika (economic restructuring) and glasnost (openness). These far-reaching reforms—and the rapid shift they brought toward a relative liberalization of both the economy and freedom of speech—created a separation between communist ideology and what many believed to be its historical institutional realization. Communists all over the world had to decide between remaining loyal to the old ideology or the new Soviet Union. These transformations left Rakah (which in 1989 readopted its old name, the ICP) perplexed, and caused significant tensions in the party ranks. It seems that nothing reflects Zayyad's deep conviction in the truth of the old communist ideology better than his tense relations with Habibi in the last years of his life. While Zayyad, like most of the other party leaders, followed the reforms with much suspicion and concern, Habibi welcomed them. "I am very happy and encouraged by what is happening in the communist movement throughout the world, and particularly in Russia," he said. "I feel that I am returning to the days of my youth—to the purity of a young man searching for social justice, courage and self-respect, for my right to be able to tell a bad person that he is bad and not be afraid."[11]

In May 1987, Habibi, then the editor in chief of *al-Ittihad*, attended a conference in Moscow commemorating the seventieth birthday of *Pravda*. He was highly impressed with Secretary General Mikhail Gorbachev's speech about the reforms and especially liked Gorbachev's statement that "it is time to eliminate the gap that separates politics from morality." Upon his return, he published his impressions from that speech in *al-Ittihad*, but was surprised when the party refused to publish his report in the Hebrew bulletin *Zo ha-Derekh*.[12] This was the beginning of an unprecedented struggle, initially far from the public eye, between the editor in chief of the party's Arabic-language organ and the rest of the party's senior leaders. In early 1989, these disagreements led the Politburo to dismiss Habibi as editor in chief of *al-Ittihad*. On March 6, following that decision, Habibi submitted to Secretary General Meir Vilner a letter of resignation from his official positions in the Politburo and the Central Committee. For the next two months, he continued to publish in *al-Ittihad*, and on April 28, he published his weekly column, "Usbu'iyyat," for the last time, signing it with his real name rather than Juhayna, his daughter's name, which he had used as a pseudonym since the 1960s. In that column, Habibi praised the reforms in the Soviet Union, connecting them with enlightenment and humanism, and ended with a message about the inevitability of change: "Life in our villages has changed profoundly from the era of using gas torches to the era of using electric lamps, and there is no way back. The days when our sleeping time was parallel to that of the beasts have gone forever."[13] Now Habibi became an optimist, while his own vision for the future was a threat to many of his colleagues.

Ten days later, in a dramatic resignation speech in front of the Central Committee, Habibi reprimanded the party's leadership for launching a witch hunt, silencing nonconformist voices, and lacking collegiality.[14] Although he did not mention Zayyad's name, he referred to him in harsh words:

> It is not easy for a person of my age and with my history to see with his own eyes and hear with his own ears new members in the leadership demanding his dismissal from his leadership position without hearing any word of defense or expression of collegial confidence from his old friends in the leadership, whom he has always considered lifelong friends and companions. It is not easy for a person of my age to hear with his own ears the fatal accusation that I established in the board of *al-Ittihad* a bloc opposing the party and to hear that the goal of my dismissal is to restore the party's control over *al-Ittihad*. For me, it was more difficult than death to witness the silence of my friends and fellows, lifelong fellows and students, in view of these deadly accusations.[15]

According to Samih Ghanadri, his son-in-law, Habibi believed that Zayyad had the power to prevent his dismissal and felt betrayed by what he considered Zayyad's passivity in the face of this development. In his view, Zayyad could have threatened to resign from the party institutions if Habibi was dismissed, as the other party leaders could not have afforded to lose them both.[16]

After that speech, Habibi left the country for two months. In his attempt to distance himself from personal conflicts and focus on political disagreements while overseas, he sent articles about perestroika to *al-Ittihad*, but the new editorial board (headed by the author Salim Jubran) refused to publish them. In September, after his return and probably as part of a reconciliation attempt, Habibi was allowed to publish an article in *al-Ittihad*, but it did not help ease the tension. Habibi published an emotional and incoherent text (he did not include it in a collection of articles from that period he published later). He protested especially the party's intolerance of those who questioned old dogmas. "Stop accusing us of heresy and infidelity," he wrote. With much sarcasm he also criticized Vilner and Tubi for remaining in their official leadership position for decades, as if only

God was allowed to decide about their replacement by ending their lives, an ironic stand for atheists: "We [the party] became religious more than the believers on this issue [of leadership] to the extent that we do not replace our leaders unless God decides to do so."[17]

In October 1989, following that article, Zayyad and Habibi exchanged letters that did not bring them any closer. After Habibi expressed his frustration with Zayyad's lack of support and compared his treatment by the party to the attack of the Israeli authorities on his People and his party, Zayyad answered:

> Since our paths crossed you have become the closest person to me, and whatever happens, your role in establishing the communist movement of our People and your sharp thought as a political leader cannot be denied. [. . .] Who knows better than you that I tried from the beginning till the end to prevent the deterioration to the current situation? [. . .] Who knows better than you that I saw the decision to replace you as the editor-in-chief of *al-Ittihad* as unjust and offensive toward you, wrong for the party, and unnecessary? I rejected it in every formulation since it emerged as an idea until its final formulation [. . .] however, between that decision and your reactions there is a deep gap, unbridgeable and unjustifiable, and they contradict the party values and the principle of proper treatment.[18]

In this last sentence, Zayyad referred mainly to Habibi's decision to attack the party leadership publicly, something unheard of in communist parties, whose leaders have always closed ranks and never exposed their internal controversies to outsiders. Furthermore, Zayyad read in Habibi's criticism a comparison between Habibi's treatment by the party leaders and the state's policy toward Arab citizens. "Did your hands and conscience not tremble when you wrote that?" he asked Habibi. Although Zayyad ended his letter with a conciliatory tone ("I look forward to meeting with you soon, with much love, Tawfiq Zayyad"), their communication stopped for a long time.

During the course of their exchange, dramatic developments were taking place in Eastern Europe. In September, a noncommunist government was sworn in in Poland, and in October, the regime in Hungary was transformed into a parliamentary multiparty democracy. In November, the Berlin Wall collapsed, and the Czechoslovakian Communist Party announced that it would relinquish its monopolistic power. On December 28, 1989, three days after the Romanian ruler

Nicolae Ceaușescu was executed, Zayyad addressed an open meeting of the Nazareth branch of the party and discussed the recent political upheavals in Eastern
Europe. He praised them as "a revolution for democracy" and for the first time
expressed public criticism of the Soviet Union, even if mild, when he described
his recent visit to the country in June and the complaints he heard from citizens
about bureaucracy. Therefore, he saw the developments in the socialist countries
as positive, but raised the concern that they were being used by the enemies of
socialism for delegitimizing the socialist idea rather than criticizing the way it
was implemented.

Where he seemed to be less flexible was on the principle of democratic centralism. Talking about this issue, his conflict with Habibi surfaced:

> A party member is allowed to express any opinion inside the party institutions
> and fight for this opinion for years, and he is allowed not to be convinced.
> When a decision is made, however, everyone is committed to it. The party,
> every party, cannot be democratic if it does not follow the majority opinion.
> Some wrong practices turned the democratic centralism into bureaucracy. We
> have to treat them from their roots [. . .] but not to eliminate democratic cen-
> tralism.[19]

During the Iraqi invasion of Kuwait and the US military intervention in January and February 1991, the political rift between Zayyad and Habibi deepened.
While Zayyad believed that defeat of the US would be a defeat of the Israeli occupation and sympathized with Iraq during the war, Habibi was outspoken in his
criticism of Saddam Hussein, and especially his decision to fire ballistic missiles
into Israel during the war. While this specific difference of opinions itself could
not have been a trigger for personal confrontation, previous tensions made it
another expression of a prolonged confrontation.

THE KEENER

In March 1991 Habibi published his novel, *Saraya, the Ogre's Daughter*, which he
had been working on since his dismissal from the board of *al-Ittihad*. The book
made an implicit but self-evident commentary on the members of the Communist Party in a chapter that builds on Plato's allegory of the cave. In the allegory,
Plato describes people who have lived chained to the wall of a cave all of their
lives. The prisoners can see shadows projected on the wall from people and ob-

jects passing in front of a fire behind them, but for them, these shadows—rather than the objects creating them—are reality. In this story, the philosopher is like a liberated ex-prisoner who can perceive the true form of reality rather than the shadows. The other prisoners do not wish to leave the cave, which is the only life they have ever known. On April 25, Habibi sent Zayyad a copy of the book in which he had written a short note: "A shared hostility could be the beginning of love or the end of love. Hostility from one side, however—I am not used to it." On May 1, Zayyad sent the copy back with a reply stating that "the pot [was] calling the kettle black" and blaming Habibi for being hateful. Habibi, abroad at the time, did not receive Zayyad's response, and his son-in-law, who received the copy, preferred not to show it to him.

That same day, Zayyad spoke at the annual First of May rally, where he dedicated much of his speech to a new ode, "The Keener," in which he made a direct reference to the ideological crisis in the party.[20] "The Keener" is an important document, regardless of its artistic quality. While the ode could be read as a personal attack on Habibi, it is much more than that. Nowhere else did Zayyad express so poignantly and emotively his frustration and disappointment about the failure of the most comprehensive attempt to establish heaven on earth, a utopian egalitarian society. Habibi most likely had become a lightning rod for this frustration, a personification of the powers that undermined communism and left Zayyad, and many devoted communists of his generation worldwide, helpless. Explicitly, the ode criticizes the keener, who is lamenting a dream that the keener believes is dead—a clear reference to Habibi as someone who had given up on the Marxist vision. The keener could also be read as the author himself, who is lamenting a lost friendship and maybe even his vanishing life-long dream—though it is doubtful that Zayyad intended this second meaning because the text is in his typical realist mode aimed at political mobilization; therefore, at the explicit level, the keener is the one who denies the Marxist principles.

As in his description of his pilgrimage to Lenin's tomb, the ode also reveals Zayyad's reliance on the symbols and vocabulary of Islamic tradition. In particular, the ode uses the same vocabulary reserved to criticize infidels:

> In the difficult times, the doubt grows
> Skepticism increases
> Suspicions prevail
> And following that—he whose determination and faith are weak
> —recoils as an apostate [murtadd].[21]

In Islamic tradition, the word *murtadd* (apostate) refers to a Muslim who has consciously abandoned the Islamic faith. It evokes memories of the Wars of Apostasy launched by the caliph Abu Bakr against rebel Arabian tribes that he charged with abandoning Islam after Muhammad died.[22] This language is evidence that what provoked Zayyad's fury was more than Habibi's violation of the tactical principle of democratic centralism. Rather, it was what he considered Habibi's betrayal of core ideological principles. The entire ode is a concentrated attack on "the apostate," who gave up on fighting for the Marxist utopia:

> The apostate is fleeing . . . from all the principles.
> Renouncing all the principles
> And he covers the shameful flee with a twist
> And verbal needlework.
> [. . .]
> The apostate flees from his trench
> From the idea of "heaven on earth"
> And the right of people to have the good which their hands create
> Like the green vegetables.
> The apostate escapes . . . from what is around him
> from his skin . . . from his tribe . . .
> From himself . . . his history . . . his principle
> From his mother . . . from his nation . . . from his People
> From his pure dream and the dream of humanity.

Although Zayyad does not mention Habibi's name, the many indirect references to him do not leave any room for doubts regarding the protagonist of his ode. For example, in several places, he criticizes the apostate's use of the term *qafs* ("cage"), which Habibi frequently used in reference to conventions that limit the intellectual freedom of party members:

> The apostate escapes . . . from all the principles
> And he names the commitment to the truth "a cage" [*qafs*]
> And he names the terrible apostasy
> Emancipation
> And openness [*infitah*].

The word *infitah* ("openness") that Zayyad uses here is commonly used as a translation of the Russian word *glasnost,* which Gorbachev adopted to describe the political reforms he led.

Not only does Zayyad blame the apostate for abandoning the dream; he holds him responsible for killing it (or at least trying to):

The apostate is acting as in the folk parable:

Kill as you like, but . . .
March in the head of the funeral
Weep like a crocodile as much as you want
Tear your black clothes
Slam your sinful chest
Pluck the remaining hair on your head
And lament.

As befits an ode written for First of May and in keeping with Zayyad's use of poetry to encourage mobilization, the ode shifts to a hopeful tone. It turns out that the dream is not dead after all:

Those who became lost in the setback are lost
But the sail
On our cruising boat always continues
Toward the sun . . . and heaven on earth.
And the ebullient dream of humankind and freedom continues
Everywhere.

THE END OF THE SOVIET UNION

In August 1991 the party faced another crisis. Some members of the Soviet government who were opposed to Gorbachev's reforms attempted to take control of the country. The coup collapsed in only two days, and Gorbachev returned to power. The failed coup d'état was the last straw that led Habibi to officially leave the party after more than five decades. During the two days between the beginning of the coup and its ultimate failure, *al-Ittihad* and the ICP's high officials welcomed the supposed new leadership in Moscow. Tawfiq Zayyad himself was not recorded at the time as adopting any position. Following these events, Habibi published an article in *Majallat al-Dirasat al-Filastiniyya* in which he expressed his satisfaction with the failure of the coup. In it, he again used the cage metaphor (and implicitly recalled the cave metaphor), likening the members of the Communist Party to birds that had lived in a cage for a long time. He describes how when one day the cage gate was opened and the birds left, some became frightened and flew back, but the cage was no longer there. Habibi also replied to Zayyad's accusations in "The Keener": "I do not feel an 'apostate' or 're-treating.' If I retreat in any way, I am retreating to the springs of my youth, which brought me to communism: justice, in all areas of justice."[23]

The metaphor of the cage that "was not there anymore" became even more poignant with the final dissolution of the Soviet Union in December 1991. These developments had put all the ICP's leaders on the defense, while Habibi celebrated: "We wanted to establish the religion of the twentieth century and it is good that the religion of the twentieth century was proven to be a failure."[24] Zayyad did not make frequent public references to the demise of the Soviet Union, but in the 1992 election campaign the communists' rivals repeatedly invoked it to taunt party members and supporters. Zayyad answered them once in an election rally in Bi'na by clarifying that his party had not been dependent on the Soviet Union: "Regarding those who try to shame us with the collapse of the Soviet Union—we were with the Soviet Union because it was supporting our issues and our relations with it were relations of respect and similarity in attitudes. However, the source of our power has been our masses and their standing on our side."[25] This description of instrumental relations belittles the emotional enthusiasm that Zayyad had expressed in his book *A Nazarian in the Red Square* two decades earlier and in many of his poems, in which the world was doing well "as long as the red star was atop the domes of Moscow."

Regarding the doubts about the validity of Marxist ideology following the collapse of socialist regimes in Eastern Europe, Zayyad adopted the consensus among the party leaders at the time and wrote: "The scientific socialism (Marxism) is our worldview, in which we believe, and we strive for its victory. Our communist party remains the tool to achieve it and we adhere to it. The failure of the Soviet regime and the regimes in Eastern Europe is a failure of a particular model and not a failure of the idea and the way."[26] In a later reflection, answering a question of the Syrian journalist Riyad Na'san Agha about the collapse of the Soviet Union, Zayyad said:

> History is developing in a vacillating way. There are vicissitudes. Obviously, we
> live now in a period of decline. We are descendants of peasants and a peasant
> never plants an olive tree and looks at it waiting for it to grow. You cannot see

how it grows. He leaves it and returns after a year or two and then he can see the growth. Humankind has developed, even in the Third World. It developed to a certain cultural level and it cannot go back. [...] Even if we are inside a thick forest, we should not lose the compass directing us toward the historical truth of the inevitable human development.[27]

After their correspondence in fall 1991, Zayyad and Habibi had no further direct personal communication. Moderation attempts by shared friends and acquaintances repeatedly failed. When the new editor of *al-Ittihad*, Nazir Majali, reinvited Habibi to write a weekly article in 1992, Zayyad was furious. Did the two ever meet again? Maybe—if not in reality, at least in the imagination and memory of people who wanted them to reconcile. On May 14, 1994, Zayyad spoke in a ceremony celebrating fifty years since the establishment of *al-Ittihad*. In his speech, he praised Habibi and his invaluable contribution to the newspaper, and the audience reacted with a loud standing ovation, reflecting the popular hope for a reconciliation between the two leaders. While this event was verified by separate testimonies of people who attended it, what followed is less clear. Nazir Majali remembered that the same evening Habibi was in the hospital, and the following day, he, Majali, convinced Zayyad to visit him, accompanied by their mutual friend, Mun'im Jarjura. On Habibi's bed, recalled Majali, the two leaders shook hands and reconciled.

This handshake may have been the end of a painful rivalry, but most likely it never happened. According to Habibi's daughter, Rawiyya, who was also his doctor, Habibi was never hospitalized before his terminal illness in 1996. Given how much her father suffered from the conflict with Zayyad, she said, he would have told her about a reconciliation. It is possible, though, that Majali confused the roles. In mid-May 1994, Mun'im Jarjura was terminally ill and was treated at the Rambam Hospital in Haifa. It is possible that Zayyad and Habibi happened to visit him at the same time and might have even politely shaken hands near his bed, a gesture that Majali interpreted as reconciliation. We will probably never know.

PERESTROIKA INSIDE THE PARTY

While the Israeli Communist Party initially seemed reluctant to sympathize with the reformers in the Soviet Union and practically excluded the supporters of this process from their ranks, the upheavals in Eastern Europe in fall 1989 triggered strong internal pressure for reforms in the party itself. On November 30, 1989, as regime instability in Eastern Europe snowballed, the three MKs of the ICP—Meir Vilner, Tawfiq Tubi, and Tawfiq Zayyad—announced their intention to resign from the Knesset in 1990 in order to allow party members of the younger generation to take the place of the more senior ones.[28] At the time they made this announcement, Habibi might have already been an outcast, but the resignation rebutted his sarcastic accusation earlier that same year that the communists let God decide about changing their leaders. It is noteworthy that Vilner and Tubi had been Knesset members since 1948, while Zayyad had served only since 1974. Nevertheless, some observers noted that the two senior members insisted that Zayyad resign with them. According to at least one observer, they were concerned that Zayyad's assertive Palestinian identification and his blatant rhetoric might hurt the public status of the ICP and the DFPE,[29] though his activity in the Knesset had dwindled and his attendance in the Knesset assembly had become rare.[30] On February 12, 1990, Zayyad submitted his resignation to the Knesset presidency, bringing to an end his sixteen consecutive years as a legislator at the national level.

In one of their correspondences after Habibi was dismissed from his role as editor, he warned Zayyad that "they are after me, but you are next in line."[31] This prediction turned out to be accurate. Although Tubi and Vilner left the Knesset, they did not relinquish their control over the party. Tubi, who was appointed secretary general in 1989, remained in that position, and before the 1992 elections, he tried to prevent Zayyad from returning to the Knesset. In that period, the party experienced the most intense internal struggle since the 1965 split, although this time, the dividing lines were related to personal alliances more than to ideological positions. At the head of the list approved by the Politburo, Tubi and his supporters put Hashim Mahamid, the former mayor of Umm al-Fahm. Tubi even came in person to Mahamid's house in Umm al-Fahm and asked him to lead the list.[32] In his political stands and tendency to provoke the Hebrew media, Mahamid was not so different from Zayyad, but he did not have the same independent power base in the DFPE (furthermore, he was not even an ICP member) and therefore was probably considered more "manageable" than Zayyad. Second on the list was the DFPE secretary, the poet and author Salim Jubran, a Christian from Nazareth, who inherited Habibi's role as the editor of *al-Ittihad*. The third, fourth, and fifth places were reserved for the party's Jewish and Druze MKs (Tamar Gozansky and Muhammad Nafa') and the Jewish trade unionist (Binyamin Gonen).[33] According to this arrangement, Zayyad was left without a realistic chance of being reelected in 1992.

Zayyad might have objected to Habibi's rebellion against democratic centralism, but soon he discovered the advantages of being able to challenge the official party line. Zayyad and his supporters anticipated the attempt of the party leadership to exclude him from the Knesset, and they worked beforehand to equip the DFPE institutions (in which the ICP was the dominant but not the only force) with more power in order to counterbalance the power of the ICP's institutions. Six months before the 1992 elections, the DFPE council had decided to democratize the selection process and hold a separate ballot on each of the first eight positions on the list for the 1992 election. When the Tubi group brought their proposed list to the DFPE's council for approval, they faced effective resistance for the first time. In the days before the council meeting, Nazareth's city hall became a headquarters from which phone calls were made to DFPE's council members, urging them to oppose the party's proposal. The Nazareth group in the DFPE objected particularly to Jubran, arguing that the party institutions should not impose on the Nazareth District, the largest district in the party, a candidate with no electoral power base in the area.[34] Salim Jubran decided to withdraw completely from the list, and shortly before the vote, Mahamid withdrew his candidacy for the first place, running instead as a single candidate for second place. Zayyad remained the only candidate and was elected automatically to lead the DFPE in the Knesset.[35] Paradoxically, perestroika, of which Zayyad was so suspicious, indirectly equipped him with unprecedented power in the party.

NEW HOPE

Although Zayyad was not the official leader of his party, at the age of sixty-three, he became the most influential political figure among Palestinians in Israel. It happened shortly after the dissolution of the Soviet Union—after "the heart of the world" stopped beating.[36] During the last two years of his life, however, Zayyad was more optimistic than he had ever been before. This optimism was related to what Zayyad saw as another inevitable process: a Palestinian-Israeli reconciliation, leading to a peace based on a two-state solution, a partial restoration of Palestinian rights, and equality between Arabs and Jews. The Oslo process, Zayyad believed, would lead ultimately to the realization of these goals.

Chapter 10

OSLO

The Sky Is the Limit

WHEREAS PERESTROIKA CHALLENGED ZAYYAD'S POLITICAL VISION, the most serious reconciliation attempt between Israelis and Palestinians, known as the Oslo Accords, seemed to confirm the political plan he and his party had championed since 1947: a two-state solution. In the first years of the state, it was impossible to separate the ICP's support of a two-state solution from the official position of the Soviet Union. This position set the party activists apart from Arab nationalists and the mainstream Palestinian national movement for many years. Zayyad himself did not argue explicitly against it, but the Palestinian literary scholar Salim al-'Atawna asserted that before 1967, Zayyad's poetry still reflected a dream to liberate Palestine.[1] After 1967, however, his poetry reflects the increasing recognition among Palestinians that the establishment of the State of Israel was irreversible. In 1980, Zayyad told a Jewish Israeli journalist, "Until today I am convinced that if the Palestinian People had back then a rational leadership, we would have had today two states. Certainly. I see the 1948 war as an Arab aggression."[2] Zayyad's statement is compatible with the traditional party line, which has commonly blamed Arab "reactionary regimes" that arguably served imperial interests when they invaded Palestine.

The two-state solution was not supposed to replace drastic reforms inside the State of Israel, which since 1948 had practiced *"Israeltheid*—Apartheid in the Israeli way," as Zayyad described it in an interview three days before his death.[3] Zayyad hoped that a Palestinian-Israeli peace agreement would create a different political atmosphere that would be more convenient for the struggle for national equality inside Israel. His support of a two-state solution, though, made him a potential ally of the Zionist Left in Israel.

RAPPROCHEMENT WITH ZIONIST LEFT PARTIES

While the tension between their Palestinian affiliation and Israeli citizenship has always presented Palestinians in Israel with daily dilemmas, the first intifada (1987–1993) emphasized the urgency of finding a solution that would ease this tension. The two-state solution had never been so popular before. For many, it was a magic formula reconciling citizenship and national sentiments, supposedly allowing Palestinians in Israel to fight for equality without being considered a security threat and the enemy's agents.

That growing sense of urgency to end the occupation might explain the rapprochement between the DFPE and Left Zionist forces in the early 1990s. On March 15, 1990, the DFPE and the Arab Democratic Party provided the crucial votes in a vote of no confidence against the Likud-led government, and then the DFPE negotiated its conditions for supporting a Labor-led government. This government was never established for other reasons, but the legacy of that attempt was an unprecedented signed document in which the Labor Party committed to a set of policies based on the DFPE's demands.[4]

Although Zayyad was not a member of the Knesset at the time, it is evident that he was ready to go even further in cooperating with Zionist parties. During the intifada years, he used to warn against a tendency to abandon cooperating with them. For example, during the Iraqi invasion of Kuwait in August 1990, the PLO leadership and some Arab Knesset members expressed unambiguous support for Saddam Hussein. MK Yossi Sarid, a major figure in the Zionist Left, wrote a column denouncing this support and concluding, "Until further notice, they can come looking for me."[5] Among Palestinians, many considered his article and that statement as disqualifying Sarid as a partner, and MK Muhammad Mi'ari from the PLP (whom Sarid named in that article) even declared, "We will not come looking for you." Zayyad criticized Sarid but argued with Mi'ari as well. "We should not pay them back with the same coin," he wrote, "Rather, we should continue the discussion and the dialogue with them and help them to awake from this nationalist whim, as they woke up from other misconceptions in the past. [...] We should not confront them with anger and withdraw our outreached hand. Rather, we should continue the dialogue and strengthen the productive cooperation."[6]

Before the 1992 election, Zayyad even supported the creation of a political bloc with Zionist parties. The alliance with the Black Panthers, which in 1977 Zayyad had been the strongest advocate of, had already broken; by 1990, the movement had dissolved, and its sole remnant was the seat held by Charlie Bitton. When Vilner, Tubi, and Zayyad resigned from the Knesset that year, Bitton refused to join them and even left the DFPE, but he remained an MK, thereby depriving the DFPE of a seat. In a rare occurrence, the veteran leadership admitted that his inclusion on the list for the fourth time in 1988 was a mistake.[7] Zayyad himself retroactively stated that the decision to join forces with the Panthers and to include Bitton in the list was the right decision in 1977 and in 1981, but in the following two elections (1984 and 1988), it was a mistake because "Charlie Bitton did not grow and did not develop any movement. [...] I would like to emphasize that our mistake regarding Bitton was not in him being a Jew but because he was only an individual who failed to develop a political force with an electoral or political weight."[8] In less formal circumstances, Zayyad reportedly said: "The Communist Party might have been unsuccessful in solving many social problems in Israel, but there is at least one social problem it did solve—that of Charlie Bitton."[9] The Black Panthers episode was a failure to mobilize Mizrahi Jews for a class struggle. The vast majority of them continued to vote for Zionist parties.

Zayyad's personal disappointment about Bitton and the failure of the Black Panthers experiment did not erode his support for a wide political front and strategic collaboration with Jewish or even Zionist forces. Months before the June 23, 1992, elections, three left-leaning Zionist parties merged into one list, Meretz. In an unpublished interview with the filmmaker Hagar Kot, Zayyad said, "I welcome the establishment of this bloc. It is an important step forward toward the unification of all the forces of peace. This agreement should have been done a long time ago, and it should include as well the DFPE and other forces." Indeed, behind the scenes, Zayyad worked on an ambitious project: uniting the three Arab lists (DFPE, Arab Democratic Party, and the PLP) together with Meretz into one list in order to "cause a change in the political map in Israel in favor of peace, equality, and democracy, as well as promoting democratic Arab-Jewish cooperation."[10] While Meretz rejected the idea out of hand, the other three parties entered negotiations, though they ultimately failed. Zayyad still attempted until the last minute to change the mind of his potential Arab partners, warning them that they might not cross the bar of 1.5 percent required to gain seats in the Knesset and that many Arab votes would be lost.[11] His efforts failed, and in the elections, the PLP gained only 0.9 percent of the votes, and more than 24,000 votes were lost.

In a way, this vision of joining forces with Zionist parties was a natural extension of the old philosophy of the front, but there is a difference between partnering with a splinter faction of the Black Panthers, which was agnostic about Zionism, and partnering with mainstream self-proclaimed Zionist parties. In this sense, the attempt to join forces with Meretz was unprecedented, and it foreshadowed the DFPE's cooperation with Yitzhak Rabin's government later that year. What certainly contributed to this development was the adoption of the two-state solution as a political program by both the PLO and significant forces in the Zionist Left, including members of the Labor Party. Zayyad saw this development as a historic victory for his party, and in public appearances following the 1992 election campaign, he frequently quoted from Psalms 122:18, "The stone which the builders rejected has become the chief cornerstone"—a reference to the Labor Party's adoption of the communist political plan after its previous rejection of it. The use of this verse has a history in the party; for example, Emile Habibi used it to praise the party in his obituary of Emil Tuma in 1985.[12] This quote also has a strong resonance in Zionist imagery, and Zayyad was surely aware of that imagery and of the subtext alluding to rapprochement.[13]

During the campaign, Zayyad had clarified that the central goal of the DFPE was to block the Likud and the extreme Right parties from establishing a government.[14] Presenting this as the major goal inevitably set the ground for collaboration with the Zionist Left parties. Indeed, in the 1992 elections, the Labor Party and Meretz together gained fifty-six seats, and the Labor Party needed the votes of the DFPE (three) and the Arab Democratic Party (two) to secure the magic number of sixty-one, which would prevent the Likud from building a coalition. Immediately after the announcement of the first results from the exit polls on the night of June 23, Zayyad told the Hebrew media that his party would consider (for the first time in its history) supporting a coalition led by the Labor Party.[15] Zayyad's statement reflected informal conversations the Labor Party and the DFPE had held before the election; then on June 28, Yitzhak Rabin phoned Zayyad and, congratulating him on the success of the DFPE in the election, told him that he considered the DFPE part of the bloc that would prevent the Likud from forming a government.

Zayyad said that his party representatives would advise the state president to charge Rabin with forming a government in the customary consultations of the president with the elected Knesset members—and so they did.[16]

On July 6, the DFPE negotiation team, led by Zayyad, met the Labor Party negotiation team, led by Rabin, to discuss the conditions for DFPE support. Neither side was interested in including the DFPE in the government. The ideological gap concerning Zionism, the obscure position of the Labor Party regarding the occupation of the West Bank and the Gaza Strip, and the ongoing bloody oppression of Palestinian resistance prevented both sides from sharing responsibility in the executive branch. During the term of that government, Zayyad explicitly excluded the possibility of joining government and criticized the Arab Democratic Party for its hypothetical readiness to do so.[17] At the same time, both the DFPE and the Labor Party were interested in maintaining a coalition that would potentially promote an Israeli-Palestinian reconciliation, which involved territorial compromise. In the meeting, Zayyad presented a set of demands related to the occupied territories, as well as the equal rights of the Palestinian citizens of Israel. While Rabin commented that the gaps between the two sides on the first issue were significant, he stated, regarding the latter, that he was "ashamed of the continuous erosion of the rights of the Arab citizens in all the fields—the legal, the economic, and the social, as well as in the fields of service and education."[18]

Accordingly, on July 12, the Labor Party sent letters to Zayyad and to the chair of the Arab Democratic Party committing to a list of concrete changes to promote equality and the integration of Israel's Arab citizens.[19] The far-reaching symbolic meaning of supporting an Israeli government led to an internal struggle in the DFPE, whose secretariat decided that same day (July 12) to abstain in the vote on the approval of Rabin's government, scheduled for July 13. On the following morning, though, it was still unclear if Rabin had a majority, since the ultra-Orthodox Shas Party conditioned its support on not being the party to provide the decisive sixty-first vote for the coalition. Now Rabin, who already had gained the support of the two Arab Democratic Party members, was dependent on convincing the DFPE to change their stand and support him.

This moment carried great symbolic weight. In 1948, Yitzhak Rabin was a high-ranking officer who had signed a command to expel tens of thousands of Palestinians from the Ramla and Lydda area. In the 1967 war, Rabin was the IDF chief of staff who imposed the occupation of the West Bank and the Gaza Strip. Rabin was the prime minister during Land Day in 1976. In 1984, he was appointed minister of defense and led a deadly policy in Lebanon that cost the lives of hundreds of Palestinians and Lebanese, leading Zayyad to name him "the cutthroat from Tel Aviv" in a 1985 Land Day rally.[20] From 1987 to 1990, still minister of defense, Rabin implemented harsh measures to suppress the first intifada. During the 1992 election campaign, the DFPE used Rabin's role as the leader of the Labor Party to discourage Arab voters from voting for the party. In an election rally in Bi'na, Zayyad said, "Young men and women: go back to history and ask your parents. Rabin is responsible for the massacres in Lydda and Ramla and the killing of hundreds inside a mosque. He is behind the policy of breaking bones. Ask who issued the orders to suppress the strike on Land Day, killing six martyrs. The same Rabin is at the head of the Labor Party list."[21]

That same Rabin sent an urgent request to Zayyad, who was brought in 1948 to substitute the working hands of the Ramla refugees (see chapter 1), the author of "Unadikum," and the leader of Land Day, asking for the DFPE support. The DFPE leadership reconsidered its previous resolution and decided, unprecedentedly, to vote in favor of the new government.[22] Officially, the DFPE, like the Arab Democratic Party, was not part of the coalition but saw itself and was described by the media as forming an "obstructing bloc" against right-wing rule. Rabin became a prime minister for the second time—this time with crucial communist and Arab support. The coalition included the Labor Party, the Left Zionist Meretz party, and the Sephardi ultra-Orthodox Shas party, while the DFPE and the Arab Democratic Party agreed to offer external support (approved the government by their vote but not included in it).

While the first term of Yitzhak Rabin as a prime minister (1974–1977) was carved into the Palestinian collective memory mainly because of land confiscation and the blood spilled on Land Day, many consider his nonconsecutive second term (1992–1995) as the "honeymoon" of the Arab citizens and the Zionist Left. At least in the realm of promoting equality between Arab and Jewish citizens, the Arab parties maximized their negotiation power and were able to divert resources toward their constituents. Regarding the broader Palestinian issue, in summer 1992 Rabin still opposed negotiating with the PLO, but he faced strong opposition to this insistence inside his own party. The doves in the Labor Party demanded that the legal ban on meeting PLO members be rescinded, and the ban was indeed removed by the Knesset in January 1993.

For Zayyad, the victory of the Labor-Meretz coalition was a reason for much optimism, as well as a confirmation of his party's position since 1948:

Today, more than ever, the political developments at both the local and global level are evidence of a historical victory of the party and its plan for solving the problem in the region based on the principle of the right of self-determination and national sovereignty in two independent states, Israeli and Palestinian, one aside the other. Therefore, "the stone which the builders rejected has become the chief cornerstone," and the plan that everyone rejected has become today the basis for the solution.[23]

CONFRONTATIONS

The right-wing opposition frequently attacked Rabin for his alliance with the anti-Zionist Arab parties. The most consistent among them was MK Rehav'am Ze'evi, a former general who established Moledet, a political party explicitly calling for a "transfer" of Arab population from the country. Ze'evi consistently referred to the government as the Rabin-Zayyad-Darawsha government and did not miss an opportunity to mention in the Knesset assembly that Rabin's government was supported by the "Arafat party."

As in previous Knesset terms, Zayyad became the main target of right-wing attacks, but this time the confrontation became even more turbulent—probably for three reasons. First, the growing presence of television cameras in the assembly increased the tendency of Knesset members from all political parties to use various kinds of provocations to increase their visibility. Second, some Israeli political parties adopted the primary system, which meant that Knesset members worked to impress their base by making bold declarations at their public appearances. Equally important was Zayyad's new status: while in the past, his party had no tangible influence on policy, this time he was de facto part of the coalition supporting the ruling government, and therefore right-wing politicians perceived him as a much stronger threat.

There was major turmoil, verging on physical violence, on November 30, 1992, when the Knesset assembly discussed the strengthening of extreme Right forces in Germany. In his speech, Zayyad argued that Germany was not alone and mentioned some other countries: "We should stand against this phenomenon in full power," he added. "In France we call him Le Pen and Le Penism. Here we call him Ze'evi." Right-wing MKs interrupted Zayyad and asked the speaker, Shevah Weiss, to halt Zayyad's speech. Weiss asked Zayyad to withdraw this comparison. Zayyad refused, and MKs from three right-wing parties, Likud, Tsomet, and Moledet, left the assembly hall. When Zayyad left the podium, some of them returned to the assembly and approached him. According to *Hadashot* reporter Amnon Levy, the ushers rescued Zayyad seconds before the eruption of a fistfight.[24] Following the event, Zayyad received death threats over the phone and was aggressively attacked in the Hebrew media. The author Haim Hefer published a venomous poem in which he named Zayyad "the last Bolshevik, a skin-head poet."[25]

This tension culminated in a turbulent discussion in the assembly on December 28, 1992, when Zayyad climbed to the podium to talk about benefits for children. Right-wing Knesset members repeatedly interrupted him, and the series of curses they subsequently exchanged covered ten pages of the minutes (the roughest slurs were omitted). Especially violent was the exchange between Zayyad and MK Ze'evi, who called Zayyad "Hitler," "Stalin," and "a terrorist." Zayyad in turn called Ze'ev "insane," a "wolf who escaped from the jungle" (*ze'ev* means "wolf" in Hebrew), and "human garbage." When Deputy Speaker Sarah Salmowitz ordered Zayyad to end his speech and leave the podium, he refused, arguing that he was not given the opportunity to deliver his speech. He rejected her request to step down, and Salmowitz announced a break in the session. The turbulent confrontation continued over the break. In one of the most memorable moments in the history of the Knesset, Zayyad called out in a choked voice to a group of right-wing MKs, "You are the crazy Right," and then, pointing to MK Ze'evi, "and this is your balls, I've got you by the balls." Later that day, the Knesset Committee decided to suspend Zayyad from the assembly for five sessions.

On the following day, Zayyad appealed the suspension and defended his position in the assembly:

> Honorable Knesset members, I will not bend, I will not be deterred by this insane attack. I have not flinched and have not bent facing physical attacks for many years. I experienced arrest and imprisonment countless times because of my political struggles. I experienced clubs landing on my head many times. I experienced assassination attempts more than once. I experienced bloody incitements, wild incitements, false charges, and slurs—against me, my party, and my political movement.

The Knesset voted and rejected Zayyad's appeal. This incident inspired Zayyad to write his only known poem in Hebrew. Titled "A Report from the Assembly Hall" and typed on an official letterhead of the Knesset, the original Hebrew version of the poem has never been published, although *al-Ittihad* published an

Arabic translation. In it, he addresses those who attacked him in the Knesset:

> You all, the insane of racism, occupation, and transfer
> I will be after you, after you—even after my death
> And finally—listen, listen—all the insane of racism
> I spent all my life fighting for peace and justice
> For equality and freedom and fraternity of Peoples
> And I will keep this way, I will not let you rest
> And about your frenzied rampage—I do not give a shit.[26]

Another strategy of the right-wing opposition to undermine the coalition was to embarrass Shas for sharing a government with Meretz, whose platform emphasized a secularist agenda. On November 2, 1992, four opposition parties submitted a no-confidence motion, based on their objection to the government's policy in various fields, in addition to specific complaints about some of the declarations of the new minister of education and the leader of the Meretz party, Shulamit Aloni. Zayyad represented his party in the discussion at the Knesset assembly, where he unambiguously defended Aloni:

> This is an attack on what the Minister Aloni represents—on openness, on social progress, on civil rights, on democratic rights, and on the real aspiration for peace. We totally reject this attack. This is a great honor for the government and for the state that they have a minister of education and culture like Aloni. We voted in favor of this government, and we will not help to topple it—and I say it even though we have severe criticism against it.[27]

Then Zayyad moved on to criticize Rabin for the lack of progress in the Israeli-Palestinian negotiations:

> Prime Minister Yitzhak Rabin does not want to be courageous [. . .] he goes one step forward, one step backward, look forward, look backward, and the end result is that he is walking in place. In the occupied territories nothing has changed, the cruel oppression continues, and collective punishment continues.

Criticizing the prime minister was certainly not new to Zayyad or to the other members of his party. This time, however, they criticized a government that was dependent on their votes and therefore they could be held somewhat responsible for its actions. Rabin's government repeatedly presented the DFPE Knesset members with serious dilemmas—most notably when it decided on December 17, 1992, to expel 415 Hamas activists from the West Bank to Lebanon, without trial, ostensibly for Hamas's assassination of an Israeli policeman days earlier. The expulsion unleashed a wave of protest and confrontation with the occupation forces in the West Bank and the Gaza Strip, who across the week killed ten Palestinians in the city of Gaza alone.

On December 24, a group of Knesset members from the DFPE and the Arab Democratic Party made a solidarity visit to the city. While there, MK Hashim Mahamid delivered a speech in which he told the crowd, "As long as the occupation continues, the struggle will continue, and in a struggle we do not mean only by a rock, but by all means available to our People."[28] Broadcast on the Israeli television, his speech provoked the public outrage so familiar to Zayyad: condemnation from the entire Zionist spectrum of Israeli politics and demands to revoke parliamentary immunity. Unlike the attacks against Zayyad in the 1970s and the 1980s, though, Arab Knesset members had unprecedented political power from 1992 to 1995. After threatening to submit a no-confidence motion to protest the expulsion, the MKs of the DFPE and Arab Democratic Party were invited to a meeting with Prime Minister Rabin on December 28. When they entered Rabin's office, he refused to shake Mahamid's hand. Zayyad announced that without a handshake, there would be no meeting, and Rabin was forced to shake Mahamid's hand. In the meeting itself, the minister of finance committed to significantly increasing the budget for projects related to the Arab population.

OSLO

While the government's new financial commitments might have contributed to the DFPE's decision to avoid the no-confidence motion, there was an even more important factor. According to a report in *Yedi'ot Aharonot* published the same day of that meeting, although Rabin publicly continued to oppose any negotiations with PLO, he did not in fact exclude it as an option and made a distinction between "extremists" and "moderates" within the PLO.[29] On January 19, 1993, the Knesset canceled the ban on meetings with PLO members, and two days later, in a phoned-in statement to an Israeli television program, Yasser Arafat invited Rabin to meet with him. Zayyad celebrated the event and demanded an urgent meeting of the Knesset assembly to discuss Arafat's statement.[30] He also sent a letter, preapproved by the Nazareth Municipal Council, to Arafat, stating that the Knesset decision is a historical political and moral victory, first and foremost for the PLO, and the noble intifada, for you personally, for the forces of peace, those who fought for a long time to cancel the law, all those who, throughout the years defied the law and suffered for that reason, and especially your friend and our friend Abie Nathan. [. . .] We will continue the struggle, Arabs and Jews, inside the Knesset and outside of it, for the formal Israeli recognition of the PLO and the beginning of negotiation with it.[31]

Although Rabin ignored Arafat's call, far-reaching developments had been taking place behind the scenes since early 1993. By early June 1993, there were reports about secret negotiations between Israeli and PLO representatives in Norway,[32] and in early September, the Israeli government confirmed that Israel and the PLO had reached an agreement on mutual recognition and a pathway to a future peace agreement, the Declaration of Principles (known later as the Oslo Accords).

A significant number of Palestinian citizens of Israel, and especially Palestinian members of the ICP, celebrated these events with euphoric enthusiasm. On September 11, the Follow-Up Committee organized a demonstration in Nazareth in support of the agreement. Representatives from both the PLO and the Israeli government were among the speakers. Eighteen years after his father, the minister Moshe Bar'am, visited Nazareth and threatened to "react severely" if the communists won the local elections (see chapter 5), the minister Uzi Bar'am spoke in a demonstration as an ally of the Arab local leaders. In the crowd, demonstrators waved both Palestinian and Israeli flags. Tawfiq Zayyad liked this joint appearance and said in his speech that it symbolized the future—two states for two Peoples. He promised that his party would support the government in any step it took toward a just peace. Zayyad ended his speech by inviting Arafat to visit Nazareth.[33]

The Declaration of Principles was officially signed in Washington, DC, on September 13, 1993, and was harshly criticized by Israeli and Palestinian opposition leaders alike. Zayyad defended the accord when he addressed the Knesset assembly in a special meeting convened to discuss and vote on the Oslo agreement. Of all Zayyad's speeches, this was probably the most "Israeli" speech. It depicted a new line of division in which he sided with the Israeli government against those on both sides who rejected reconciliation, dubbing the opposition leader, Benjamin Netanyahu, "Bibi Hamasiyahu" (a reference to the Palestinian Islamist Hamas movement, who rejected the agreement) and describing his speech as confused, shallow, and petty. He dismissed the power of the opposition to the agreement:

> The objectors there and here cannot stop the necessary development. They cannot stop peace. This big rock, the rock of peace, already started rolling down from the top of the mountain and there is no power that can stop it. Knesset members, we are still in the beginning, we are still in the tunnel but we are confident that the light is at the end of the tunnel, even if we do not see it yet, and we know that we have already begun the first step toward the right direction. There are obstacles, and there will be more in the future—but we shall overcome them.[34]

Then Zayyad outlined the four issues that the Declaration of Principles had not yet resolved: the status of Jerusalem, which should be divided into two capital cities that maintained peaceful cooperation; the Palestinian refugees, for whom any solution should be based on their right to return to their homeland; the right of the Palestinian People to a state, which Israel should recognize; and borders, which should be along the 1967 line. Zayyad took credit, in the name of his party, for envisioning and enabling the agreement: "This great achievement—we are its father and mother—since 1948 [...] this was our political program, which advocated the right for self-determination and national sovereignty for both sides." Zayyad also celebrated his party's decision to provide external support for the government and repeated his promise to support any step the government would take toward a just peace. He explained the special investment of the Arab citizens of Israel in peace:

> While every side in this conflict, the Israeli side and the Palestinian side, has an interest in peace in the Middle East, we, the Arab population in Israel, have a double interest: once as part of the state, and once as part of the Arab Palestinian People. Honorable members of the Knesset, two days before the historical event, there was a mass demonstration of the Arab population in Nazareth. In this demonstration, two flags were raised, the Israeli flag and the Palestinian flag, side by side—and this is a symbol of the future, pointing to the inevitable just peace.

Then Zayyad did something he had never done before: he read his own poetry (translated into Hebrew) from the Knesset podium. Since becoming an MK,

Zayyad had separated his poetry from his parliamentary work. The revolutionary enthusiasm of his poetry was surely foreign to the house of Israeli legislators and incompatible with the pragmatic and calculated approach he adopted there. Because he excluded his Palestinian patriotic poetry, he probably felt that his pro-peace poetry should also stay out of the assembly hall. The Declaration of Principles allowed a rare moment of convergence between his poetic charisma and what he believed to be the vision of most Israeli Knesset members at the time.

"Allow me," he prefaced the reading, "one more minute to read from a poem I wrote for Abie Nathan almost two years ago after he was sentenced to six months in prison because he met Yasser Arafat." He continued:

> Give the flower, the bee, the kiss, and the shining smile in the eyes, the
> right to speak.
> Give the sun, the top of the green mountain, and the trees, the right
> to speak.
> Give the sea and the sea waves, the corals, the forest, and the nightingale, the right to speak.
> Give the school, the field of seeds, and the factory, the right to speak.
> Give the morning dew, the moon in love, and the bird, the right to
> speak.
> Give the future, carried on the wings of seagulls, on lilac scent, the
> right to speak.
> Give Peace Now, the right to speak.[35]

Interestingly, when Prime Minister Rabin presented the accord to the assembly an hour earlier, he had also invoked the sun, ending his speech by calling on Knesset members to "let the sun shine." During the eleven-hour meeting, Zayyad also occupied himself with his recent hobby—drawing. His sketch (see figure 3) portrays the faces of Arafat and Rabin looking at each other in the middle of a chaotic swirl. Two small suns are shining around them, but a vulture is flying above.

On October 6, 1993, Rabin and Arafat met in Cairo for their first working meeting. Publicly, Rabin continued to convey mixed messages. In an interview with the *Jerusalem Post* that same day, he declared that the meeting in Cairo reflected the new strategic partnership with the PLO. At the same time, he remained committed

FIGURE 3. A sketch Zayyad drew during the discussion on the Knesset on the Oslo Accords, March 21, 1993.
Source: Tawfiq Zayyad Institute.

to his old positions: "No Palestinian state, [and] Jerusalem must remain united under Israeli sovereignty and be our capital forever."[36] Zayyad preferred to look at the glass as half full. In his speech at the Knesset assembly on October 11, he added another metaphor to his optimistic vision, emphasizing that the direction of history has turned: "It was a 180-degree turn. With this turn of the wheel, we entered a new highway, full of relaxation, full of greenery, fresh air, and a glowing hope for the establishment of a just, comprehensive, and stable peace, of which we have dreamed for decades [...] I am proud to say that our political movement is the mother and father of this political solution."[37]

As the leader of the DFPE in the Knesset and the major player in establishing the obstructing bloc, Zayyad became the Arab politician most identified with the Oslo process. The "Oslo euphoria" therefore surely bolstered the popular appeal of both the DFPE and Zayyad personally, overshadowing the demise of the Soviet Union two years earlier. When Zayyad ran against six other candidates in the December 1993 municipal elections, he was elected mayor for the fifth time and increased his share of the total vote from 57.6 percent in 1989 to 62.5 percent. The Nazareth Front increased its representation in the municipal council from ten to eleven seats.

MINES ON THE ROADS

In the year following the signing of the first Oslo Accords, the process faced major potholes. First, immediately after the agreement was signed, Shas left Rabin's coalition, making him even more dependent on Arab votes and more vulnerable to the delegitimizing efforts of the opposition. Zayyad, who probably hoped that sharing a coalition with Shas was the beginning of renewed Mizrahi-Arab rapprochement would later expressed his hope that Shas would return to the coalition, while at the same time he strongly opposed the inclusion of the mostly Ashkenazi right-wing Tsomet party in that coalition.[38]

The more severe deterioration in the popular support of the Oslo process began on February 25, 1994, when an American Israeli Far Right activist opened fire on a large number of Palestinian Muslims who had gathered to pray inside the mosque at the Cave of the Patriarchs in Hebron, killing twenty-nine. The massacre triggered a wave of demonstrations and riots on both sides of the Green Line. Following a demonstration of a thousand Arab citizens in Nazareth on February 26, some youngsters started throwing stones at the police, who reacted harshly. As in the past, some demonstrators assumed that Zayyad's parliamentary immunity would make his house a safe shelter. Once again, it turned out that Zayyad's immunity was limited and fragile, as policemen broke into the house.

Earlier that day, Zayyad had been speaking to the crowd. He blamed the government, and especially its insistence on a long "interim stage" in the process, for the massacre:

> Why should we wait long years before the final settlement? Do they think that we will live these years in a vacuum? No, there is no vacuum—it will be filled with massacres and violence. Nobody can stop the historical development, and the Palestinian state will be established. The Israeli occupation of the Palestinian territories, as well as of south Lebanon and the Golan Heights, will be ended—so why should we wait? [. . .] We pay with bloodshed, not only Arab blood but Jewish blood as well. [39]

The validity of Zayyad's warning became painfully clear in April when Hamas retaliated by killing thirteen Israelis and injuring more than a hundred in two suicide bombings in buses in Israeli cities. The killing of Palestinians and Israelis undermined the popular support of the process on both sides, but the leadership seemed determined to implement the accords as planned.

In May 1994, Israel withdrew its military forces from most of the Gaza Strip and the city of Jericho as part of the implementation of the Oslo agreements, and the Palestinian Authority was established. The Palestinian Authority was founded as an interim self-government body, with limited autonomy in defined domains, and it was supposed to function until the final agreement was signed, within five years. Many supporters of a two-state solution considered its creation as a step in the right direction. For the DFPE leaders, this development was further proof that the establishment of the obstructive bloc had been the right decision. The Hebron massacre, on the one hand, and the implementation of the agreement on the other, intensified the tension between the basic elements of Zayyad's rhetoric and politics at the time: protecting the government from the attempt of the right-wing parties to topple it and criticizing that same government for the interim stage and appeasement of the settlers.

On June 28, the Knesset assembly discussed the report of the commission of inquiry appointed to investigate the massacre in Hebron. Zayyad described the report as a "failure," stating that its major sin was disconnecting the massacre at the Cave of the Patriarchs from the political reality around it and ignoring the causal relations between the two: "The most important thing in the report is the exoneration of other responsible forces. Exoneration of the occupation, exoneration of settlers, of the extreme right, exoneration of the military, the government, and the general policy."[40] He implied, though, that he still had some trust in the judgment of the prime minister, who was "more realistic when he declared that it is not possible to guarantee that a massacre like this will not happen again. He knows what he is talking about because he knows that the occupation and the endurance of the conflict are the greenhouse for these things." The report, Zayyad said, would be soon forgotten; however "what will endure is the cry of the victims, the victims of the occupation and colonization in Hebron and in other places. This will be the cry: 'End the occupation, end the bloodshed.'"

These were Zayyad's last words on the Knesset podium.

ACCIDENT ON THE WAY TO JERUSALEM

If the Oslo Accords aimed at restoring Palestinian rights, at least partially, the moment that most strongly symbolized that restoration was the return on July 1, 1994, of Yasser Arafat to Palestine as the chairman of the new Palestinian Authority. Since the 1930s, Palestinian leaders had been driven into exile abroad, and for many, Arafat's return represented the beginning of the reversal of that trend. Zayyad surely considered Arafat's return a major landmark in the Palestinian struggle: "The significance of Arafat's visit is immense. First, it affirms the right of the Palestinian People to return to their homeland. Second, it is a drive for the unification of the Palestinian People around the Palestinian Authority and in supporting the peace process in its entirety."[41]

Two days after Arafat's arrival, Zayyad led a delegation of the DFPE to Gaza to meet him. They met late at night at the Palestine Hotel, where Arafat was staying in the first days of his arrival. Zayyad invited him to visit Nazareth, and the two shared with the other attendees the story of their first meeting in Berlin in 1973, which had remained a secret until that moment.

That night, Zayyad returned to Jerusalem for his parliamentary work. Na'ila, who accompanied him to Gaza, continued from Tel Aviv by herself to Nazareth. This was the last time she saw her husband. Zayyad stayed at the Ramada Renaissance Hotel and spent the next evening dining informally with other Knesset members: Hashim Mahamid from his party, Walid Sadiq from Meretz, and Nawaf Musalha from the Labor Party. At the end of the evening, Zayyad discussed transportation arrangements for the following morning, as he intended to be in Jericho to welcome Arafat on his first visit to the city. Since being elected to the Knesset,

Zayyad was usually accompanied in his travels by his parliamentary assistant and nephew, Nidal Sliman, who served also as a driver. That night, though, Sliman was in Nazareth, and Zayyad did not want to bother him. He tried to persuade Mahamid to go with him to Jericho, but Mahamid had another commitment at the Knesset scheduled for the same morning. Walid Sadiq said that he would pick up Zayyad and they would drive together to Jericho. However, when Sadiq arrived at Zayyad's hotel room, he did not find him; Zayyad had left earlier, alone, in his own car.[42]

That day, Zayyad did not manage to meet Arafat in person, but he did find time to read his poem "Unadikum" in front of an improvised crowd of Palestinian policemen. He attended Arafat's public appearance with the rest of the audience, and after it ended, he ran into Sadiq at around 5:00 p.m. and invited him for a drink.[43] Sadiq was tired, however, and declined. Zayyad left Jericho shortly after that. At 5:15 p.m., on the uphill and curvy road leading from Jericho to Jerusalem, Zayyad was driving behind two cars, including a slow-moving truck, and tried to pass them both in one stretch. He hit a van coming from the other direction, its driver also from Nazareth. When the paramedics removed him from the car, he was still alive, but he died shortly after.

EPILOGUE

Put my neck
In the black hanging rope
Put my dead body
In a grave within a grave
But I,
From the power of my love for my homeland
I will not die and will not vanish
I will forever be renewed
As long as a flower sprouts in my land
As long as in my homeland a rock remains
As long as a cloud hovers in the horizon
As long as soil survives in the land
I shall live, I shall live
In a flowing breeze
Inside a flower
In the scent of the za'atar
In the wild weeds
I will be renewed
Every morning, every minute
In the flute of a shepherd

In the humming of a mother
In a poet's violin
In the sunlight
[...]
I will remain forever and ever
I will be renewed in the homeland of the ancestors
I shall meet the triumph and the sun of the free people.[1]

ON JULY 6, 1994, BLACK FLAGS WERE RAISED ON UTILITY POLES across Nazareth and above the roofs of many of the city's houses. Businesses were closed, and the walls were covered with Tawfiq Zayyad's pictures and obituary notices. Sounds of church bells and muezzins' prayers filled the streets. Thousands of people crowded in the narrow street in front of Zayyad's house, waiting for his coffin. When it finally arrived in the black car, dozens of arms carried it inside his house to allow his family a private farewell. Then Zayyad's coffin was carried from his house, while the men who packed the alleys of the Eastern Neighborhood accompanied it with the rhythmic slogan, borrowed from the intifada repertoire: "Oh martyr, rest in peace, we will continue the struggle." The coffin was brought to the House of Friendship, the communist headquarters in Nazareth, for mourners to pay their respects. Faris, Tawfiq Zayyad's youngest son, spread the communist red scarf on his father's chest. One by one, mourners approached the open coffin; some touched Zayyad or kissed his head, many of them crying. The eulogies took more than two hours, and then the coffin was carried to Fountain Square next to the Church of the Annunciation and from there to the Mosque of Peace, where Zayyad's archrival, Kamal Khatib, delivered a religious sermon. The funeral procession then continued to the city hall, where it stopped for a moment of silence before heading to its last destination at the Muslim cemetery.

PALESTINIAN LEADER AND ISRAELI LEGISLATOR

Tawfiq Zayyad died at the most optimistic moment of the Oslo process, days after Yasser Arafat returned to Palestine and began to build what many believed was the beginning of the first Palestinian government. At the time, many considered Zayyad's funeral a step toward his vision of a just Palestinian-Israeli reconciliation. *Al-Ittihad* directly referenced this vision in the headline of its report about the funeral: "In his death he brought together representatives of two governments from two states of two Peoples."[2] Indeed, near Zayyad's coffin, ministers in the Israeli government gathered together with high-ranking officials in the PLO. The Palestinian Authority's designated minister of welfare, Intisar al-Wazir (the widow of Abu Jihad, the Palestinian leader assassinated by Israel six years earlier), shook the hand of Israel's minister of tourism, Uzi Bar'am. Among those who eulogized Zayyad were the Knesset Speaker, Shevah Weiss; Israel's deputy prime minister, Moshe Shahal; and the minister of housing in the Palestinian Authority, Zakariya al-Agha. Telegrams of condolences were sent by leaders from both sides—including President Ezer Weizman, Prime Minister Yitzak Rabin, King Hussein of Jordan, and Yasser Arafat, who was prohibited from attending any official event inside the Green Line—as well as by the Jewish Mizrahi poet Erez Bitton; the secretary general of the Popular Front for the Liberation of Palestine, George Habash; and many Palestinian prisoners held for years in Israeli prisons. The offices of the Democratic Front of the Liberation of Palestine in both Damascus and Gaza also sent letters. President Weizmann followed the telegram with a visit at Zayyad's house in Nazareth three days after the funeral. So did Jibril Rajub, then the head of the Palestinian Preventive Security.

This diversity was an indication of the complicated position of Palestinians within Israel, of Zayyad's own centrality in the attempts to maintain a delicate equilibrium in this contested sphere, and of the spirit of optimism that was common during the first two years of the Oslo process. Zayyad was clearly aware of the weaknesses of the process and used every opportunity to warn against the lack of clear Israeli commitments regarding the Palestinian refugees, the settlements, and Jerusalem, as well as a Palestinian state and its borders. In an interview with the Palestinian French journalist Samir 'Abdallah three days before his death, Zayyad referred to these issues as "mines on the roads." He believed, though, that the agreement shook political reality and provided a real opportunity for partly restoring Palestinian rights, the implementation of a two-state solution (even though the accords did not specify that), and the maintenance of a viable peace in the region.

Since Zayyad's death in 1994, the two-state solution has become a slogan that various actors have adopted to denote different—and sometimes contradictory—political visions. This is why it is important to clarify Zayyad's interpretation of the term. He did not see it as a formula aimed at separating Israelis and

Palestinians, an interpretation that gained momentum among Zionist centrist politicians only after Zayyad's death. In 1947, the Nazareth branch of the National Liberation League supported the UN partition plan, which was anything but a separation plan. It called for economic union between the proposed states, which were supposed to have a joint currency and joint economic development and preserve "freedom of transit and visit for all residents and citizens of the other State."[3] Later, Zayyad and his party considered the two-state solution an attractive formula because it was supposed to solve the tension between Palestinian national identification and Israeli citizenship.

While Israeli commentators frequently misread Zayyad's struggle for justice for Palestinians as fanatic nationalism, his willingness to be part of the Israeli system frustrated some Palestinian observers. In his party, Zayyad did not share the tendency of senior leaders like Meir Vilner and Tawfiq Tubi to nurture a non-Zionist civic Israeli pride. Unlike his cosmopolitanism, his Israeliness was largely utilitarian and passionless. The "Israeli" element of his identity was never part of his self-identification or self-presentation. In many ways, his election to the Israeli legislative house depleted him of his poetic Eros. Until then, his poetry was an important political tool that was highly compatible with an antiestablishment message and long-term national and universalist aspirations.

In the Knesset, he had to communicate in Hebrew, a language that he used mainly instrumentally and without creative aspirations. The Knesset was also a sphere of constant compromise, whose official symbols deny the existence of a Palestinian identity; at the same time, it was a necessary arena for defending Palestinian interests. His Knesset speeches were loaded with dry facts and statistics, and his unplanned verbal exchanges over the podium were frequently considered "unparliamentary." Poetry was unfit for this environment, and in his many years as a member of the Knesset (1974–1990, 1992–1994), he did not write poetry (with the exception of the satirical poem in Hebrew about Ze'evi). Nor did he include poetry in his addresses to the Knesset assembly, with the notable exception being his reading, during a September 1993 discussion of the Oslo agreements, from a Hebrew translation of his pro-peace poem dedicated to the Jewish Israeli peace activist Abie Nathan.

Zayyad's consistent support for Arab-Jewish cooperation was never an attempt to develop a shared national identity with Jewish Israelis. He sought bridges to Jewish Israelis because of his belief in a shared humanity, shared class affiliation, and, in the case of Mizrahi Jews, shared experience of ethnically based discrimination.

In this context, his cosmopolitanism was unambiguous and passionate, and it was not always easy for Arab audiences outside Israel to digest. It was only in spring 1994, at the height of the Oslo process and parallel to Israeli-Syrian negotiations, that Syrian television aired an interview with Zayyad. The interviewer, Syrian journalist Riyad Naʿsan Agha, asked him about his opinion on Jewish Israeli authors. He answered:

> The ideological mainstream in Israeli culture is hostile toward Arabs. It distorts the Arab's image, describing him as a killer with a knife ambushing the Jew [. . .] but there are Jewish authors and poets who are at the top of solidarity with Palestinian rights because they understand that justice for the Palestinian People is an interest of the Israeli People, which has also paid a price for this bad situation for decades. This is in addition to a general humanist perspective. There are some [Israeli] literary works, plays, novels, and poetry that we are proud of, and we are developing our relations with these people. This is the other face, the democratic and humanist face. [. . .] There is a conflict between two cultures. However, there is also a conflict, which we are interested in developing, and this is the conflict between every democratic culture and every nationalist chauvinist culture inside the culture of each People. [. . .] There are Jewish authors whose friendship, I swear on my honor, I am proud of, and I consider them a million times more humanist than some Arabs.[4]

MARXISM AS A MORAL COMPASS

It is not surprising that the tendency to equate Zayyad with Jesus resurfaced after his death. For example, the Jordanian poet Jiryis Samawi said, "Tawfiq Zayyad was the son of Nazareth who painfully carried his cross and his People's cross to Golgotha, in order to enter a better future of salvation and liberation."[5] While in his life, Zayyad rejected comparisons with Jesus, his religious-like conviction and a sense of destiny guided his political way. Here, however, both Zionist and Palestinian observers have mostly underappreciated the centrality of Marxist faith in Zayyad's worldview. The Palestinian national movement emphasized his supreme patriotism and has selectively incorporated his poetry into the national canon, marginalizing his more class-oriented poems.[6] Therefore, the river of condolence letters and telegrams sent after his death from Palestinians outside Israel highlighted his struggle to defend Palestinian rights but almost always ignored his Marxism. Meanwhile, Zionist observers tended to dismiss Zayyad's

Marxist universalist vision as a superficial cover for his Arab and Palestinian nationalism.[7]

Yet Zayyad was ready to pay in hard political and personal currency to defend his Marxist faith. He scolded Gamal Abdel Nasser, probably the most popular figure among Palestinians at the time, when he adopted an anticommunist stance in 1959; three decades later, he sacrificed his friendship with Emile Habibi when he believed that Habibi abandoned his faith in Marxism. After Zayyad's death, Habibi wrote that nothing ever hurt him more than the disagreement with Zayyad.[8] Even the collapse of the Soviet Union was for Zayyad a temporary decline in an inevitable process of human development toward equality and justice.

As his utopian and eschatological vocabulary shows, Marxism for Tawfiq Zayyad was a messianic religion. When the late Yossi Sarid (then a minister in Rabin's government) eulogized Zayyad in the Knesset, he said, "Peace, brotherhood, and equality were his God, and he did not have any other Gods before them."[9] Sarid captured in this sentence the explanation for the strength of Zayyad's secularism, echoing Ernst Bloch's dialectical understanding of religion and secularism: Marxist secular religion was Zayyad's "*transcendence* [italics in original] without transcendence." It provided him with meaning, purpose, faith, and hope. And it did not leave room for any other religion. His dream about justice and his unshakable faith in the power of hungry people to achieve it were what he owned.

> *What I own*
> I am a simple person.
> I have never carried a machine gun on my shoulders,
> I never pulled a trigger
> In my life.
> I do not own anything except
> My music
> And a feather for drawing my dreams
> And a bottle of ink.
> I do not own even daily bread,
> And my stomach is barely satisfied.
> I do own my unshakable faith
> And passion
> . . . the universe will be swept away, if facing a hungry People.[10]

Acknowledgments

I COULD NOT HAVE ACCOMPLISHED THIS BOOK WITHOUT THE GEN-erosity, goodwill, and talent of many. First, it began as a joint project with my friend Issam Aburaya, and our many conversations shaped my thinking about Zayyad's life and poetry. Although Issam withdrew from the project, his contribution to it is invaluable. Tawfiq Zayyad's family members, especially his wife, Na'ila, his daughters, Wahiba and 'Ubur, his brother, Musbah, and his nephews, Nidal Sliman and Yihya Dahamsha, opened their hearts to me, shared endless stories, and provided important personal documents. So did Adib Abu Rahmun, the co-manager of the Tawfiq Zayyad Institute in Nazareth and Zayyad's long-time political partner. I am grateful as well for a very long list of people who knew Zayyad and shared their memories with me and to those who helped to create important contacts: Yossi Algazy, Nazim Badir, Charlie Bitton, 'Abd al-Malik Dahamsha, Suhayl Diab, Nabila Espanioli, Samih Ghanadri, Binyamin Gonen, Samiah Hakim, Marzuq Halabi, Fathi Furani, Farid Ghanim, Tamar Gozansky, Raik Jarjura, Ramiz Jaraysi, As'ad Kanana, Avshalom Kave, Ibrahim 'Abd al-Khaliq, Samira Khouri, Violet Khouri, the late Felicia Langer, the late Hashem Mahamid, Nazir Majali, 'Isam Makhul, Ibrahim Malik, Faruq Mawassi, Ayman 'Uda, Nabil 'Uda, Michal Sela, Muhammad 'Ali Taha, and Micha Vilner.

The translation of poetry from Arabic to English has been especially challeng-ing, and I am grateful for Aida Bamia for generously and skillfully translating some of the poems included in this book, and for my friend, the linguist Youssef Haddad, for his excellent advice regarding my own translations. Conversations with my friends 'Imad Khamaysi, Eric Kligerman, Yael Shenker, and Raef Zreik helped me articulate my ideas in their theoretical and historical contexts. Film director Hagar Kot provided a valuable recorded interview with Zayyad, and Daniel Ziss assisted with obtaining and translating documents from the Security Services Archive in Prague. My two research assistants, Nareeman Jamal and Mi'ad Hasan, helped me sift through thousands of issues of *al-Ittihad* newspapers. I am grateful to Joel Beinin and Maha Nassar who read closely and carefully through an earlier version of the manuscript and provided invaluable comments.

My wife, Michelle, closely read part of the manuscript, and her comments helped me significantly to clarify my ideas. Friends and colleagues read some chapters and provided helpful comments: Adey Almohsen, Ahmad Agbaria, Orna Akad, Leena Dallasheh, Lior Sternfeld, and Himmat Zu'bi. The responsibility for the content of this book, however, is mine. The contribution of Stanford University Press editors Kate Wahl and Leah Pennywark, as well as the language editor Allison Brown and the copy editor Bev Miller was vital and significantly improved the quality of this book. The research was supported by the Humanities Scholarship Enhancement Fund, granted by the College of Liberal Arts and Sciences at the University of Florida. Finally, I am grateful for Michelle, Tal, and Noah for their love, the secret ingredient of my writing.

PROLOGUE

1. The word *sha'b* in Arabic (*shu'ub* in plural) means a body of persons united by a common culture or tradition, such as the Palestinian people. Throughout this book, I have translated it as *People* (capitalized) to distinguish it from people in general.

2. Tawfiq Zayyad, "'Ila ayna yadhhab ma nadfa'?" [Where are our payments going?], *al-Jadid* 1, no. 11 (September 1954). Translation by Aida Bamia.

3. Maha Nassar, *Brothers Apart: Palestinian Citizens of Israel and the Arab World* (Stanford: Stanford University Press, 2017), 58–64.

4. Ibid., 10.

5. Ibid.

6. In rare cases, some of them (most notably, Rashid Husayn) joined the socialist Zionist Mapam, but he was expelled from the party later.

7. See Khaled Furani, *Silencing the Sea: Secular Rhythms in Palestinian Poetry* (Stanford: Stanford University Press, 2012); Hanna Abu Hanna, *Rihlat al-Bahth 'an al-Turath* (Haifa: al-Wadi, 1994), and Adina Hoffman, *My Happiness Bears No Relation to Happiness: A Poet's Life in the Palestinian Century* (New Haven: Yale University Press, 2009).

8. Tamir Sorek, *Palestinian Commemoration in Israel: Calendars, Monuments, and Martyrs* (Stanford: Stanford University Press, 2015), 13–18.

9. Honaida Ghanem, *Reinventing the Nation: Palestinians Intellectuals in Israel* [in Hebrew] (Jerusalem: Magnes Press, 2009), 70–71.

10. Talal Asad, *Formations of the Secular: Christianity, Islam, Modernity* (Stanford: Stanford: Stanford University Press, 2003.

11. See, for example, Jules Monnerot, *Sociology and Psychology of Communism* (Boston: Beacon Press, 1976); Walter Benjamin, *Walter Benjamin: Selected Writings, 1938–1940* (Cambridge, MA: Belknap Press of Harvard University Press, 2003); Karl Löwith, *Meaning in History: The Theological Implications of the Philosophy of History* (Chicago: University of Chicago Press, 1957); Raymond Aron, *In Defense of Decadent Europe* (Chicago: Regnery/Gateway, 1979).

12. Hannah Arendt, "A Reply to Eric Voegelin," in *The Portable Hannah Arendt*, ed. Peter Baehr (New York: Viking Press, 2000).

13. Ernst Bloch, *Atheismus Im Chritentum: Zur Religion Des Exodus Und Des Reichs* (Frankfurt: Springer-Verlag, 1968), 23.

14. Warren S. Goldstein, "Messianism and Marxism: Walter Benjamin and Ernst Bloch's Dialectical Theories of Secularization," *Critical Sociology* 27, no. 2 (2001).

15. Ernst Bloch, *Atheism in Christianity: The Religion of the Exodus and the Kingdom* (London: Verso, 2009), 224. Walter Benjamin suggests a similar, though less sociological, dialectic of secularization.

16. In 1973 the ICP already claimed control over the municipal council of Yafat al-Nasira (a town of 5,000 at the time), but Nazareth was the first city where a communist became mayor.

17. See Tamir Sorek, *Arab Soccer in a Jewish State: The Integrative Enclave* (Cambridge: Cambridge University Press, 2007); Sorek, *Palestinian Commemoration in Israel.*

18. For a discussion of Israeli orientalists, see Dan Rabinowitz, *Antropologyah Ve-ha-Falastinim* [in Hebrew] (Ra'ananah: Ha-Merkaz le-ḥeker ha-hevrah ha-'Arvit, 1998); Gil Eyal, *The Disenchantment of the Orient: Expertise in Arab Affairs and the Israeli State* (Stanford: Stanford University Press, 2006).

19. 'Izz al-Din al-Manassira, "Muqadamma: Tawfiq Zayyad—al Sha'ir, al-Sha'b wal-Qadiya," in *Diwan Tawfiq Zayyad*, ed. 'Izz al-Din al-Manassira (Beirut: Dar al-'Awda, 1970); Avraham Yinon, "Tawfiq Zayyad: 'We Are the Majority Here,'" in *The Arabs in Israel: Continuity and Change*, ed. Aharon Layish (Jerusalem: Magness Press, 1981); Salim al-'Atawna, *Tawfiq Zayyad, Dirasa Tahliliya fi Intajihi al-Adabi* (Beersheeba: Kaye Academic College of Education, 2017); Nu'aima al-Ahmad, *Tawfiq Zayyad—al-Sha'ir al-Munadil* (Haifa: Maktabat Kul Shee, 2018); Salma K. Jayyusi, *Anthology of Modern Palestinian Literature* (New York: Columbia University Press, 1992); Jamil Kitani, *Al-Lugha al-Tahridiyya lada Tawfiq Zayyad wa-Masa'il 'Ukhra fi*

Shiʿrihi (Baqa al-Gharbiyya: Al-Qasemi College, 2011); Habib Bulus, *Al-Wathaʾiq al-Harir* (Nazareth: Tawfiq Zayyad Institute, 2000).

20. Sasson Somekh, quoted in Amos Karmel, "Politika ve-ha-Shira," *Yediʿot Aharonot*, April 13, 1995.

21. Tawfiq Zayyad, "Diwan ʿAshiq min Falastin li-Mahmud Darwish, " in *Dirasat fi al-Adab al-Falstini al-Mahali*, ed. Nabih al-Qasim (Acre: Dar al-Aswar, 1987), 142.

22. Mutlu K. Blasing, *Nâzım Hikmet: The Life and Times of Turkey's World Poet* (New York: Persea Books, 2013).

CHAPTER 1

1. Nazareth Municipality, *Al-Faris—Tawfiq Zayyad, al-Insan, al-Qaʾid, al-Shaʿir* (Nazareth: al-Hakim, 1994).

2. Ibid., 10–12.

3. *Kol ha-ʿAm*, June 3, 1958.

4. Ibid.

5. Sandy M. Sufian, *Healing the Land and the Nation: Malaria and the Zionist Project in Palestine, 1920–1947* (Chicago: University of Chicago Press, 2008), 64.

6. Rashid Khalidi, *Palestinian Identity: The Construction of Modern National Consciousness* (New York: Columbia University Press, 1997).

7. Maha Nassar, *Brothers Apart: Palestinian Citizens of Israel and the Arab World* (Stanford: Stanford University Press, 2017), 21–22, 33–34.

8. Roman Szporluk, *Communism and Nationalism: Karl Marx versus Friedrich List* (New York: Oxford University Press, 1988).

9. Chad F. Emmet, *Beyond the Basilica: Christians and Muslims in Nazareth* (Chicago: University of Chicago Press, 1995).

10. Fred Halliday, "Early Communism in Palestine," *Journal of Palestine Studies* 7, no. 2 (1978): 162–169

11. Musa Budeiri, *The Palestine Communist Party 1919–1948: Arab and Jew in the Struggle for Internationalism* (Chicago: Haymarket Books, 2010); Shmuel Dothan, *Adumim: Ha-Miflagah Ha-Komunistit be-Erets-Yisraʾel* (Kefar-Saba: Shevna ha-sofer, 1991); Jacob Hen-Tov, *Communism and Zionism in Palestine during the British Mandate* (New Brunswick, NJ: Transaction Publishers, 1974).

12. Dothan, *Adumim*, 197–200.

13. Ibid., 178–179.

14. Ibid.

15. Ibid., 551.

16. Yehoshua Porath, *The Palestine Arab National Movement: From Riots to Rebellion* (London: Frank Cass, 1977).

17. Leena Dallasheh, "Nazarenes in the Turbulent Tide of Citizenships: Nazareth from 1940 to 1966" (PhD diss., New York University, 2012), 53.

18. Ahmad Marwat, *Al-Nasira—A'alam wa-Shakhsiyat 1800–1948* (Acre: Mu'assasat al-Aswar, 2009), 128–129

19. Dallasheh, "Nazarenes in the Turbulent Tide of Citizenships," 54. On the role of Fu'ad Nassar in nurturing political consciousness among the young generation, see Mun'im Jarjura, *Qamh Wa-Zawan* (Haifa: Dar 'Arabesk, 1994),138.

20. Interview conducted by the poet Naim Araidi at the Cultural Institute in Nazareth, December 26, 1992. Film provided by the Tawfiq Zayyad Institute; *Al-Faris*, 9. Zayyad himself provided some of the details of this story in an interview with 'Aql al-'Awit, *al-Ittihad*, February 26, 1988.

21. *Al-Faris*, 9.

22. An interview conducted by the poet Naim Araidi at the Cultural Institute in Nazareth, December 26, 1992. Film provided by the Tawfiq Zayyad Institute.

23. *Al-Ittihad*, February 25, 1983.

24. Salim Tamari, Munir Fakhr al-Din, and Muhannad Abd al-Hamid, "Hanna Abu Hanna: Rihlat Al-Adab wa-l-Siyasa wa-l-Muqawama," *Majalat al-Dirasat al-Falastiniyya* 105 (2016): 92–109.

25. Each of the three teachers taught in multiple cities simultaneously, and the dates they arrived in Nazareth are unclear. The poet Hanna Abu Hanna remembers that they came during the revolt in 1938, when he was in fourth grade (Tamari, al-Din, and al-Hamid, "Hanna Abu Hanna," 97). This date, however, is incompatible with biographical publications about Shahin, who most likely had not begun teaching in Nazareth before 1942 (Shahin completed high school in Nablus in 1939 and graduated from the Arab College in Jerusalem in 1942; http://www.nablus-city.net/?page=details&cat=9&newsID=2220), but it is possible that the two other teachers, who came from villages near Nazareth, taught there earlier. On the affiliation of Shahin and Khuri with the National League for Liberation, see Ahmad Marwat, *Al-Nasira—A'alam wa-Shakhsiyat 1800–1948* (Acre: Muassasat al-Aswar, 2009), 197.

26. Zachary Lockman, *Comrades and Enemies: Arab and Jewish Workers in Palestine* (Berkeley: University of California Press, 1996); Dallasheh, "Nazarenes in the Turbulent Tide of Citizenships."

27. Dallasheh, "Nazarenes in the Turbulent Tide of Citizenships," 44.

28. Ibid., 40.

29. Ibid., 41.

30. Ibid, 44–46.

31. Joel Beinin, *Was the Red Flag Flying There? Marxist Politics and the Arab-Israeli Conflict in Egypt and Israel, 1948–1965* (Berkeley: University of California Press, 1990), 42.

32. Budeiri, *The Palestine Communist Party*, 108.

33. Abigail Jacobson, "Between Ideology and Practice, National Conflict and Anti-Imperialist Struggle: The National Liberation League in Palestine," *Nations and Nationalism* 25, no. 4 (2019): 1412–1431.

34. Ibid.

35. "Al-Shuyu'iyya wa-l-qawmiyya," *al-Ittihad*, October 1, 1944.

36. Dallasheh, "Nazarenes in the Turbulent Tide of Citizenships," 50.

37. Jarjura, *Qamh Wa-Zawan*, 81 (according to one account, the true founder of the bookstore was Fu'ad Nassar himself, for the purpose of developing political consciousness in the city).

38. "Mun'im jarjura—al-munadil aladhi lam talun lahu kana," *al-Ittihad*, March 2, 1979.

39. David Halevi, "Tawfıq Zayyad, 'Od nitsba' otakh be-adom, moledet," *Monitin*, February 1981, 34–38.

40. Bingbing Wu, "Secularism and Secularization in the Arab World." *Journal of Middle Eastern and Islamic Studies (in Asia)* 1, no. 1 (2007): 55–65.

41. Abied Alsulaiman, "The Adaptation of the Terms 'Laicism,' 'Secularism' and 'Laïcité' in Arabic," *Journal of Internationalization and Localization* 3, no. 1 (2016); Talal Asad, *Formations of the Secular: Christianity, Islam, Modernity* (Stanford: Stanford: Stanford University Press, 2003), 206–207.

42. Khalidi, *Palestinian Identity*, 37–39, 86.

43. Ibid., 115.

44. Laura Robson, *Colonialism and Christianity in Mandate Palestine* (Austin: University of Texas Press, 2011), 96.

45. Ibid., 64; Adnan Abu-Ghazaleh, "Arab Cultural Nationalism in Palestine during the British Mandate," *Journal of Palestine Studies* 1, no. 3 (1972): 64; Beverley Milton-Edwards, *Islamic Politics in Palestine* (London: I. B. Tauris, 1999), 20; Baruch Kimmerling and Joel Migdal, *The Palestinian People: A History* (Cambridge, MA: Harvard University Press, 2003).

46. Charles Taylor, *A Secular Age* (Cambridge, MA: Harvard University Press, 2009), 2.

47. *Al-Faris*, 11.

48. Haya Kadmon, "Prisat shalom lohemet mi-natseret," *Kol ha-'Am*, June 11, 1958.

49. Interview with As'ad Kannana, August 12, 2015.

50. Talal Asad, *Formations of the Secular: Christianity, Islam, Modernity* (Stanford: Stanford University Press, 2003), 16,

51. Hasan Al-Banna, *What Is Our Message?* 5th ed. (Lahore, Pakistan: Islamic Publications, 1995), 31.

52. Khalil Sakakini, *Yawmiyat Khalil al-Sakakini: Yawmiyat, Rasa'il, Ta'ammulat: Al-Kitab Al-Awal*, ed. Akram Musallam (Ramallah: Markaz Khalil al-Sakakini al-Thaqafi: Mu'assasat al-Dirasat al-Muqaddasiyah, 2003).

53. Ishaq Musa Husayni, *Khalil Al-Sakakini: Al-Adib Al-Mujaddid* (Jerusalem: Markaz al-Abhath al-Islamiyya, 1989).

54. Susan Laila Ziadeh, "A Radical in His Time: The Thought of Shibli Shumayyil and Arab Intellectual Discourse (1882–1917)" (PhD diss., University of Michigan, 1991), 267.

55. Sakakini, *Yawmiyat Khalil al-Sakakini*, 158.

56. Asad, *Formations of the Secular*, 196.

57. For example, *al-Karmil*, October 21, 1921, August 16, 1929.

58. Asad, *Formations of the Secular*, 197

59. Tamir Sorek, *Palestinian Commemoration in Israel: Calendars, Monuments, and Martyrs* (Stanford: Stanford University Press, 2015), 28–29.

60. *Al-Karmil*, March 22, 1924, 1.

61. *Filastin*, March 7, 1924.

62. Mona Hassan, *Longing for the Lost Caliphate: A Transregional History* (Princeton, NJ: Princeton University Press, 2017), 174–178.

63. Awad Halabi, "Liminal Loyalties: Ottomanism and Palestinian Responses to the Turkish War of Independence, 1919–22, "*Journal of Palestine Studies* 41, no. 3 (2012).

64. Abied, "The Adaptation of the Terms 'Laicism.'"

65. Azzam Tamimi, "The Origins of Arab Secularism," in *Islam and Secularism in the Middle East*, ed. Azzam Tamimi and Jon L. Espositio (New York: New York University Press, 2000), 17.

66. See, for example, *Filastin*, March 7, 1924; *al-Karmil*, March 22, 1924.

67. Najati Sidqi, *Mudhakkirat Najati Sidqi* [The memoirs of Najati Sidqi] (Beirut: Mu'assasat al-Dirasat al-Filastiyya, 2001), 47.

68. Musa Budeiri, *Shuyu'iyun fi Falastin: Shathaya Ta'rikh Munsa* [Communists in

Palestine: Fragments of a forgotten narrative] (Ramallah: MUWATIN—The Palestinian Institute for the Study of Democracy, 2013), 58–59.

69. Dalia Karpel, "A Revolutionary Life," *Haaretz*, December 9, 2004.

70. Dothan, *Adumim*, 401.

71. Budeiri, *The Palestine Communist Party*, 137–138.

72. See "al-Ittihad al-Sufiaty wa-l-din," *al-Ittihad*, June 4, 1944.

73. Narjis Tawhidi Far, *Abu al-'Ala' al-Ma'arri: Dirasah fi Mu'taqadatihi al-Diniyya* (Beirut: Dar Sadir, 2011), 79–84.

74. Reynold A. Nicholson, *Studies in Islamic Poetry* (Cambridge: Cambridge University Press, 1969), 173.

75. Matthew Reynolds, "Introduction," in Abu l-'Ala al-Ma'arri, *The Epistle of Forgiveness* (New York: NYU Press, 2016).

76. The source of the story is Naila Zayyad.

77. Dallasheh, "Nazarenes in the Turbulent Tide of Citizenships."

78. *Al-Faris*, 12.

79. Budeiri, *The Palestine Communist Party*, 234.

80. Dothan, *Adumim*, 500.

81. Interview conducted by Musa Budeiri with Fahmi al-Salfiti, in Budeiri, *Shuyu'iyun fi Falastin*, 235.

82. "A Communist View of the Middle East" [unsigned interview with Tawfiq Zayyad], *MERIP Reports*, no. 55 (March 1977): 18–20.

83. Peretz Kidron, "Truth Whereby Nations Live," in *Blaming the Victims: Spurious Scholarship and the Palestinian Question*, ed. Edward Said and Christopher Hitchens (London: Verso, 1988), 87.

84. Benny Morris, *The Birth of the Palestinian Refugee Problem Revisited* (Cambridge: Cambridge University Press, 2004), 418–420.

85. Mustafa Abbasi, "Kibush Natseret: Ha-'Ir he-'Aravit She-Sarda et ha-Milhama," *'Iyonim bi-Tkumat Yisra'el* 20 (2010).

86. Geremy Forman, "Military Rule, Political Manipulation, and Jewish Settlement: Israeli Mechanisms for Controlling Nazareth in the 1950s," *Journal of Israeli History* 25, no. 2 (2006).

87. Charles S. Kamen, "After the Catastrophe I: The Arabs in Israel, 1948–51," *Middle Eastern Studies* 23, no. 4 (1987): 475.

88. About this policy, see Shira Robinson, *Citizen Strangers: Palestinians and the Birth of Israel's Liberal Settler State* (Stanford: Stanford Univesrsity Press, 2014).

89. See "Geirushim hamoniyyim shel toshvei natseret," *Kol ha-'Am*, November 22, 1949.

90. Interview by 'Aql al-'Awit, *al-ittihad,* February 26, 1988.

91. "Hamonei Natseret qamu lehagen 'al ha-tsedek," *Kol ha-'Am*, November 28, 1949.

92. Dallasheh, "Nazarenes in the Turbulent Tide of Citizenships," 61.

93. Danna Piroyansky, *Ramle Remade: The Israelisation of an Arab Town, 1948–1967* (Haifa: Pardes, 2014).

94. See Tamar Gozansky, *Mizrahi Communists: The Struggle against Ethnic Discrimination and for Housing Rights* (Haifa: Pardes, 2018), 43. The presence of Tawfiq Zayyad in Ramle after the war was confirmed also by Adib Abu Rahmun and Naila Zayyad.

95. Letter by Intelligence Services to the Ministry of Religions, December 20, 1948, "'Avodat Po'alim mi-natseret be-lod ve-ramle," Israel State Archive, RG49/297/16.

96. Letter from Avraham Kidron from the Intelligence Services to Minister of Minorities, December 19, 2018. Israel State Archive, RG49/297/16.

CHAPTER 2

1. Shira Robinson, *Citizen Strangers: Palestinians and the Birth of Israel's Liberal Settler State* (Stanford: Stanford Univesrsity Press, 2014), 68–112.

2. Cary Nelson, *Revolutionary Memory: Recovering the Poetry of the American Left* (London: Routledge, 2001). Greg Dawes, *Aesthetics and Revolution: Nicaraguan Poetry, 1979–1990* (Minneapolis: University of Minnesota Press, 1993).

3. See Salma K. Jayyusi, *Trends and Movements in Modern Arabic Poetry,* vol. 2 (Leiden: Brill, 1977), 655; 'Izz al-Din al-Manassira, "Muqadamma: Tawfiq Zayyad—al-Sha'ir, al-Sha'b wal-Qadiya," in *Diwan Tawfiq Zayyad*, ed. 'Izz al-Din al-Manassira (Beirut: Dar al-'Awda, 1970).

4. Socialist realism is an artistic style developed in the Soviet Union and is characterized by the glorified depiction of communist values.

5. Hanna Abu Hanna, *Rihlat Al-Bahth 'an Al-Turath* (Haifa: al-Wadi, 1994), 108.

6. Maha Nassar, *Brothers Apart: Palestinian Citizens of Israel and the Arab World* (Stanford: Stanford University Press, 2017), 71.

7. Honaida Ghanem, *Reinventing the Nation: Palestinians Intellectuals in Israel* [in Hebrew] (Jerusalem: Magnes Press, 2009).

8. See, for example, an interview with 'Aql al-'Awit, *al-Ittihad,* February 26, 1988.

9. Salim Al-'Atawna, *Tawfiq Zayyad, Dirasa Tahliliya fi Intajihi al-Adabi* (Beersheeba: Beersheeba Kaye Academic College of Education, 2017), 133.

10. 'Izz al-Din al-Manassira, "Muqadamma: Tawfiq Zayyad—al-Sha'ir, al-Sha'b

wal-Qadiya," in *Diwan Tawfiq Zayyad*, ed. 'Izz al-Din al-Manassira (Beirut: Dar al-'Awda, 1970).

11. Ibid.; Avraham Yinon, "Tawfiq Zayyad: 'We Are the Majority Here'"; Salim Jubran, "Tawfiq Zayyad fi al-Diwan: 'Ashuddu 'ala' Ayadikum' Sha'ir Ya'arifu Sahr al-Basata," in *Dirasat fi al-Adab al-Filastini al-Mahali*, ed. Nabih al-Qasim (Acre: Dar al-Aswar, 1987), 72 (originally published in *al-Jadid* in May 1967).

12. Leena Dallasheh, "Nazarenes in the Turbulent Tide of Citizenships: Nazareth from 1940 to 1966" (PhD diss., New York University, 2012), 45–46.

13. Ibid., 57–59.

14. "A Communist View of the Middle East" [interview with Tawfiq Zayyad], *Merip Reports*, no. 55 (March 1977): 18–20; Moshe Kohn, "Red Mayor for Jerusalem," *Jerusalem Post*, December 19, 1975, 10–11.

15. "Ha-mishtara patha be-esh 'al haganat muvtalim be-Natseret," *Kol ha-'Am*, February 23, 1950; "Hafgana komonistit 'Arvit be-Natseret," *Ma'ariv*, February 23, 1950.

16. Israel State Archive, Prime Minister Advisor for Arab Affairs, GL-17109/44.

17. "A Communist View of the Middle East."

18. Y. Kinarot, "Natser lo ba le-'ezrat tawfiq zayyad," *Ma'ariv*, June 17, 1957, 4.

19. Nazareth Municipality, *Al-Faris—Tawfiq Zayyad, al-Insan, al-Qa'id, al-Sha'ir* (Nazareth: al-Hakim, 1994), 14, 22.

20. Ervand Abrahamian, *Iran between Two Revolutions* (Princeton, NJ: Princeton University Press, 1982), 266.

21. Tawfiq Zayyad, "'Abadan," *Ashuddu 'ala Ayadikum* (Acre: Matba'at Abu Rahmun, 1994), 150. My translation.

22. "Al-Nassira tastaqbilu abtal 'Abadan," *al-Ittihad*, October 20, 1951.

23. Tawfiq Zayyad interviewed by 'Aql al-'Awit, *al-Ittihad*, February 26, 1988.

24. Ahmad H. Sa'di, "Control and Resistance at Local-Level Institutions: A Study of Kafr Yassif's Local Council under the Military Government," *Arab Studies Quarterly* 23, no. 3 (2001): 31–47; Tawfiq Kana'na, *Dhikrayat Khityar lam Tamut Ajyaluhu* [Memoirs of an old man whose generation has not died], 'Arraba, self-published, n.d., 25–28; Forman, "Military Rule, Political Manipulation, and Jewish Settlement."

25. Tawfiq Zayyad, "Where Are Our Payments Going?" (Ila ayna yadh-hab ma nadfa'?), *al-Jadid*, 1, no. 11 (September 1954): 18–20. Translation by Aida Bamia.

26. "Anshei maki sharim ve-rokdim be-hutsut Natseret," *ha-Herut*, April 14, 1954.

27. Geremy Forman, "Military Rule, Political Manipulation, and Jewish Settlement: Israeli Mechanisms for Controlling Nazareth in the 1950s," *Journal of Israeli History* 25, no. 2 (2006).

28. Mustafa Abbasi, "Kibush Natseret: Ha-'Ir he-'Aravit She-Sarda et ha-Milhama," *'Iyonim bi-Tkumat Yisra'el* 20 (2010).

29. Dallasheh, "Nazarenes in the Turbulent Tide of Citizenships," 151.

30. Ibid.; Forman, "Military Rule, Political Manipulation, and Jewish Settlement."

31. Ilana Kaufman, *Arab National Communism in the Jewish State* (Gainesville: University Press of Florida, 1997), 50.

32. "On the Situation on the Nazareth Party Organization," in "Letters to the Districts," Nazareth District 1960–1964, ICP collection, Yad Tabenkin Archive.

33. Kaufman, *Arab National Communism in the Jewish State*, 43–44.

34. "Small dictators" probably refers to Saliba Khamis. Although the report recommended that Khamis continue to serve as the branch secretary, it seems that instability in the Nazareth branch continued, because in December 1953, at the opening of the party campaign for the local election, Tawfiq Zayyad was mentioned as the branch secretary and the speaker who opened the inaugural meeting (*al-Ittihad*, December 4, 1953). Two years later, Khamis was described in the press again as the branch secretary.

35. Y. Kinarot, Y. "Natser lo ba le-'ezrat Tawfiq Zayyad," *Ma'ariv*, June 17, 1957, 4.

36. Ibid.

37. For details about these activists and their protest, see Kana'na. *Dhikrayat Khityar lam Tamut Ajyaluhu*, 25–28.

38. *Al-Ittihad*, May 7, 1954.

39. "Pkudat hityatsvut li-shnei havrei maki be-Natseret," *Davar*, May 4, 1954.

40. Sarah Osacky-Lazar, "He-'Arvim ba-'Asor ha-Rishon," in *Yisrael ba-'Asor ha-Rishon,* vol. 6, ed. Binyamin Neuberger (Ra'anana: Open University, 2001–2011), 54.

41. *'Al ha-Mishmar,* May 25, 1954, 3.

42. Forman, "Military Rule, Political Manipulation, and Jewish Settlement."

43. Minutes of First Nazareth Municipal Council Meeting; "Mahalakh ha-yeshivah ha-rishonah shel ha-nivharim la-mo'etzah" [The first meeting of elected council members], June 9, 1954, Israel State Archive, G-5431/16, 'Iriyat Natzeret—part 1.

44. "Pratikol ha-yeshiva ha-rishona shel 'Iriyat Natseret," Israel State Archive, G-5431/16, "Iriyat Natzeret—part 1" (this second version of the meeting minutes was written by Moshe Ruah himself).

45. Ibid.

46. Ibid.

47. Ibid.

48. Dallasheh, "Nazarenes in the Turbulent Tide of Citizenships," 204.

49. Forman, "Military Rule, Political Manipulation, and Jewish Settlement."

50. Dallasheh, "Nazarenes in the Turbulent Tide of Citizenships."

51. Q. Menahem, "Natseret—hevlei leida shel 'iriya hadasha," *Davar*, July 2, 1954, 7.

52. Memorandum from the Meeting of the Minority Department at the Ministry of Interior, July 7, 1954, "Local Authorities," Israel State Archive-PMO-ArabAffairs-Advisor-000ev5c.

53. Dallasheh, "Nazarenes in the Turbulent Tide of Citizenships," 219–220.

54. *Al-Ittihad*, January 15, 1957, 1.

55. "Miflaga Komonistit Yisraelit—Mehoz Natseret," Yad Tabenkin Archive, 10–16/14/8.

56. Y. Kinarot,. "Natser lo ba le-'ezrat Tawfiq Zayyad," *Ma'ariv*, June 17, 1957, 4.

57. *Al-Ittihad*, December 2, 1955, 1.

58. Tamir Sorek, *Palestinian Commemoration in Israel: Calendars, Monuments, and Martyrs* (Stanford: Stanford University Press, 2015), 30–31.

59. See Alan Davies, *The Crucified Nation: A Motif in Modern Nationalism* (Eastbourne, UK: Sussex Academic Press, 2010), 89–107.

60. *Al-Ittihad*, April 10, 1956.

61. "Mithadesh mishpat 'asqan 'Aravi shel maki ha-ne'esham bi-tqifat shotrim," *Ma'ariv*, December 19, 1956.

62. "Ushar zikui Zayyad mi-Natseret," *Ma'ariv*, August 20, 1958, 3.

63. The opening line of the ode "Hasd al-Jamajim" [The harvest of skulls]. First published in *al-Jadid* 4, no. 1 (1957): 25–30. Translation by Aida Bamia.

64. For a detailed outline of the Kafr Qasim massacre, see Rubik Rosenthal, "Who Killed Fatma Sarsur," in *Kafr Kassem: Myth and History* [in Hebrew], ed. R. Rosenthal (Tel Aviv: Hakibbutz Hame'uhad, 2000). For the political role of the Kafr Qasim commemorations, see Shira Robinson, "Local Struggle, National Struggle: Palestinian Responses to the Kafr Qasim Massacre and Its Aftermath, 1956–1966," *International Journal of Middle East Studies* 35, no. 3 (2003), and Sorek, *Palestinian Commemoration in Israel*.

65. Salim Al-'Atawna, *Tawfiq Zayyad, Dirasa Tahliliya fi Intajihi al-Adabi* (Beersheeba: Beersheeba Kaye Academic College of Education, 2017), 133, 165.

66. Translation by Aida Bamia.

67. My translation.

68. Sharif Yunis, *Nida' al-Sha'b : Ta'rikh Naqdi lil-Idyulujiya al-Nasiriyya* (Cairo: Dar al-Shuruq, 2012).

69. Panayiotis J. Vatikioti, *Nasser and His Generation* (London: Croom Helm, 1978), 275–277.

70. Maha Nassar, *Brothers Apart: Palestinian Citizens of Israel and the Arab World* (Stanford: Stanford University Press, 2017), 50.

71. Ghazi Falah, "Israeli 'Judaization' Policy in Galilee," *Journal of Palestine Studies* 20, no. 4 (1991).

72. Dallasheh, "Nazarenes in the Turbulent Tide of Citizenships," 223.

73. "Lan takun al-Nasira janub Afriqya jadida," *al-Ittihad*, January 22, 1957.

74. Kaufman, *Arab National Communism in the Jewish State*, 87.

75. The Histadrut, the general federation of the working unions in Israel, worked closely with the government and the ruling party. Until 1966, the Histadrut included only Jewish workers.

76. Mapam was a socialist-Zionist party that was relatively successful among Palestinians in Israel.

77. Ibid.

78. "3 hodshei ma'atsar," *Kol ha-'Am*, May 12, 1958.

79. Elie Rekhess, *The Arab Minority in Israel: Between Communism and Arab Nationalism, 1965–1991* [in Hebrew] (Tel-Aviv: Ha-Kibutz He-Meuhad, 1993), 31.

80. Tawfiq Zayyad, "We Have a People Who Knows the Way," *al-Jadid*, May 1960, 8–10.

81. "Rashei maki be-Natseret ne'etsru ha-layla," *Ma'ariv*, April 30, 1958, 1.

82. Central Committee of the Israeli Communist Party, *Ha-Emet 'al Meora 'ot Ha-1 be-May be-Natseret* [The truth about the First of May events in Nazareth] (Israeli Communist Party, 1958), 3–4.

83. Zayyad, "We Have a People Who Knows the Way."

84. Ibid.

85. Ibid.

86. Ibid. See also *Kol ha-'Am*, "hishtolelut ha-mimshal ha-tsvai nimshekhet," May 4, 1958; Joel Beinin, *Was the Red Flag Flying There? Marxist Politics and the Arab-Israeli Conflict in Egypt and Israel, 1948–1965* (Berkeley: University of California Press, 1990), 202; Dallasheh, "Nazarenes in the Turbulent Tide of Citizenships," 73–74.

87. Tawfiq Zayyad, "We Have a People Who Knows the Way."

88. *Kol ha-'Am*, June 3, 1958.

89. Zayyad might be referring here to some Palestinian communists who were persecuted in 1948. For example, the Egyptian forces that occupied territories in the south of the country arrested some NLL activists; Imil Tuma was arrested in Lebanon in April 1948 and confined for five months. See Musa al-Budairi, "Iqrar nil-Dhanb: Imil Tuma wal-Taqsim aladhi lam Yahdath," *Bidayat*, no. 18–19 (2017/2018).

90. *Kol ha-'Am*, June 3, 1958.

91. Haya Kadmon, "Prisat shalom lohemet mi-natseret," *Kol ha-'Am*, June 11, 1958.

92. Ibid.

93. Letter from Hanna Abu Hanna to Naila Zayyad, May 2, 1999.

94. Tawfiq Zayyad's interview with the poet Na'im 'Araidi at the Cultural Institute in Nazareth, December 26, 1992. Film provided by the Tawfiq Zayyad Institute.

95. Tawfiq Zayyad, "Behind the Bars," *Ashuddu 'Ala Ayadikum*, 17. Translated by Aida Bamia.

96. *Al-Jadid*, 6, 1958, 38–40.

97. Tawfiq Zayyad, "The Reward for the Victory," *Kalimat Muqatila* (Acre: Matba'at Abu Rahmun, 1994), 56. Translated by Aida Bamia.

98. Avraham Yinon, "Tawfiq Zayyad: 'We Are the Majority Here,'" in *The Arabs in Israel: Continuity and Change*, ed. Aharon Layish (Jerusalem: Magness Press, 1981).

99. Muhammad Ibrahim Huwar, *Al-Qabd 'ala al-Jamr: Tajribat al-Sijn fi al-Shi'r al-Mu'asir* (Beirut: al-Mu'assasa al-'Arabiyya li-l-Dirasat wa-l-Nashr, 2004).

100. Interview conducted by Issam Aburaya with Tawfiq Kana'na, June 29, 2015.

101. Tawfiq Zayyad, "Oh My People, Oh Branch of My Peers," *Ashuddu 'Ala Ayadikum*, 37–38. Translated by Aida Bamia.

102. Minutes of the Politburo Meeting, September 21, 1958, National Library of Israel (NLI), Communist Party Archive, V 1272 3 15. It is unclear what happened to the initiative to send Zayyad to Poland.

103. *Al-Ittihad*, October 14, 1958.

104. Interview with Muhammad 'Ali Taha, July 16, 2015.

CHAPTER 3

1. Joel Beinin, *Was the Red Flag Flying There? Marxist Politics and the Arab-Israeli Conflict in Egypt and Israel, 1948–1965* (Berkeley: University of California Press, 1990), 97.

2. Ibid., 201.

3. Anouar Abdel-Malek, "Nasserism and Socialism," *Socialist Register* 1, no. 1 (1964).

4. Tawfiq Zayyad, "'Abadan," *Ashuddu 'ala Ayadikum* (Acre: Matba'at Abu Rahmun, 1994), 7–8. My translation.

5. Beinin, *Was the Red Flag Flying There?* 216. See also Maha Nassar, *Brothers Apart: Palestinian Citizens of Israel and the Arab World* (Stanford: Stanford University Press, 2017), 94–97.

6. Maha Tawfik Nassar, "Affirmation and Resistance: Press, Poetry and the For-

mation of National Identity among Palestinian Citizens of Israel, 1948–1967" (PhD diss., University of Chicago, 2006), 198–199; Honaida Ghanem, *Reinventing the Nation: Palestinians Intellectuals in Israel* [in Hebrew] (Jerusalem: Magnes Press, 2009).

7. Ghanem, *Reinventing the Nation*.

8. *Al-Ittihad*, March 1959, quoted in Nassar, *Brothers Apart*, 97.

9. Hanna Abu Hanna, quoted in Adina Hoffman, *My Happiness Bears No Relation to Happiness: A Poet's Life in the Palestinian Century* (New Haven: Yale University Press, 2009) , 264.

10. *Ha-'Olam ha-Zeh*, April 1, 1959. The report cites lines translated to Hebrew from Zayyad's poem that arguably appeared in *al-Ittihad*, but I could not find this poem anywhere. It is possible that the trigger for the anger toward Zayyad was "One of the Agents," whose publication fits the date referred to by *ha-'Olam ha-Zeh*.

11. Beinin, *Was the Red Flag Flying There?* 215–216.

12. Nassar, *Brothers Apart*, 97.

13. Pierre Clermont, *Le Communisme à Contre-Modernité* (Paris: Presses universitaires de Vincennes, 1993).

14. Johann P. Arnason, "Communism and Modernity," *Daedalus* 129, no. 1 (2000).

15. This is especially evident in the writing of the Palestinian educator Khalil al-Sakakini: Khalil Sakakini and Akram Musallam, *Yawmiyat Khalil al-Sakakini: Yawmiyat, Rasa'il wa-Ta'ammulat—al-Kitab al-Awal* (Ramallah: Markaz Khalil al-Sakakini al-Thaqafı : Mu'assasat al-Dirasat al-Muqaddasiyah, 2003). See also the discussion about Sakakini in Noah Haiduc-Dale, *Arab Christians in British Mandate Palestine: Communalism and Nationalism, 1917–1948* (Edinburgh: Edinburgh University Press, 2013), 35–36.

16. Weldon Matthews, *Confronting an Empire, Constructing a Nation: Arab Nationalists and Popular Politics in Mandate Palestine.* (London: Bloomsbury Academic, 2006), 260.

17. Musa Budeiri, *The Palestine Communist Party 1919–1948: Arab and Jew in the Struggle for Internationalism* (Chicago: Haymarket Books, 2010).

18. Hanna Abu Hanna, *Rihlat Al-Bahth 'an al-Turath* (Haifa: al-Wadi, 1994), 107.

19. Charles Taylor, *A Secular Age* (Cambridge, MA: Harvard University Press, 2009).

20. Ts. David, "Le-Haveri Tawfıq," *Kol ha-'Am*, June 21, 1957.

21. *Al-Jadid*, June 7, 1958, 39.

22. Nassar, *Brothers Apart*, 51.

23. Tawfıq Zayyad, "Ila 'umal aata al-mudribin," *Ashuddu 'ala Ayadakum*, 120. Translated by Aida Bamia.

24. *Kol ha-'Am*, August 16, 2016.

25. Zayyad, "al-Manashir al-muhtaraqa," *Ashuddu 'ala Ayadakum*, 31. Translated by Aida Bamia.

26. Ibid., 122–123. My translation.

27. The Sixth Meeting of the Central Committee, May 23, 1962, INL, Communist Party Archive, V 1272 3 231.

28. Tawfiq Zayyad, *Nasrawi fi al-Saha al-Hamra* (Nazareth: Al-Nahda, 1972), 10–13.

29. Mun'im Jarjura, *Qamh wa-Zawan* (Haifa: Dar 'Arabesk, 1994), 110.

30. My interview with Suhayl Diab, July 29, 2015.

31. *Al-Ittihad*, October 17, 1957.

32. A letter to Musbah Zayyad, February 25, 1963.

33. Mervyn Matthews, *Education in the Soviet Union: Policies and Institutions since Stalin* (London: Taylor & Francis, 2012), 185.

34. My interview with As'ad Kananeh, August 12, 2015.

35. Tawfiq Zayyad to his parents, January 17, 1963.

36. Walter Benjamin, *Walter Benjamin: Selected Writings, 1938–1940* (Cambridge, MA: Belknap Press of Harvard University Press, 2003), 401.

37. Zayyad, *Nasrawi fi al-Saha al-Hamra'*, 8–9.

38. Zayyad, "Amam Darih Linin," *Ashuddu 'ala Ayadikum*, 66–67. Translated by Aida Bamia.

39. Sa'id Bin Nasir al-Ghamdi, *Al-Inhiraf Al-'Aqdi fi Adab al-Hadatha wa-Fikruha* (Jeddah: Dar al-andalus al-khdraa, 2003), 253, 392, 532.

40. "Syrian Poet Adonis Says Poetry 'Can Save Arab World,'" *Daily Star Lebanon*, September 27, 2016, http://www.dailystar.com.lb/Arts-and-Ent/Culture/2016/Sep-27/373857-syrian-poet-adonis-says-poetry-can-save-arab-world.ashx.

41. Eviatar Zerubavel, "The French Republican Calendar: A Case Study in the Sociology of Time," *American Sociological Review* 42, no. 6 (1977).

42. Zayyad, *Nasrawi fi al-Saha al-Hamra'*, 45.

43. Ibid., 46.

44. Ibid., 47.

45. Tawfiq Zayyad, *Hal Al-Dunya: Qisas Qasirah* (Beirut: Dar al-Quds, 1970), 6.

46. Ibid.

47. Ibid., 10.

48. 'Adel al-Asta, "Tawfiq Zayyad as a Teller and as a Critic," https://staff.najah.edu/media/sites/default/files/_دايز_قاصِوأناقدأ.pdf.

49. Salim Al-'Atawna, *Tawfiq Zayyad, Dirasa Tahliliya fi Intajihi al-Adabi* (Beer-

sheeba: Beersheeba Kaye Academic College of Education, 2017); Nu'aima al-Ahmad, *Tawfiq Zayyad—al-Sha'ir al-Munadil* (Haifa: Maktabat Kul Shee, 2018).

50. Bin Nasir al-Ghamdi, *Al-Inhiraf Al-'Aqdi*, 517.

51. "Piskei din hamurim be-natseret," *Zo ha-Derekh*, August 26, 1964.

52. The source of this story is Nazir Majali who heard it from both Emile Habibi and Zayyad's father-in-law, Yusuf Sabbagh.

53. Ilana Kaufman, *Arab National Communism in the Jewish State* (Gainesville: University Press of Florida, 1997), 86–87.

CHAPTER 4

1. Erving Goffman, *The Presentation of Self in Everyday Life* (Garden City, NY: Doubleday, 1959), 31.

2. Nazareth Municipality, *Al-Faris—Tawfiq Zayyad, al-Insan, al-Qa'id, al-Sha'ir* (Nazareth: al-Hakim, 1994), 22.

3. Berl Belati, *Ba-Ma'avak 'al ha-Kiyum ha-Yehudi: Li-Demuto Shel Mosheh Sneh* (Jerusalem: Y. Markus 1981), 125–135. See also Ilana Kaufman, *Arab National Communism in the Jewish State* (Gainesville: University Press of Florida, 1997), 35; Yair Bauml, *A Blue and White Shadow: The Israeli Establishment's Policy and Action among the Arab Citizens. The Formative Years: 1958–1968* (Haifa: Pardes, 2007), 263–269; Elie Rekhess, *The Arab Minority in Israel: Between Communism and Arab Nationalism 1965–1991* [in Hebrew] (Tel-Aviv: Ha-Kibutz He-Meuhad, 1993), 32–34.

4. *Zo ha-Derekh*, May 24, 1972.

5. Minutes of the Twenty-Fourth session of the Central Committee, March 9, 1972, NLI, Communist Party Archive/ V 1272 3 232.

6. Al-Arabiyya interview in 1993, https://www.youtube.com/watch?v=Q28O1Lm-8VzU.

7. Salma K. Jayyusi, *Trends and Movements in Modern Arabic Poetry* (Leiden: Brill, 1977), 665.

8. Tawfiq Zayyad, "Ashuddu 'ala Ayadikum," *Ashuddu 'ala Ayadikum* (Acre: Matba'at Abu Rahmun, 1994), 40–41. (Translation from Abdelwahab M. Elmessiri, *The Palestinian Wedding: A Bilingual Anthology of Contemporary Palestinian Resistance Poetry* (Washington, DC: Three Continents Press, 1982), 191.

9. Imil Tuma, "Al-Shi'r al-'Arabi al-Thawri fi Isra'il," *al-Jadid* 12, no. 1 (1965): 5–8. It is worth mentioning that Zayyad disliked Tuma, and he expressed this view in a meeting of the Central Committee in the early 1970s. It is possible that the tension between the two goes back to that episode.

10. Translated by Sharif Elmusa and Jack Collom, in Salma K. Jayyusi, *Anthology of Modern Palestinian Literature* (New York: Columbia University Press, 1992), 327.

11. "Ughniyat 15 'Ayar," *Falastin*, May 15, 1966.

12. Tawfiq Zayyad, "On the Trunk of an Olive Tree," translated by Abdelwahab Elmessiri in Elmessiri, *The Palestinian Wedding*, 55.

13. Ghassan Kanafani, *Adab Al-Muqawamah Fi Filasṭin Al-Muhtallah, 1948–1966* (Beirut: Dar al-Adab, 1966).

14. Ibid., 27.

15. Muhammad al-Jaza'iri, "Al-Muqawama bi-l-kilma fi Shi'r Tawfiq Zayyad," *al-Aadab* 15, no. 10 (1967).

16. *Al-Tariq*, 10–11, no. 28, (November–December 1968).

17. Fadwa Tuqan, a Palestinian poet from Nablus (1917–2003).

18. Fatah, the Palestinian National Liberation Movement, was a political movement established in 1959, and in the late 1960s, it operated the largest Palestinian guerrilla group.

19. Edouard Saab, "L'omniprésence en Jordanie des organizations Palestiniennes," *Le Monde*, December 7, 1968.

20. See, for example, Emile Habibi, "Unadikum," *al-Ittihad*, June 7, 1968, and "Adab al-muqawama," *al-Ittihad*, March 21, 1969.

21. Tawfiq Zayyad, "Al-Shi'r al-'Arabi al-Thawri fi isra'il," *al-Jadid*, October 8–9, 1966, 5–10.

22. Y. A. "Mulahathat awalia hawla: al-Shi'r al-'Arabi al-Thawri fi Isra'il,'" *Sawt al-Sha'ab*, October 1966, 10–11.

23. 'Adel al-Asta, "Tawfiq Zayyad as a Teller and as a Critic," https://staff.najah.edu/media/sites/default/files/أدقانوأَصِساق_دايز.pdf.

24. Zayyad, "Diwan 'Ashiq Min Falastin li-Mahmud Darwish," originally published in *al-Jadid* (December 1966).

25. Tawfiq Zayyad, "Khutwa ila al-khalf, 'ashr ila al-'amam," *Sujana al-Hurriyya* (Acre: Matba'at Abu Rahmun, 1994), 40.

26. "La taqulu li," *Kalimat Muqatila*, 1.

27. Ibid. Translation by Yousef Haddad.

28. Azmi Bishara, "The Arabs in Israel: Reading a Fragmented Political Discourse," in *Between the 'Me' and the 'Us,'"* [in Hebrew] ed. 'Azmi Bishara. Jerusalem: Van Leer Institute, Ha-kibbutz Ha-meuchad, 1999.

29. Minutes of the Eighteenth Session of the Central Committee, April 25, 1971, NLI, Communist Party Archive/V 1272 3 27; Minutes of the Twenty-Second Session

of the Central Committee, November 27, 1971, NLI/Archives/V 1272 3 232; Minutes of Twenty-Fourth Session of the Central Committee, March 9, 1972. NLI, Communist Party Archive, V 1272 3 232.

30. Minutes of the Twenty-Fourth Session of the Central Committee, March 9, 1972, NLI Communist Party Archive V 1272 3 232.

31. See Ehud Ya'ari, "Ha-kav ha-adom shel Rakah," *Davar*, February 16, 1973; Rekhess, *The Arab Minority in Israel*, 42–43.

32. Minutes of the Eleventh Meeting of the Central Committee, May 15–16, 1969 NLI Communist Party Archive /V 1272 3 25/.

33. *Al-Ittihad*, May 8, 1970. My translation.

34. Tawfīq Zayyad, *Ughniyyat al-Thawra wa-l-Ghadab* (Beirut: Dar al-Awda, 1970).

35. See a discussion of that omission in Avraham Yinon, "Tawfiq Zayyad: 'We Are the Majority Here,'" in *The Arabs in Israel: Continuity and Change*, ed. Aharon Layish (Jerusalem: Magness Press, 1981).

36. I do not know who is responsible for the first translation, which I found among Zayyad's personal documents. For the published translation, see ibid.

37. "Nehsaf ta fatah," *Davar*, July 25, 1971.

38. Ehud Ya'ari, "Ha-kav ha-adom shel Rakah," *Davar*, February 16, 1973.

39. My interview with Binyamin Gonen, August 17, 2015. See also Binyamin Gonen, *Hayim Adumim: Tahanot be-Hayey Komonist Yisraeli* (Haifa: Pardes, 2009), 90.

40. "Tawfik Zayyad," KR-635119 MV, file opened July 5, 1973, closed June 18, 1974, Security Services Archive in Prague.

41. Minutes of the Eighth Session of the Central Committee, September 15–16, 1973, NLI Communist Party Archive V1272 3 55.

42. On July 8, 1972, Israel assassinated the author Ghassan Kanafani and his niece by a bomb planted in his car.

43. Kamal Nasir was a Palestinian writer, assassinated during an Israeli raid on Beirut in April 1973, alongside dozens of other PLO members, including two of its senior leaders, Kamal Adwan and Muhammed Youssef al-Najjar.

44. Tafwiq Zayyad in an Interview with the poet Naim Araidi at the Cultural Institute in Nazareth, December 26, 1992. Film provided by the Tawfiq Zayyad Institute.

45. Tawfiq Zayyad, "Al-'Ubur al-Kabir," *al-Ittihad*, October 4, 1974, 2.

46. Danny Rubinstein, "Simhat ha-Gvura ve-ha-Tsliha," *Davar*, March 24, 1974.

47. Yoel Dar, *Davar*, October 15, 1974. My translation.

48. Moshe Dor, "Dma'ot ha-Simha shel Tawfiq Zayyad," *Ma'ariv*, October 18, 1984.

49. Minutes of the Fifteenth Session of the Central Committee, October 19, 1974, NLI Communist Party Archive, V 1272 3 37.

50. Ibid.

51. See Rekhess, *The Arab Minority in Israel*.

52. Minutes of the First Session of the Central Committee, February 8, 1969, NLI, Communist Party Archive, V 1272 3 23.

53. "Ha-Ve'ida ha-16 shel ha-Miflaga," *Zo ha-Derekh*, February 5, 1969.

54. Ibid.

55. Kaufman, *Arab National Communism in the Jewish State*, 94.

56. Press release of the Knesset Committee, November 5, 1974.

57. "Tguva Harifa shel Si'at Rakah," *Zo ha-Derekh*, November 13, 1974.

58. Ilyas Nasr Allah, *Shahadat 'Ala al-Qarn al-Filastini al-Awwal* [Testimonies on the first century of Palestine] (Beirut: Dar al-Farabi, 2016), 319.

59. The full Arabic text, "'Ubur aakhir 'ala al-'Ubur al-Kabir" [Another crossing, beyond the "The Great Crossing"], was published December 6, 1974, in *al-Ittihad*. Lecture notes provided by the Tawfiq Zayyad Institute. Quotes from the Hebrew speech appeared in "Tawfiq Zayyad: lo Nishba'ti ba-Knesset Emunim la-Kibush," *Ma'ariv*, November 12, 1974.

60. During the war, vehicles' lights in Israel were painted blue to reduce their visibility.

61. The translation from Hebrew to English is mine.

62. I did not trace the original request, but Barzilai's letter of response is available at the Tawfiq Zayyad Institute collection.

63. *Zo ha-Derekh*, July 2, 1975.

CHAPTER 5

1. Emile Habibi (signed as Juhaina), "Ma'arakat al-Nasira," November 13, 1970.

2. Quotes from the Shabak assessment appear in a letter from the adviser for Arab affairs, Shmuel Toledano, to Prime Minister Golda Meir: Israel State Archive, "Iriyat Natseret," G-6501/20, ISA-PMO-PrimeMinisterBureau-000327l, December 4, 1970.

3. Eli Eyal, "Natseret: Rakah mul kol ha-sh'ar," *Ma'ariv*, December 4, 1970.

4. *Al-Ittihad*, December 7, 1970.

5. Minutes of the First Meeting of the Central Committee, July 6, 1972, NLI Communist Party Archive V1272 3 29.

6. "Ha-Mahaloket be-Rakah 'asuya leharaif," *Davar*, December 15, 1972.

7. Elie Rekhess, *The Arab Minority in Israel: Between Communism and Arab Nationalism 1965–1991* [in Hebrew] (Tel-Aviv: Ha-Kibutz He-Meuhad, 1993), 102.

8. *Al-Ittihad*, August 21, 1973.

9. Henry Rosenfeld and Majid Al-Haj, *Arab Local Government in Israel* (Boulder, CO: Westview Press, 1990), 126–136.

10. Rekhess, *The Arab Minority in Israel*.

11. Naor Bar-Nir, "Madu'a shruya 'iriyat natseret be-mashber?" *Zo ha-Derekh*, April 12, 1974.

12. *Al-Ittihad*, May 25, 1974.

13. Ibid., June 28, 1974.

14. Ibid., July 26, 1974 September 3, 1974

15. "Invitation to the Palestine Liberation Organization," 2268th Plenary Meeting of the UN Assembly, October 14, 1974. https://undocs.org/en/A/RES/3210(XXIX).

16. For example, celebration of Dimitrov's seventy-fifth birthday in *Zo ha-Derekh*, June 18, 1957.

17. Yoel Dar, "Leha'arikh kehunat ha-va'ada he-qrua'h," *Davar*, October 15, 1974.

18. In a discussion at his office on January 29, 1975, Prime Minister Yitzhak Rabin said explicitly, "We concluded that if we conduct the elections on time, we almost certainly ensure the failure of the lists not affiliated with Rakah," Israel State Archive, Discussion Minutes, "Prime Minister Diaries," a-6/7020.

19. Ibid.

20. Ibid.

21. Daniel Bloch, "ha-Sakana she-bi-nfilat natseret li-yedey Rakah," *Davar*, November 25, 1975.

22. My interview with Ra'iq Jarjura, one of the leaders of the Association of Academics, July 26, 2017.

23. Nazareth Municipality, *Al-Faris—Tawfiq Zayyad, al-Insan, al-Qa'id, al-Sha'ir* (Nazareth: al-Hakim, 1994), 26; Suhayl Diab, "Fikr Jabhat al-Nasira al-Dimokratiyya," December 5, 2015, http://www.aljabha.org/index.asp?i=96142.

24. My interview with Nabil 'Oda, July 28, 2017.

25. Minutes of the Twenty-Second Session of the Central Committee, December 13–14, 1975, Communist Party Archive, V 1272 3 139, Minutes of the Central Committees Meetings, National Library.

26. Rekhess, *The Arab Minority in Israel*, 102.

27. *Al-Ittihad*, November 4, 1975. See also this suggestion at *Davar*'s editorial from October 27, 1975.

28. *Davar*, November 19, 1975.

29. *Zo ha-Derekh*, December 3, 1975.

30. Yosef Algazi, "Lekah ha-bhirot be-natseret," *Zo ha-Derekh*, December 17, 1975.

31. Ibid.

32. My interview with Suhayl Diab. July 29, 2015.

33. *Yedi'ot Aharonot*, December 10, 1975.

34. My interview with Suhayl Diab. July 29, 2015.

35. Zayyad's speech on the Eighteenth Congress of the Communist Party, *Zo ha-Derekh*, January 19, 1977.

36. *Al-Ittihad*, December 23, 1975.

37. Faysal Daraj, "Tawfiq Zayyad—sha'ir al-waqi'iyya al-muqatila," *Shu'un falastiniyya* 53–54 (January–February 1976): 96–108.

38. 'Isa al-Su'aibi, "Fi daw intikhabat al-nasira, " *Shu'un falastiniyya* 53–54 (January–February 1976): 216–220.

39. "Toledano mazhir mi-yad hazaka," *Davar*, December 14, 1975.

40. Yosef Algazi, "Lekah ha-bhirot be-natseret," *Zo ha-Derekh*, December 17, 1975.

41. Yosef Algazi, "Mo'etset natseret 'omedet lehikanes le-tafqida," *Zo ha-Derekh*, December 24, 1975.

42. *Davar*, December 22, 1975.

43. "Rosh 'iriya natseret: Misrad Ha-Pnim Mekapeah otanu," *Davar*, August 1, 1976.

44. *Davar*, August 2, 1977; "Ushar taktsiv 'Iriyat Natseret," *Davar*, August 28, 1977.

45. See Minutes of Meeting No. 292 of the Eighth Knesset Plenum, May 17, 1976, https://fs.knesset.gov.il/8/Plenum/8_ptm_253392.pdf.

46. Minutes of the Twenty-Fourth Meeting of the Central Committee, March 20, 1976, Israeli National Library, V 1272 3 141.

47. Ibid.

48. Ahmad H. Sa'di, "The Koenig Report and Israeli Policy towards the Palestinian Minority, 1965–1976: Old Wine in New Bottles," *Arab Studies Quarterly* 25, no. 3 (2003): 51–61. The document itself reflected internal struggles in the Israeli establishment; see Yitzhak Reiter, *National Minority, Regional Majority: Palestinian Arabs Versus Jews in Israel* (Syracuse, NY: Syracuse University Press, 2009), 45–46; Gadi Algazi, "The Deep State Is Speaking: The Koenig Report, 1976," *Tarabut*, http://www.tarabut.info/he/articles/article/koenig-report-1976/.

49. Reiter, *National Minority, Regional Majority*, 46.

50. Algazi, "The Deep State Is Speaking."

51. Letter from the Advisor on Arab Affairs to Prime Minster, July 15, 1976. Israel State Archive, GL-7430/4.

52. Reiter, *National Minority, Regional Majority*, 49.

53. An appendix to a letter from the Adviser on Arab Affairs, Binyamin Gur Aryeh, to the Director of the Ministry of Education, Eliezer Shmueli, February 26, 1981, Israel State Archive, GL-14517/8.

54. Ilanda Kaufman, *Arab National Communism in the Jewish State* (Gainesville: University Press of Florida, 1997), 100.

55. Minutes of Meeting No. 292 of the Eighth Knesset, Knesset Plenum, May 17, 1976, https://fs.knesset.gov.il/8/Plenum/8_ptm_253392.pdf.

56. Zayyad's speech in Minutes of Meeting No. 9 of the Ninth Knesset, Knesset Plenum, July 6, 1977, https://fs.knesset.gov.il/8/Plenum/8_ptm_253558.pdf.

57. *Al-Faris*, 30.

58. "Iftitiah 'urs al-'amal wal-karameh al-thani fi-l-Nasira," *al-Ittihad*, August 12, 1977.

59. "Nitan tsav ha-oser piturey menahel beit ha-sefer ve-sgano be-natseret," *Davar*, June 3, 1976.

60. "Takalot kalot bi-ftihat shnat ha-limudim," *Davar*, September 2, 1976.

61. Letter from Moshe Sharon to Aharon Barak, April 25, 1976; Israel State Archive, "Arab Education," GL-17998/5.

62. See a letter from Ezra Kopelevitz, director of the Arab Department in the Ministry of Education to the legal adviser of the Ministry, June 19, 1978. Israel State Archive, "Arab Education," GL-17998/5.

63. Tamir Sorek, *Palestinian Commemoration in Israel: Calendars, Monuments, and Martyrs* (Stanford: Stanford University Press, 2015), 175.

64. Kaufman, *Arab National Communism in the Jewish State*.

65. "Iriyat Natseret metakhnenet hakamat universita 'aratvit," *Davar*, September 14, 1980.

66. *Al-Ittihad*, October 31, 1980.

67. Yoel Dar, "Hikukhim be-natseret" *Davar*, March 26, 1976.

68. See the exchange of accusations between Zayyad and Habib in the Thirteenth Session of the Central Committee, November 16–17, 1978, , NLI Communist Party Archive V1272 3 114. It is noteworthy that at the time, Arab councilwomen were rare. As late as 1989, there were only three Arab councilwomen in Israel, among them Samyah Hakim, the first councilwomen in Nazareth who was elected that same year in the front list. Hanna Herzog, *Gendering Politics: Women in Israel* (Ann Arbor: University of Michigan Press, 2010), 175.

69. Minutes of the Politbureau discussion, March 23, 1977, NLI/The Communist Party Archive, V 1272 3 105.

70. Rosenfeld and Al-Haj, *Arab Local Government in Israel*, 69.

71. The title of an article in the PLP *Al-Watan* bulletin, October 25, 1984.

72. *Al-Ittihad*, April 16, 1986.

73. *Al-Sinara*, February 5, 1988. Zayyad's deputy, Ramiz Jeraysi, spent almost an entire council meeting refuting the allegations.

74. *Al-Watan*, October 28, 1988; Lutfi Mash'ur, editorial, *Al-Sinara*, October 7, 1988.

75. Tawfiq Zayyad, *Ana min hadhihi al-Madina wa-Qasa'id Jadida Ukhra* (Acre: Matba'at Abu Rahmun, 1994), 29. My translation.

CHAPTER 6

1. Minutes of the Twenty-Second Session of the Central Committee, December 13–14, 1975, NLI, Communist Party Archive, V 1272 3 139.

2. For detailed account of the developments that led to the March 30 strike, see Nabih Bashir, *The Land Day: Betwixt and Between—National and Civic* [in Arabic] (Haifa: Mada al-Carmel (in Arabic), 2006), and Elie Rekhess, *'Arviyey Yisrael ve-Hafka'at ha-Karka'ot ba-Galil* (Tel Aviv: Shilo'ah Institute, 1977).

3. For detailed description of the political mobilization before Land Day, see Rekhess, *'Arviyey Yisrael ve-Hafka'at ha-Karka'ot ba-Galil* and Bashir, *The Land Day*.

4. Rekhess, *'Arviyey Yisrael*, 18.

5. *Al-Ittihad*, May 5, June 27, 1975.

6. Ibid., October 31, 1975.

7. Ibid., February 20, 1976.

8. Ehud Ya'ari and Yoel Dar, "ha-Memshala lo tisog mi-tokhnit ha-hafqa'ot," *Davar*, March 7, 1976.

9. Yoel Dar, *Davar*, March 26, 1976.

10. Uri Standel, *Haaretz*, March 31, 1976.

11. *Al-Ittihad*, March 21, 1999.

12. Yoel Dar, "Rashei Ha-rashuyot ba-migzar he-'arvi neged ha-shvita," *Davar*, March 26, 1976. *Al-Ittihad* did not report about the results of the vote.

13. Rekhess, *'Arviyey Yisrael*, 28.

14. According to Jamal Tarabiyya, then the mayor of Sakhnin, the vote was open. *Al-Ittihad*, March 21, 1999.

15. See a discussion of the different versions at Bashir, *The Land Day*, 76.

16. Meir Vilner, "Yom ha-Adama ha-Rishon," 'Arakhim, February 1996.

17. Bashir, *The Land Day*, 76. Some details are based on my personal communication with Nabih Bashir.

18. Yoel Dar, "Hitya'atsuyot be-dereg bahir," *Davar*, 28, 1976.

19. Rekhess, 'Arviyey Yisrael, 5.

20. Yoel Dar, "Benatseret nivlemu ha-hitpar'uyot," *Davar*, March 31, 1976.

21. Ibid.

22. "Galilee Battles Indicate End to Docility of Israel's Arabs," *International Herald Tribune*, April 1, 1976.

23. Yoel Dar, "Benatseret."

24. Vilner, "Yom ha-Adama ha-Rishon."

25. Minutes of the Twenty-Fifth Meeting of the Central Committee, April 9, 1976, INL, Communist Party Archive, V 1272 3 140.

26. Rekhess, 'Arviyey Yisrael, 22.

27. Zayyad's speech at the Eighteenth Congress of the Communist Party, *Zo ha-Derekh*, January 19, 1977.

28. See Danny Rubinstein, "Mimadaf ha-sfarim ba-shtahim," *Davar*, January 9, 1979.

29. Ehud Ya'ari, "Reshamim mi-ve'idat Rakah," *Davar*, December 31, 1976.

30. My interview with Samih Ghanadri, July 30, 2017.

31. *Zo ha-Derekh*, April 12, 1976.

32. Uri Standel, *Haaretz*, March 31, 1976.

33. Haim Guri, *Davar*, June 13, 1981.

34. Yehoshu'a Bitsur, "Briha mi-hitmodedut," *Ma'ariv*, November 10, 1985.

35. *Al-Ittihad*, May 4, 1976.

36. Dabke is an Arab folk dance common in the Levant countries.

37. Hora is a type of circle dance originating in the Balkans and Eastern Europe that played a foundational role in modern Israeli folk dancing.

38. Zayyad: "O ezrahim mele'im, o hishtaykhut le-medina aheret," *Haaretz*, May 4, 1976. Haim Nahman Bialik is considered the "national poet" in Zionist terminology. His poems have been taught in both Jewish and Arab schools.

39. This statement was recorded by the researcher Elie Rekhes and appeared in Rekhess, 'Arviyey Yisrael, 39. The press reports provided only a paraphrased version.

40. The Movement for Greater Israel, a political organization in Israel during the late 1960s and 1970s, called on the Israeli government to keep the areas that Israel captured in the 1967 war and to settle them with Jewish populations.

41. *Davar*, May 4, 1976.

42. "Be-Hag sameah berekh Zayyad be-mesiba li-khvod yom ha-'atsmaut," *Davar*, May 3, 1976.

43. *Ma'ariv*, June 9, 1980. I could not gain access to the speech as it was originally broadcast, so I cannot determine how accurate the quotation in *Ma'ariv* was.

44. Ibid.

45. Ibid.

46. Israel Landers, "ha-shiryun shel ha-hakim," *Davar*, June 17, 1980.

47. Elie Rekhess, *The Arab Minority in Israel: Between Communism and Arab Nationalism, 1965–1991* [in Hebrew] (Tel-Aviv: Ha-Kibutz He-Meuhad, 1993), 112–117.

48. Yosef Tsuri'el, "Tsavei rituk neged pe-'ilei Rakah 'aravim," *Ma'ariv*, June 9, 1980.

49. *Al-Ittihad*, June 10, 1980.

50. Minutes of the 341st session of the Ninth Knesset Plenum, June 9, 1980.

51. An irregular session of the Central Committee, June 12, 1980, NLI/ Communist Party Archive, V 1272 3 147.

52. A letter from the attorney general to the minister of justice, June 26, 1980, Israel State Archive, 4329/3-A.

53. "Law for the Amendment of the Prevention of Terrorism Ordinance," Knesset Archive, https://fs.knesset.gov.il//9/law/9_ls1_290968.PDF.

54. "Seventh division" (*liga zayn*) is a reference to soccer and its divisional system, with the seventh division being a very low division—indeed, lower than any existing one. Furthermore, Zayyad's choice of terms carried a vulgar sexual denotation: in Hebrew, *zayn* is the seventh letter of the alphabet but is also used to mean "dick."

55. Minutes of the 361st Session of the Ninth Knesset Plenum, July 28, 1980.

56. Avraham Yinon, "Tawfiq Zayyad: 'We Are the Majority Here,'" in *The Arabs in Israel: Continuity and Change*, ed. Aharon Layish (Jerusalem: Magness Press, 1981), 213.

57. David Halevi, "Tawfiq Zayyad, 'Od nitsba' otakh be-adom, moledet," *Monitin*, February 1981, 34–38.

58. Ehud Ya'ari, "Milhemet behirot ba-migzar he-'arvi," *Davar*, February 11, 1977.

59. Sami Shalom Chetrit, *Intra-Jewish Conflict in Israel: White Jews, Black Jews* (London: Routledge, 2010), 81–140.

60. Minutes of the Second Session of the Central Committee, January 22, 1977, NLI, Communist Party Archive, V 1272 3 141.

61. Rekhess, *The Arab Minority in Israel*, 64, 214.

62. Third Session of the Central Committee, February 25–26, 1977, NLI/ Communist Party Archive, V 1272 3 141.

63. *Zo ha-Derekh*, March 23, 1977.

64. Ibid., *Zo ha-Derekh*, March 9, 1977.

65. Ibid., February 9, 1977.

66. Tamar Gozansky, *Mizrahi Communists: The Struggle against Ethnic Discrimination and for Housing Rights* (Haifa: Pardes, 2018), 178.

67. Ilana Kaufman, *Arab National Communism in the Jewish State* (Gainesville: University Press of Florida, 1997), 152–153.

68. *Yedi'ot Aharaonot*, February 18, 1983.

69. Nazareth Municipality, *Al-Faris—Tawfiq Zayyad, al-Insan, al-Qa'id, al-Sha'ir* (Nazareth: al-Hakim, 1994), 19–20.

70. Yoel Dar, "Nimtse'ah ha-mekhonit ha-gnuva," *Davar*, May 15, 1977.

71. Ha-Levi, "Tawfiq Zayyad."

72. Ian Lustick, *Arabs in the Jewish State* (Austin: University of Texas Press, 1980).

73. Yitzhaq Ben Horin, "Rakah: Targil 'al hevel dak be-natseret," *Ma'ariv*, December 2, 1980.

74. Ibid.

75. See Shmuel Segev, "Mi-Shfar'am le-Natseret," *Ma'ariv*, December 5, 1980; "Congress be-Natseret," *Ma'ariv*, December 2, 1980; "Mu'tamar al-jamahir al-'arabiyya," *al-Ittihad*, September 16, 1980.

76. Yitzhak Ben-Horin, "Rosh 'iriyat Natseret nehkar," *Ma'ariv*, November 2, 1980.

77. *Ma'ariv*, December 2, 1980.

78. Daliah Ravikovitz, "Hatuna 'al heshbon ha-memshalah," *Ma'ariv*, December 8, 1980.

79. Ha-Levi, "Tawfiq Zayyad."

CHAPTER 7

1. David Halevi, "Tawfiq Zayyad, 'Od nitsba' otakh be-adom, moledet," *Monitin*, February 1981.

2. *Davar*, August 24, 1980.

3. *Ma'ariv*, August 22, 1980.

4. Yoel Dar, "Natseret hit'orerea mi-tardemata," *Davar*, September 4, 1980.

5. Minutes of the Eighty-Seventh Session of the Tenth Knesset Plenum, May 19, 1982.

6. "Hadhihi hawiyyatuna al-wataniyya wa-l-insaniyya," *al-Ittihad*, August 24, 1982.

7. Estimates of those massacred have ranged from roughly three hundred to as many as three thousand people. See Linda A. Malone, "The Kahan Report, Ariel Sha-

ron and the Sabra-Shatilla Massacres in Lebanon: Responsibility under International Law for Massacres of Civilian Populations," *Utah Law Review* 1985, no. (1985): 373–433.

8. *Al-Ittihad*, September 24, 28, 1982.

9. Minutes of Meeting No. 128 of the Tenth Knesset Plenum, October 27, 1982.

10. Public opinion polls managed by Sammy Smooha showed that the percentage of Arab citizens of Israel who considered the Palestinian identity (by itself or within combinations such as "Israeli Palestinian" or "Palestinian Arab") was significantly higher in 1985, as compared with 1980. Sammy Smooha, "The Advances and Limits of the Israelization of Israel's Palestinian Citizens," in *Israeli and Palestinian Identities in History and Literature*, ed. Kamal Abdel-Malek and David C. Jacobson (New York: St. Martin's Press, 1999), 19.

11. Elie Rekhess, *The Arab Minority in Israel: Between Communism and Arab Nationalism, 1965–1991* [in Hebrew] (Tel-Aviv: Ha-Kibutz He-Meuhad, 1993), 130–132.

12. "Arafat Ihel le-Vilner be-Hatslaha," *Haaretz*, July 12, 1984.

13. *Al-Ittihad*, July 16, 1984.

14. Shefi Gabai, "Shnayim ohazim be-ashaf," *Ma'ariv*, July 13, 1984.

15. *Al-Ittihad*, July 16, 1984.

16. Moshe Dor, "ha-Hod ha-Leumi," *Ma'ariv*, July 15, 1984.

17. Matti Golan, "Mahaze mevish," *Haaretz*, July 12, 1984.

18. Minutes of Meeting No. 108 of the Politburo, August 2, 1984; Minutes of the Politburo of the Israeli Communist Party, 1983–1984, NLI, Communist Party Archive, V 1272 3 42.

19. *Al-Ittihad*, July 16, 1984.

20. Ibid., July 20, 1984.

21. 'Atallah Mansur, "Miflaga le'umit la-'aravim," *Haaretz*, July 30, 1984, 9.

22. Minutes of Meeting No. 109 of the Politburo, August 12, 1984, Minutes of the Politburo of the Israeli Communist Party, 1983–1984, NLI, Communist Party Archive, V 1272 3 42.

23. See Vilner's remarks in Meeting No. 123 of the Politburo: Minutes of the Politburo of the Israeli Communist Party, 1983–1984, February 14, 1985, NLI, Communist Party Archive, V 1272 3 42.

24. *Al-Ittihad*, September 16, 1987.

25. Minutes of Municipal Council Meeting No. 26, December 16, 1987, Abu Salma Library, Nazareth.

26. Asher Arian, "A Report: Security and Political Attitudes in Israel: 1986–1991," *Public Opinion Quarterly* 56, no. 1 (1992).

27. *Al-Ittihad*, December 20, 1987.

28. Ibid., January 24, 1988.

29. Ibid.

30. Ibid., February 14, 1988.

31. My interview with Nazir Majali, July 28, 2017.

32. Avino'am Bar Yosef, "lisgirat bete'on Rakah kadmu hazharot," *Ma'ariv*, March 25, 1988.

33. Speech in the DFPE Acre district meeting, *Al-Ittihad*, March 4, 1988.

34. *Al-Ittihad*, April 11, 1988.

35. Speech in the opening event of the 1989 local elections campaign, February 17, 1988; film provided by the Tawfiq Zayyad Institute.

36. *Al-Ittihad*, February 18, 1991.

37. Gideon Richer, "Hakim me'idim 'al 'atsmam," *Yedi'ot Aharonot*, March 9, 1978.

38. Filmed interview by Samir 'Abdallah with Tawfiq Zayyad, July 2, 1994; raw footage provided by the Tawfiq Zayyad Institute.

39. *Al-Ittihad*, July 13, 1988.

40. Minutes of Meeting No. 157 of the Tenth Knesset Plenum, January 4, 1983.

41. *Al-Ittihad*, February 25, 1983.

42. My interview with 'Ubur Zayyad, August 7, 2017.

43. In 1982, Arab mayors, Arab parliament members, and representatives of extraparliamentary Arab organizations established the Follow-Up Committee (FUC) to coordinate the collective action of Palestinians in Israel. Since 1988, the FUC has been the major forum for making decisions about nationwide strikes and demonstrations.

44. See *Btselem* data: "Fatalities in the first Intifada," https://www.btselem.org/statistics/first intifada tables.

45. Zayyad, *Ana min hadhihi al-Madina*, 46. My translation.

46. *Al-Ittihad*, May 26, 1991.

47. Tawfiq Zayyad, *Ana min hadhihi al-Madina*, 52–59. My translation.

48. Ibid., 61–73. My translation.

49. Mahmud Darwish, "Akhir Aswat al-'Asifa," *al-Ittihad*, July 8, 1994.

CHAPTER 8

1. Moshe Kohn, "Red Mayor for Jerusalem," *Jerusalem Post*, December 19, 1975, 10–11.

2. Mahmud Darwish, "Akhir Aswat al-'Asifa," *al-Ittihad*, July 8, 1994.

3. Khatib provided a full reference for the interview with Zayyad—*Kol ha-'Emek*

ve-ha-Galil, January 14, 1994—but I could not find that issue and I rely on Khatib's description of the interview.

4. Khatib is referring to an incident that took place on December 30, 1993. MK Haim Dayyan from the right-wing Tsomet Party reported that he saw Zayyad driving under influence in the parking lot of the Ramada Hotel in Jerusalem, hit two cars, and drive away. Zayyad denied the allegations, arguing that while backing out of a parking space, he had a minor accident and then had a friendly chat with the other driver in which he promised to cover the cost. See *al-Ittihad,* January 3, 1994.

5. Kamal Khatib, *Sawt al-Haq wal-Huriyya,* January 21, 1994.

6. Ziad Abu-Amr, *Islamic Fundamentalism in the West Bank and Gaza: Muslim Brotherhood and Islamic Jihad* (Bloomington: Indiana University Press, 1994), 4.

7. Alisa Rubin-Peled, *Debating Islam in the Jewish State: The Development of Policy toward Islamic Institutions in Israel* (Albany: State University of New York Press, 2001), 131–132.

8. Issam Aburaiya, *Developmental Leadership: The Case of the Islamic Movement in Umm Al-Fahim, Israel* (Worcester, MA: International Development and Social Change, Clark University, 1991), 132–136.

9. Ibid., 108.

10. Interview with Ibrahim 'Abd al-Khaliq, one of the four founders of the library, January 28, 2018.

11. Interview with 'Abd al-Malik Dahamsha, August 2, 2017.

12. "Al-Shaikh 'Abdallah Nimr Darwish," *al-Sinnara,* April 8, 1988.

13. Reuven Paz, "The Islamic Movement in Israel and the Municipal Election of 1989," *Jerusalem Quarterly* 53 (1990), 3–26.

14. Ibid.

15. Ibid.

16. See, for example, Vilner's remarks in Meeting No. 108 of the Central Committee, August 2, 1984, NLI, Communist Party Archive, V 1272 3 42, Minutes of the Politburo of the Israeli Communist Party, 1983–1984.

17. Meeting No. 132 of the Politburo, June 6, 1985, NLI, Communist Party Archive, V 1272 3 42, Minutes of the Politburo of the Israeli Communist Party, 1983–1984.

18. *Al-Ittihad,* May 2, 1988.

19. Jahiliyyah, "the age of ignorance," is an Islamic concept referring to the period of time and state of affairs in Arabia before the advent of Islam.

20. A speech in the opening event of the 1989 local elections campaign, February 17, 1988; film provided by the Tawfiq Zayyad Institute.

21. *Al-Ittihad*, February 18, 1989.

22. Ariela Ringel-Hoffman, *Yedi'ot Aharonot*, July 7, 1994.

23. Ibid.

24. My conversation with Na'ila Zayyad, January 31, 2018.

25. My conversation with Adib Abu Rahmun, January 31, 2018.

26. Mazal Mu'alem, "Tawfiq Zayyad tove'a," *Ma'ariv*, May 7, 1990.

27. Mazal Mu'alem, "Makot bein rosh 'iriyat Natseret le-havrei mo'atsa," *Ma'ariv*, December 16, 1990.

28. Tamir Sorek, *Arab Soccer in a Jewish State: The Integrative Enclave* (New York: Cambridge University Press, 2007).

29. Minutes of Nazareth City Hall Meeting: Seventh Meeting, June 6, 1989; Fifteenth Meeting, March 15, 1990; Twenty-Eighth Meeting, March 14, 1991.

30. *Al-Ittihad,* December 26, 1985, 6.

31. Minutes of the Twelfth Meeting of the Nazareth City Hall, January 4, 1990. Although the municipality did celebrate the major Muslin holidays ('Eid al-Fitr and 'Eid al-Adha), Christmas celebrations were much more pronounced and visible.

32. Tamir Sorek, "Calendars, Martyrs, and Palestinian Particularism under British Rule," *Journal of Palestine Studies* 43, no. 1 (2013). 6–23.

33. Minutes of the Eighth Meeting of the Nazareth City Hall, August 4, 1989.

34. Minutes of the Thirty-Second Meeting of the Nazareth City Hall, August 22, 1991.

35. Minutes of the Thirtieth Meeting of the Nazareth City Hall, June 12, 1991.

36. Tamir Sorek, *Palestinian Commemoration in Israel: Calendars, Monuments, and Martyrs* (Stanford: Stanford University Press, 2015), 48–64.

37. Based a videotape of the event, provided by the Tawfiq Zayyad Institute.

38. A speech Zayyad delivered during the Nineteenth Conference of the Nazareth District of the Communist Party, December 7–8, 1990. The quote is based on a videotape from the event, provided by the Tawfiq Zayyad Institute.

39. Tawfiq Zayyad, "Harb al-khalij wal-jadl al-dini," *Al-Ittihad*, March 5, 1991.

40. Leila Ahmed, *Women and Gender in Islam: Historical Roots of a Modern Debate* (New Haven: Yale University Press, 1992), 232.

41. Rema Hammami, "Women, the Hijab and the Intifada," *Middle East Report* 20, no. 3 & 4 (1990), 24–28.

42. *Al-Ittihad*, April 2, 1990.

43. A reference to the biblical story about the creation of Eve and also to a popular idiom that belittles women based on that story.

44. *Al-Ittihad*, July 3, 1990.

45. Ibid., March 29, 1991.

46. Kamal Khatib, "Yawm al-mar'a al-'alami bayna al-wahm wal-Haqiqa," *Sawt al-Haq wal-Huriyya*, March 12, 1993.

47. The details of the event are described in *al-Ittihad*, March 31, 1993.

48. "Tawfiq Zayyad wa-a'awanuhu yufajirun ijtima' al-tadamun," *Sawt al-Haq wal-Huriyya*, April 2, 1993.

49. News of the Israeli Broadcast Authority, n.d.

50. Ra'id Salah, "Rasa'il Haq 'ala man yabhath 'an al-Haq," *Sawt al-Haq wal-Huriyya*, April 9, 1993.

51. 'Abdallah Nimr Darwish, "Wali 'Ahd Asyadikum," *Sawt al-Haq wal-Huriyya*, April 9, 1993.

52. "Shaykh" is an honorific title for a tribal leader and in some contexts a religious leader.

53. "Tawfiq Zayyad (1991)," https://www.youtube.com/watch?v=4A9fkAVqfoM, retrieved July 19, 2019. Although the title refers to Land Day 1991, Zayyad's reference to certain events in his speech leads to the conclusion that it took place on the First of May 1993.

CHAPTER 9

1. From my interview with Samih Ghanadri, who heard the story from the lawyer 'Abd al-Hafiz Darawsha, a shared friend who attended the party, July 30, 2017.

2. "Sikhsukh harif parats be-tsameret Rakah," *Davar*, October 18, 1974.

3. My Interview with Nazir Majali, July 28, 2017.

4. *Al-Ittihad*, December 28, 1976.

5. Emile Habiby, *The Secret Life of Saeed: The Pessoptimist* (Northampton, MA: Interlink Books, 2002).

6. Ibid., 12.

7. Tawfiq Zayyad, "Ila 'umal musku," *Ashuddu 'ala Ayadikum* (Acre: Matba'at Abu Rahmun, 1994), 22–27.

8. Tawfiq Zayyad, "Kilmat shukr li-l-najm al-ahmar," *Sujana Al-Huriyya* (Acre: Matba'at Abu Rahmun, 1994), 99–100. My translation.

9. My interview with Violet Khuri, Habib Khuri's wife who witnessed the conversation, December 21, 2018.

10. Adina Hoffman, *My Happiness Bears No Relation to Happiness: A Poet's Life in the Palestinian Century* (New Haven: Yale University Press, 2009), 310.

11. David Rudge, "Former Knesset Member Emile Habibi Says the Old Way of Think-ing Is Over," *Jerusalem Post*, October 27, 1989.

12. Habibi told this story at his speech of resignation from the party's institutions on May 8, 1989. See Emile Habibi, *Nahwa 'alam bi-la aqfas* (Haifa: Maktab wa-Mak-tabat Kull Shay, 1993), 22.

13. Imil Habibi, "al-Rabi' fi biladina," *Al-Ittihad*, May 28, 1989.

14. Habibi, *Nahwa 'alam bi-la aqfas*, 10–27.

15. Ibid., 12–13.

16. My interview with Samih Ghanadri, Emile Habibi's brother-in-law, July 30, 2017.

17. Imil Habibi, "Kabush wa-kabsh al-fida,'" *Al-Ittihad*, September 22, 1989.

18. Letter from Tawfiq Zayyad to Emile Habibi, October 19, 1989, provided by the Tawfiq Zayyad Institute.

19. *Al-Ittihad*, December 31, 1989.

20. A keener is a professional female mourner who wails or sings during funerals.

21. "Al-Nadaba," *Al-Ittihad*, July 5, 1991. My translation.

22. Salim Al-'Atawna, *Tawfiq Zayyad, Dirasa Tahliliya fi Intajihi al-Adabi* (Beer-sheeba: Beersheeba Kaye Academic College of Education, 2017), 121–122.

23. Imil Habibi, "Risala min al-Watan: hawl 'alam bila aqfas," *Majalat al-Dirasat al-Falastiniyya* 2, no. 7 (1991).

24. From the movie *The Old World Shall Be Destroyed*, directed by Hagar Kot (1993).

25. *Al-Ittihad*, May 31, 1992.

26. Tawfiq Zayyad, "'An al-hizb wa-l-jabha," *al-Iittihad*, October 9, 1992.

27. Riyad Na'san Agha's interview with Tawfiq Zayyad in the program Shuhud al-'Aser, spring 1994.

28. *Al-Ittihad*, December 2, 1989.

29. My interview with Nazim Badir, who was then the secretary of the DFPE in the Knesset.

30. "Aluf ha-He'adruyot: Tawfiq Zayyad," *Yedi'ot Aharonot*, February 14, 1989.

31. My interview with Samih Ghanadri, July 30, 2017.

32. My interview with Hashim Mahamid, July 20, 2016.

33. Kaufman, *Arab National Communism in the Jewish State* (Gainesville: University Press of Florida, 1997), 120.

34. Ibid., 121.

35. *Al-Ittihad*, April 12, 1992.

36. Tawfiq Zayyad, *Nasrawi fi al-Saha al-Hamra* (Nazareth: Al-Nahda, 1972), 8.

CHAPTER 10

1. Salim Al-'Atawna, *Tawfiq Zayyad, Dirasa Tahliliya fi Intajihi al-Adabi* (Beersheeba: Beersheeba Kaye Academic College of Education, 2017), 103–104.

2. David Halevi, "Tawfiq Zayyad , 'Od nitsba' otakh be-adom, moledet," *Monitin*, February 1981.

3. Samir Abdallah's interview of Tawfiq Zayyad in an unpublished film, July 2, 1994, Tawfiq Zayyad Institute.

4. "Ha-Heskem 'Im Hadash," *Haaretz*, June 5, 1990.

5. Yossi Sarid, "She-yehapsu oti," *Haaretz*, August 17, 1990.

6. Tawfiq Zayyad, "The Gulf War (5)," *Al-Ittihad*, November 18, 1991.

7. Adina Kaufman, *Arab National Communism in the Jewish State* (Gainesville: University Press of Florida, 1997), 120.

8. Nazir Majali interviews Zayyad, *Al-Ittihad*, April 30, 1992.

9. Amir Zohar, "ha-Yahafokh panter 'oro?" *Haaretz*, September 18, 2007.

10. Letter from Zayyad to Muhammd Mi'ari and an identical letter to 'Abd al-Wahab Darawsha, May 12, 1992, Tawfiq Zayyad Institute.

11. Ibid.

12. *Al-Ittihad,* September 6, 1985.

13. One of the first Zionist settlements, Rosh Pinna was named after this verse.

14. Nazir Majali interviews Zayyad, *al-Ittihad*, April 30, 1992.

15. *Haaretz*, June 24, 1992.

16. *Yedi'ot Aharonot*, June 29, 1992

17. A filmed interview of Tawfiq Zayyad by Nazir Majali from late November 1994, "al-Qa'id al-Rahil Tawfiq Zayyad," *Ehna-TV*, http://www.ehna.tv/play/6066/?fbclid=I-wARoDm5vXyPGjR7ceAz4g-vEjHHg37oV-I8htWgsDbspRJsNe5kn4X-jrDG4.

18. "Rabin: Akhjal min hadm huquq al-muwatinin al-'Arab," *al-Ittihad*, July 7, 1992.

19. *Haaretz*, July 13, 1992.

20. *Al-Ittihad*, March 31, 1985.

21. Ibid., May 31, 1992.

22. See ibid., July 14, 1992.

23. Tawfiq Zayyad, "'An al-hizb wal-jabha wa-l-imana al-suhufiyya," *al-Ittihad*, October 9, 1992.

24. *Hadashot*, December 1, 1992.

25. Haim Hefer, "The Last Bolshevik," *Yedi'ot Aharnont*, December 4, 1992.

26. Tawfiq Zayyad, "A Report from the Assembly Hall," document provided by the Tawfiq Zayyad Institute.

27. Minutes of the Eighteenth Meeting of the Thirteenth Knesset Plenum, November 2, 1992.

28. *Yedi'ot Aharonot*, December 24, 1992.

29. Shaked, Roni, "Pgishat Rabin 'im ha-hakim ha-'arvim," December 28, 1992.

30. *Al-Ittihad*, January 23, 1993.

31. Ibid., January 24, 1994.

32. Pinhas 'Inbari, *'Al ha-Mishmar*, June 2, 1993.

33. *Al-Ittihad*, September 12, 1993.

34. Minutes of Meeting No. 129 of the Thirteenth Knesset Plenum, September 21, 1993.

35. Minutes of Meeting No. 129 of the Thirteenth Knesset Plenum, September 21, 1993. My translation. The original poem in Arabic ended with the line: "Give Abie Nathan, the people's conscience, the right to speak." Zayyad replaced it with, "Give Peace Now the right to speak," probably as a gesture toward the Zionist left-wing movement, carrying this name.

36. David Makovsky, "Rabin: Let's Talk about Success, Not Failure," *Jerusalem Post*, October 6, 1993.

37. Minutes of meeting No. 132 of the Thirteenth Knesset Plenum, October 11, 1993.

38. "Al-Qa'id al-Rahil Tawfiq Zayyad," *Ehna-TV*, n.d. (c. November 1994).

39. *Al-Ittihad*, February 27, 1994.

40. Minutes of Meeting No. 235 of the Thirteenth Knesset Plenum, June 28, 1993.

41. Interview in *al-Ittihad*, July 1, 1994.

42. Ariela Ringer-Hoffman, *Yedi'oth Aharonot*, July 7, 1994.

43. "MK Tawfiq Zayyad Was Killed," *Yedi'ot Aharonont*, July 6, 1994.

EPILOGUE

1. Tawfiq Zayyad, "Fi kul shay A'ishu," *Sujana Al-Huriyya* (Acre: Matba'at Abu Rahmun, 1994), 16–18. My translation.

2. *Al-Ittihad*, July 7, 1994.

3. Resolution 181 (II), Future Government of Palestine, November 29, 1947, https://undocs.org/en/A/RES/181(II)

4. Riad Na'asan Agha interviews Zayyad in the program *Shuhud al-'Aser*, Spring 1994.

5. A program on Jordanian television, covered by *al-Ittihad*, July 17, 1994.

6. See, for example, the collection of Zayyad's poems published by the Ministry of Culture of the Palestinian National Authority: Tawfiq Zayyad, *Ana min hadhihi al-Watan: Mukhtarat Shi'riyya* (Ramallah: Bayt al-Shi'r, 2016).

7. Avraham Yinon, "Tawfiq Zayyad: 'We Are the Majority Here,'" in *The Arabs in Israel: Continuity and Change*, ed. Aharon Layish (Jerusalem: Magness Press, 1981).

8. Imil Habibi, "Inna baqun 'ala al-'Ahd," *al-Ittihad*, July 8, 1994.

9. Minutes of Meeting No. 242 of the Thirteenth Knesset Plenum, July 13, 1994.

10. Tawfiq Zayyad, "Aladhi amluku," *Kalimat Muqatila* (Acre: Matba'at Abu Rahmun, 1994), 11.

Bibliography

Abbasi, Mustafa. "Kibush Natseret: Ha-'Ir He-'Arvit She-Sarda Et Ha-Milhama." *'Iyonim bi-Tkomat Yisra'el* 20 (2010): 101–21.

Abdel-Malek, Anouar. "Nasserism and Socialism." *Socialist Register* 1, no. 1 (1964).

Abrahamian, Ervand. *Iran between Two Revolutions.* Princeton, NJ: Princeton University Press, 1982.

Abu-Amr, Ziad. *Islamic Fundamentalism in the West Bank and Gaza: Muslim Brotherhood and Islamic Jihad.* Bloomington: Indiana University Press, 1994.

Abu-Ghazaleh, Adnan. "Arab Cultural Nationalism in Palestine during the British Mandate." *Journal of Palestine Studies* 1, no. 3 (1972): 37–63.

Abu Hanna, Hanna. *Rihlat Al-Bahth 'an Al-Turath* [A journey in search of heritage]. Haifa: al-Wadi, 1994.

———. *Mahr Al-Buma: Sira* [Dowry of the owl: A life]. Haifa: Maktabat kull shay', 2004.

Aburaiya, Issam. *Developmental Leadership: The Case of the Islamic Movement in Umm Al-Fahim, Israel.* Worcester, MA: International Development and Social Change, Clark University, 1991.

Ahmed, Leila. *Women and Gender in Islam: Historical Roots of a Modern Debate.* New Haven, CT: Yale University Press, 1992.

Al-Ahmad, Nu'aima *Tawfiq Zayyad—Al-Sha'ir Al-Munadil.* Haifa: Maktabat Kul Shee, 2018.

Al-'Atawna, Salim. *Tawfiq Zayyad: Dirasa Tahliliyya fi Intajihi Al-Adabi.* Beersheba: Kaye Academic College of Education, 2017.

Al-Banna, Hasan. *What Is Our Message?* 5th ed. Lahore, Pakistan: Islamic Publications, 1995.

Al-Budayri, Musa. "Iqrar Bil-Dhanb: Imil Tuma Wal-Taqsim Aladhi Lam Yahdath." *Bidayat*, no. 18–19 (2017/2018): 201–216.

Al-Jaza'iri, Muhammad. "Al-Muqawama bil-Kilma fi Shi'r Tawfiq Zayyad." *al-Aadab* 15, no. 10 (1967): 18–22.

Al-Manassira, 'Izz al-Din. "Muqadamma: Tawfiq Zayyad, Sha'ir al-Sha'b wal-Qadiya." In *Diwan Tawfiq Zayyad*, edited by al-Manassira 'Izz al-Din. Beirut: Dar al-'Awda, 1970.

Alsulaiman, Abied. "The Adaptation of the Terms 'Laicism,' 'Secularism' and 'Laïcité' in Arabic." *Journal of Internationalization and Localization* 3, no. 1 (2016): 1–17.

Arendt, Hannah. "A Reply to Eric Voegelin." In *The Portable Hannah Arendt*, edited by Peter Baehr, 157–164. New York: Viking, 2000.

Arnason, Johann P. "Communism and Modernity." *Daedalus* 129, no. 1 (2000): 61–90.

Aron, Raymond. *In Defense of Decadent Europe.* Chicago: Regnery/Gateway, 1979.

Asad, Talal. *Formations of the Secular: Christianity, Islam, Modernity.* Stanford, CA: Stanford University Press, 2003.

Bashir, Nabih. *The Land Day: Betwixt and between—National and Civic.* [In Arabic.] Haifa: Mada al-Carmel, 2006.

Bauml, Yair. *A Blue and White Shadow: The Israeli Establishment's Policy and Action among the Arab Citizens. The Formative Years: 1958–1968.* Haifa: Pardes, 2007.

Beinin, Joel. *Was the Red Flag Flying There? Marxist Politics and the Arab-Israeli Conflict in Egypt and Israel, 1948–1965.* Berkeley: University of California Press, 1990.

Belati, Berl. *Ba-Ma'avak 'al Ha-Kiyum Ha-Yehudi: Li-Demuto Shel Mosheh Sneh.* Jerusalem: Y. Markus 1981.

Benjamin, Walter. *Walter Benjamin: Selected Writings, 1938–1940.* Cambridge, MA: Belknap Press of Harvard University Press, 2003.

Bin Nasir al-Ghamdi, Sa'id. *Al-Inhiraf Al-'Aqdi fi Adab al-Hadatha wa-Fikruha.* Jeddah: Dar al-andalus al-khdraa, 2003.

Bishara, 'Azmi. "The Arabs in Israel: Reading a Fragmented Political Discourse." In *Between the 'Me' and the 'Us,'* edited by 'Azmi Bishara. [In Hebrew.] Jerusalem: Van Leer Institute, Ha-kibbutz Ha-meuchad, 1999.

Blasing, Mutlu K. *Nâzım Hikmet: The Life and Times of Turkey's World Poet.* New York: Persea Books, 2013.

Bloch, Ernst. *Atheism in Christianity: The Religion of the Exodus and the Kingdom.* London: Verso, 2009.

———. *Atheismus Im Chritentum: Zur Religion Des Exodus Und Des Reichs*. Frankfurt: Springer-Verlag, 1968.

Budeiri, Musa. *The Palestine Communist Party 1919–1948: Arab and Jew in the Struggle for Internationalism*. Chicago: Haymarket Books, 2010.

———. *Shuyu'iyun fi Falastin: Shathaya Ta'rikh Munsa* [Communists in Palestine: Fragments of a forgotten narrative]. Ramallah: MUWATIN—Palestinian Institute for the Study of Democracy 2013.

Bulus, Habib. *Al-Watha'iq Al-Harir*. Nazareth: Tawfiq Zayyad Institute, 2000.

Central Committee of the Israeli Communist Party. *Ha-Emet 'al Me'ora'ot ha-1 be-May Be-Natseret* [The truth about the First of May events in Nazareth]. Israeli Communist Party, 1958.

Chetrit, Sami Shalom. *Intra-Jewish Conflict in Israel: White Jews, Black Jews*. London: Routledge, 2010.

Clermont, Pierre. *Le Communisme À Contre-Modernité*. Paris: Presses universitaires de Vincennes, 1993.

Dallasheh, Leena. "Nazarenes in the Turbulent Tide of Citizenships: Nazareth from 1940 to 1966." PhD diss., New York University, 2012.

———. "Political Mobilization of Palestinians in Israel: The Al-Ard Movement." In *Displaced at Home: Ethnicity and Gender among Palestinians in Israel*, edited by Rhoda Ann Kanaaneh, Isis Nusair, and Lila Abu-Lughod, 21–48. Albany, NY: SUNY Press, 2010.

Davies, Alan. *The Crucified Nation: A Motif in Modern Nationalism*. Eastbourne, UK: Sussex Academic Press, 2010.

Dawes, Greg. *Aesthetics and Revolution: Nicaraguan Poetry, 1979–1990*. Minneapolis: University of Minnesota Press, 1993.

Dothan, Shmuel. *Adumim: Ha-Miflagah Ha-Komunistit Be-Erets-Yisra'el*. Kefar-Saba: Shevna ha-Sofer, 1991.

Elmessiri, Abdelwahab M. *The Palestinian Wedding: A Bilingual Anthology of Contemporary Palestinian Resistance Poetry*. Washington, DC: Three Continents Press, 1982.

Emmet, Chad F. *Beyond the Basilica: Christians and Muslims in Nazareth*. Chicago: University of Chicago Press, 1995.

Falah, Ghazi. "Israeli 'Judaization' Policy in Galilee." *Journal of Palestine Studies* 20, no. 4 (1991): 69–85.

Far, Narjis Tawhidi. *Abu al-'Ala' Al-Ma'arri : Dirasah fi Mu'taqadatihi Al-Diniyah*. Beirut: Dar Sadir, 2011.

Forman, Geremy. "Military Rule, Political Manipulation, and Jewish Settlement: Israeli Mechanisms for Controlling Nazareth in the 1950s." *Journal of Israeli History* 25, no. 2 (2006): 335–359.

Furani, Khaled. *Silencing the Sea: Secular Rhythms in Palestinian Poetry.* Stanford: Stanford University Press, 2012.

Galliher, John F., Wayne Brekhus, and David P. Keys. *Laud Humphreys: Prophet of Homosexuality and Sociology.* Madison: University of Wisconsin Press, 2006.

Ghanem, Honaida. *Reinventing the Nation: Palestinians Intellectuals in Israel.* [In Hebrew.] Jerusalem: Magnes Press, 2009.

Goffman, Erving. *The Presentation of Self in Everyday Life.* Garden City, NY: Doubleday, 1959.

Goldstein, Warren S. "Messianism and Marxism: Walter Benjamin and Ernst Bloch's Dialectical Theories of Secularization." *Critical Sociology* 27, no. 2 (2001): 246–281.

Gonen, Binyamin. *Hayim Adumim:Tahanot be-Hayey Komonist Yisraeli.* Haifa: Pardes, 2009.

Gozansky, Tamar. *Mizrahi Communists: The Struggle against Ethnic Discrimination and for Housing Rights.* Haifa: Pardes, 2018.

Habibi, Imil. "Risala Min Al-Watan: Hawl 'Alam bila Aqfas." *Majalat al-Dirasat al-Falastiniyya* 2, no. 7 (1991): 223–228.

Habiby, Emile. *The Secret Life of Saeed: The Pessoptimist.* Northampton, MA: Interlink Books, 2002.

Haiduc-Dale, Noah. *Arab Christians in British Mandate Palestine: Communalism and Nationalism, 1917–1948.* Edinburgh: Edinburgh University Press, 2013.

Halabi, Awad. "Liminal Loyalties: Ottomanism and Palestinian Responses to the Turkish War of Independence, 1919–22." *Journal of Palestine Studies* 41, no. 3 (2012): 19–37.

Halliday, Fred. "Early Communism in Palestine." *Journal of Palestine Studies* 7, no. 2 (1978): 162–169.

Hammami, Rema. "Women, the Hijab and the Intifada." *Middle East Report* 20, no. 3 and 4 (1990): 24–28.

Hassan, Mona. *Longing for the Lost Caliphate: A Transregional History.* Princeton, NJ: Princeton University Press, 2017.

Hen-Tov, Jacob. *Communism and Zionism in Palestine during the British Mandate.* New Brunswick, NJ: Transaction Publishers, 1974.

Herzog, Hanna. *Gendering Politics: Women in Israel.* Ann Arbor: University of Michigan Press, 2010.

Hoffman, Adina. *My Happiness Bears No Relation to Happiness: A Poet's Life in the Palestinian Century*. New Haven: Yale University Press, 2009.

Husayni, Ishaq Musa. *Khalil Al-Sakakini: Al-Adib Al-Mujaddid*, Jerusalem: Markaz al-Abhath al-Islamiyya, 1989.

Huwar, Muhammad Ibrahim. *Al-Qabd 'Ala Al-Jamr: Tajribat Al-Sijn fi al-Shi'r al-Mu'asir.* [In Arabic.] Beirut: al-Mu'assasah al-'Arabiyah lil-Dirasat wa-al-Nashr, 2004.

Jarjura, Mun'im. *Qamh Wa-Zawan.* [In Arabic.] Haifa: Dar 'Arabesk, 1994.

Jayyusi, Salma K. *Anthology of Modern Palestinian Literature.* New York: Columbia University Press, 1992.

———. *Trends and Movements in Modern Arabic Poetry*, vol. 2. Leiden: Brill, 1977.

Jubran, Salem. "Tawfiq Zayyad fi al-Diwan: Ashuddu 'Ala Ayadikum, Sha'er Ya'arifu Sahr Al-Basata." In *Dirasat fi al-Adab al-Falstini al-Mahali*, edited by Nabih al-Qasim. Acre: Dar al-Aswar, 1987.

Kamen, Charles S. "After the Catastrophe I: The Arabs in Israel, 1948–51." *Middle Eastern Studies* 23, no. 4 (1987): 453–495.

Kana'ana, Tawfiq. *Dhikrayat Khityar lam Tamut Ajyaluhu* [Memoirs of an old men whose generations have not died.]. 'Araba: Self publication, n.d.

Kanafani, Ghassan. *Adab Al-Muqawamah fi Filastin Al-Muhtallah, 1948–1966.* Beirut: Dar al-Adab, 1966.

Kaufman, Ilana. *Arab National Communism in the Jewish State.* Gainesville: University Press of Florida, 1997.

Kayyali, Abd al-Wahhab. *Palestine: A Modern History.* London: Croom Helm, 1978.

Khalidi, Rashid. *Palestinian Identity: The Construction of Modern National Consciousness.* New York: Columbia University Press, 1997.

Kidron, Peretz. "Truth Whereby Nations Live." In *Blaming the Victims: Spurious Scholarship and the Palestinian Question*, edited by Edward Said and Christopher Hitchens, 85–96. London: Verso, 1988.

Kimmerling, Baruch, and Joel Migdal. *The Palestinian People: A History.* Cambridge, MA: Harvard University Press, 2003.

Kitani, Jamil. *Al-Lugha Al-Tahridiyya lada Tawfiq Zayyad wa-Masa'il 'Ukhra fi Shi'rihi.* Baqa' al-Gharbiyya: Al-Qasemi College, 2011.

Lockman, Zachary. *Comrades and Enemies: Arab and Jewish Workers in Palestine.* Berkeley: University of California Press, 1996.

Löwith, Karl. *Meaning in History: The Theological Implications of the Philosophy of History.* Chicago: University of Chicago Press, 1957.

Lustick, Ian. *Arabs in the Jewish State.* Austin: University of Texas Press, 1980.

Malone, Linda A. "The Kahan Report, Ariel Sharon and the Sabra-Shatilla Massacres in Lebanon: Responsibility under International Law for Massacres of Civilian Populations." *Utah Law Review* 1985, no. 2: 373–433.

Marwat, Ahmad. *Al-Nasira—A'alam wa-Shakhsiyat 1800–1948.* Acre: Mu'assasat al-Aswar, 2009.

Matthews, Mervyn. *Education in the Soviet Union: Policies and Institutions since Stalin.* London: Taylor & Francis, 2012.

Matthews, Welodn. *Confronting an Empire, Constructing a Nation: Arab Nationalists and Popular Politics in Mandate Palestine.* London: Bloomsbury Academic, 2006.

Milton-Edwards, Beverley. *Islamic Politics in Palestine.* London: I. B. Tauris, 1999.

Monnerot, Jules. *Sociology and Psychology of Communism.* Boston: Beacon Press, 1976.

Morris, Benny. *The Birth of the Palestinian Refugee Problem Revisited.* Cambridge: Cambridge University Press, 2004.

Nassar, Maha Tawfik. "Affirmation and Resistance: Press, Poetry and the Formation of National Identity among Palestinian Citizens of Israel, 1948–1967." PhD diss., University of Chicago, 2006.

Nassar, Maha. *Brothers Apart: Palestinian Citizens of Israel and the Arab World.* Stanford: Stanford University Press, 2017.

Nasr Allah, Ilyas. *Shahadat 'Ala al-Qarn al-Filastini al-Awwal* [Testimonies on the first century of Palestine]. Beirut: Dar al-Farabi, 2016.

Nazareth Municipality. *Al-Faris—Tawfiq Zayyad, al-Insan, al-Qa'id, Al-Sha'ir i.* Nazareth: al-Hakim, 1994.

Nelson, Cary. *Revolutionary Memory: Recovering the Poetry of the American Left.* New York: Routledge, 2001.

Nicholson, Reynold A. *Studies in Islamic Poetry.* Cambridge: Cambridge University Press, 1969.

Osacky-Lazar, Sarah. "He-'Arvim ba-'Asor ha-Rishon." In *Yisrael ba-'Asor ha-Rishon,* vol. 6, edited by Binyamin Neuberger. Ra'anana: Open University, 2001–2011.

Paz, Reuven. "The Islamic Movement in Israel and the Municipal Election of 1989." *Jerusalem Quarterly* 53 (1990): 3–26.

Piroyansky, Danna. *Ramle Remade: The Israelisation of an Arab Town, 1948–1967.* Haifa: Pardes Publishing, 2014.

Porath, Yehoshua. *The Palestine Arab National Movement: From Riots to Rebellion.* London: Frank Cass, 1977.

Reiter, Yitzhak. *National Minority, Regional Majority: Palestinian Arabs versus Jews in Israel.* Syracuse, NY: Syracuse University Press, 2009.

Rekhess, Elie. *The Arab Minority in Israel: Between Communism and Arab Nationalism 1965–1991*. [In Hebrew.] Tel-Aviv: Ha-Kibutz he-Me'uhad, 1993.

———. *'Arviyey Yisrael ve-Hafka'at ha-Karka'ot ba-Galil*. Tel Aviv: Shilo'ah Institute, 1977.

Reynolds, Matthew. "Introduction." In Abu l-'Ala al-Ma'arri, *The Epistle of Forgiveness*. New York: NYU Press, 2016.

Robinson, Shira. *Citizen Strangers: Palestinians and the Birth of Israel's Liberal Settler State*. Stanford: Stanford University Press, 2014.

———. "Local Struggle, National Struggle: Palestinian Responses to the Kafr Qasim Massacre and Its Aftermath, 1956–1966." *International Journal of Middle East Studies* 35, no. 3 (2003): 393–416.

Robson, Laura. *Colonialism and Christianity in Mandate Palestine*. Austin: University of Texas Press, 2011.

Rodrigue, Aron. *French Jews, Turkish Jews: The Alliance Israélite Universelle and the Politics of Jewish Schooling in Turkey, 1860–1925*. Bloomington: Indiana University Press, 1990.

Rosenfeld, Henry, and Majid Al-Haj. *Arab Local Government in Israel*. Boulder, CO: Westview Press, 1990.

Rosenthal, Rubik. "Who Killed Fatma Sarsur." In *Kafr Kassem: Myth and History*, edited by R. Rosenthal, 11–86. [In Hebrew.] Tel Aviv: Ha-Kibbutz ha-Me'uhad, 2000.

Rubin-Peled, Alisa. *Debating Islam in the Jewish State: The Development of Policy toward Islamic Institutions in Israel*. Albany: State University of New York Press, 2001.

Sa'di, Ahmad H. "Control and Resistance at Local-Level Institutions: A Study of Kafr Yassif's Local Council under the Military Government." *Arab Studies Quarterly* 23, no. 3, (2001): 31–47.

———. "The Koenig Report and Israeli Policy towards the Palestinian Minority, 1965–1976: Old Wine in New Bottles." *Arab Studies Quarterly* 25, no. 3 (2003): 51–61.

Sakakini, Khalil. *Yawmiyat Khalil al-Sakakini: Yawmiyat, Rasa'il, Ta'ammulat: al-Kitab al-Awal*. Edited by Akram Musallam. Ramallah: Markaz Khalil al-Sakakini al-Thaqafı: Mu'assasat al-Dirasat al-Muqaddasiyya, 2003.

———. *Yawmiyat Khalil al-Sakakini: Yawmiyat, Rasa'il, Ta'ammulat: al-Kitab al-Thani*. Edited by Akram Musallam. Ramallah: Markaz Khalil al-Sakakini al-Thaqafı: Mu'assasat al-Dirasat al-Muqaddasiyya, 2003.

Sidqi, Najati. *Mudhakkirat Najati Sidqi*. [The memoirs of Najati Sidqi.] Beirut: Mu'assasat al-Dirasat al-Filastiyya, 2001.

Smooha, Sammy. "The Advances and Limits of the Israelization of Israel's Palestinian

Citizens." In *Israeli and Palestinian Identities in History and Literature*, edited by Kamal Abdel-Malek and David C. Jacobson, 9–33. New York: St. Martin's Press, 1999.

Sorek, Tamir. *Arab Soccer in a Jewish State: The Integrative Enclave*. Cambridge: Cambridge University Press, 2007.

———. "Calendars, Martyrs, and Palestinian Particularism under British Rule." *Journal of Palestine Studies* 43, no. 1 (2013): 6–23.

———. *Palestinian Commemoration in Israel: Calendars, Monuments, and Martyrs*. Stanford: Stanford University Press, 2015.

Szporluk, Roman. *Communism and Nationalism: Karl Marx Versus Friedrich List*. New York: Oxford University Press, 1988.

Tamimi, Azzam. "The Origins of Arab Secularism." In *Islam and Secularism in the Middle East*], edited by John Espositor and Azzam Tamimi, 13–28. New York: New York University Press, 2000, 17.

Tamari, Salim, Munir Fakhr al-Din, and Muhannad Abd al-Hamid. "Hanna Abu Hanna: Rihlat Al-Adab Wal-Siyasa Wal-Muqawama." *Majalat al-Dirasat al-Falastiniyya* 105 (2016): 92–109.

Taylor, Charles. *A Secular Age*. Cambridge, MA: Harvard University Press, 2009.

Vatikiotis, Panayiotis J. *Nasser and His Generation*. London: Croom Helm, 1978.

Wu, Bingbing. "Secularism and Secularization in the Arab World." *Journal of Middle Eastern and Islamic Studies (in Asia)* 1, no. 1 (2007): 55–65.

Yinon, Avraham. "Tawfiq Zayyad: 'We Are the Majority Here.'" In *The Arabs in Israel: Continuity and Change*, edited by Aharon Layish, 213–240. [In Hebrew.] Jerusalem: Magness Press, 1981.

Yunis, Sharif. *Nida' al-Sha'b : Ta'rikh Naqdi lil-Idyulujiyya al-Nasiriyya*. Cairo: Dar al-Shuruq, 2012.

Zayyad, Tawfiq. *Ana Min Hadha Al-Watan: Mukhtarat Shi'riyya*. Ramallah: Bayt al-Shi'r, 2016.

———. *Ana min hadhihi al-Madina wa-Qasa'id Jadida Ukhra*. Acre: Matba'at Abu Rahmun, 1994.

———. *Ashuddu 'Ala Ayadikum*. Acre: Matba'at Abu Rahmun, 1994.

———. "Diwan 'Ashiq min Falastin li-Mahmud Darwish." In *Dirasat fi al-Adab al-Falstini al-Mahali*, edited by Nabih al-Qasim. Acre: Dar al-Aswar, 1987.

———. *Hal al-Dunya: Qisas Qasira*. [In Arabic.] Beirut: Dar al-Quds, 1970.

———. ""Ila Ayna Yadhhab ma Nadfa'?" [Where are our payments going?] *Al-jadid* 1, no. 11 (September 1954): 18–20.

———. *Kalimat Muqatila.* Acre: Matba'at Abu Rahmun, 1994.

———. *Nasrawi fi al-Saha al-Hamra.* Nazareth: Al-Nahda, 1972.

———. *Sujana al-Huriyya.* Acre: Matba'at Abu Rahmun, 1994.

———. *Ughniyyat Al-Thawra Wa-Al-Ghadab.* [In Arabic.] Beirut: Dar al-Awda, 1970.

Zerubavel, Eviatar. "The French Republican Calendar: A Case Study in the Sociology of Time." *American Sociological Review* 42, no. 6 (1977): 868–877.

Stanford Studies in Middle Eastern
and Islamic Societies and Cultures

Joel Beinin and Laleh Khalili, editors

EDITORIAL BOARD
Asef Bayat, Marilyn Booth, Laurie Brand, Timothy Mitchell,
Jillian Schwedler, Rebecca L. Stein, Max Weiss

Lightning Source UK Ltd.
Milton Keynes UK
UKHW040917160321
380214UK00011B/412

9 781503 612730